Return: To the Land of Durga

(Part 3 of *The Eden Trilogy*)

Lesley Ann Eden

Strategic Book Publishing and Rights Co.

Copyright © 2012

All rights reserved – Lesley Ann Eden

No part of this book may be reproduced or transmitted in any form or by any means, graphic, electronic, or mechanical, including photocopying, recording, taping, or by any information storage retrieval system, without the permission, in writing, from the publisher.

Strategic Book Publishing and Rights Co.
12620 FM 1960, Suite A4-507
Houston, TX 77065
www.sbpra.com

ISBN: 978-1-61897-937-7

Book Design: Suzanne Kelly

Dedication

To you and everyone who has dared to accompany me on my adventures, both physical and paranormal.

This last journey in the trilogy will test your belief further, beyond knowing, giving you a brief glimpse into the shadowland of darker energies where together we can ascend into a higher consciousness, which is our true heritage. Thank you for believing in me and taking me into your heart.

Table of Contents

Introduction vii
1. Back 1
2. Ghost 21
3. Chennai to Pondcherry—Lost Paradise 37
4. Tsunamika 55
5. Madurai and Memories 70
6. Cinderella Chiffon 85
7. Blue Mountains 105
8. Tiger Hill 124
9. Thread Needle Garden 137
10. Screaming Walls 149
11. Postcard Back from the Future 165
12. Infinity Tea, Nonesuch Tea 180
13. Night Terror 195
14. *Uranus Ureignus* 210
15. Russian Doll 227
16. Invader 241
17. Beyond Knowing 256
18. Return 274

Introduction

Have you ever ventured far from the arid, dusty heat of the Indian plains to the quiet calm of the foothills of the Nilgiris and followed the snake pass beyond the palm trees, up and up through craggy rocks where waterfalls breach the rich red earth? Have you gone up where monkeys swing from tree to tree spying on travellers and still farther up, where the clouds rest on tree tops, like fluffy nests and where the air is clear and a hazy sun plays hide and seek in forest glades? If so, you will know the pulse of the mountain people and a welcome like no other.

In the Blue Mountains, you will find a haven where the atmosphere is cool like a sea swirl and lighter than a leaf blown on the wind, refreshing all weary visitors exhausted from the burdensome heat in the cities below, where fumes claw at throats like splintered glass and dust cakes nostrils in black grime. In the hills you can breathe deeply and inhale the eucalyptus and jasmine scent curling downwards from the mountain crest, wafting on the evening breeze, as mist folds like white dunes floating below in grey shadows around the temples.

There you will experience magical twilight as the sun softly falls behind the mountain tops and the evening fires glow red hot by the roadside and where, in one swift blink, the purple sky seeps into inky blotches, dotted with silver beacons. Stray dogs call plaintively to each other through thick forests, and the dingoes howl in the stillness as the moon watches. It is where fireflies set alight burning bushes like ruby jewels trailing luminescent halos of bright sparks across the dense jungle. It is a place where time is different and set apart from the rest of the world. It is where silence is profoundly grave.

Far away, in the winter grey daze of England, the silence of the hills haunts me and invades my thoughts, beckoning and calling through the rough terrain of routine existence. The remembered peace of the hills cuts deep and seeps through the din of the traffic, hacking through screaming children's cries echoing down careworn corridors. I crave the heady stillness of the Blue Mountains and long to smell pungent spices sizzling in a pan of ghee, as their aroma wafts through open windows in the early evening. Craggy rocks disappear in an amethyst haze as night descends, and I yearn to sleep surrounded by the night symphony as it begins its gentle overture of soft cricket clicking until dawn. I long to sleep drifting in and out of dreams with citronella oil lingering on my pillow, its lemony balm warding off the nightly attack of droning mosquitoes. I need to return to the rare place where the descending chill of the wind rolls from the mountains before the sun rises and whispers around dark corners where the tree Bhutas loiter, waiting to latch their disembodied spirits onto unsuspecting souls. You must heed the warning of the hill people never to wander near the forest glades as night approaches, for the Bhutas will attach their unearthly form to your being and haunt you until daylight. You ask yourself,

'How will I know such a spectre when the beings appear like humans?' You will know them, I am told, because they wear their feet backwards!

I know a place in the Nilgiris where English roses bloom and scent the morning dew with forgotten fragrance of a lost era. I know a little taste of England set in a hill station where lavender and thyme thrive. I know a garden where chrysanthemums bloom nodding their busy heads, smiling in the golden morning, peering from behind a blazing coverlet of marigolds with fiery orange and canary yellow faces. I know a patch of herbs hewn from English soil, lovingly transported across the seas to rest on the top of a hill overlooking the dreamy valley below. I know a garden where sweet English pansies and jasmine fuse in delicate profusion. Once upon a lifetime I knew it all so well; I wonder if, after all these years, it is as it was.

I recall caring hands that planted and watered seeds and harvested the bounty to adorn tabletops and windowsills. I remember a beautiful, genteel, old woman with bright blue eyes and coiffed silver hair, but she is long gone and rests in peace on Tiger Hill, in the Blue Mountain sanctuary of past souls—"ashes to ashes dust to dust." She lies next to her beloved husband in a tranquil graveyard like any other in rural England, except that wild bison jump over tea plants and destroy the crops and kill anyone who traverses their pathway. I will journey back to the Land of Durga, to the Nilgiris, to dig away the ravages of time and clear away mossy lichen that encrusts her name. I will place flowers on her grave. I will find her again through a veil of sorrow and replace tears with a smile. I will find you, dear Great Granny.

CHAPTER I

Back

"Hello, Mum, I've just seen an amazing price for air tickets to India, and you know how we've always wanted to go back; well, this might be our chance. The special offer lasts until the end of the weekend: What do you think?" urged my son over the phone.

"That would be great, darling, but . . . ."

"There's an educational project in Tamil Nadu. We could raise money for schools."

My mind conjured visions of unbearable monsoon heat, unclean accommodation, insects, mosquitoes, and stomach bugs—everything I dreaded. "It's a wonderful idea, but I don't think I could face it. At the moment all I want is rest and comfort and a five star hotel on my travels."

When I put down the phone, my words rebounded. Was I being selfish? A flood of pride for my son's idea washed over my conscience. Two years stuck in a loveless marriage culminating in a recent divorce had left me afraid to be adventurous again. I had been tethered to the confines of my home, travelling no farther than my work, which made me fearful to step out beyond my comfort zone. Had I lost my sense of adventure down a sluggish drain of complacency? In the quiet of the early evening, sitting in my conservatory watching the light slowly drift to another world, I began to allow possibilities to fall into my mind. Could I dare to step into the unknown again? Was I prepared to wrestle with my paranoia of insects, filth and scampering creatures? The night was heavy with doubt that I could tolerate such a trip pressing into my safe world; but curiosity tantalised me.

Through sips of fruity wine in the loneliness of the evening, I gained strength to throw my reservations out of the window, including the excuse of my age, having been advised by my youngest daughter that sixty is the new forty. I began to plan my fund raising projects, but behind the still quiet strings of certainty, the pulse beat to the tune of "what ifs" conflicting with a delicious awareness of new possibilities. I had longed to return to India for many years and I argued with myself that the travelling wouldn't be difficult every day. With my son's good planning, we could cosset ourselves on parts of the journey by staying in some lovely places. I tempted myself with the excitement of adventure and unwittingly, before I had time to change my mind, I found my passport and phoned my son.

The weeks quickly passed in planning and executing fund raising activities. I began a poetry competition for children and an end of term show. Branden organised a whole series of fund raising projects at his school. Together the outcome exceeded all expectations and we felt at ease with our desire for adventure.

Now it is early morning, as I sip coffee, counting down the days for my departure, ticking my compulsory injections off my list and noting medicines required for Tamil Nadu. I remember the injections for my Guatemalan expedition that made me sick but in retrospect, I was glad to have had the protection after encountering stomach bugs, mosquito bites and the threat of being bitten by a rabid dog. Without the protection of the antibodies, things might have been much worse. The sharp taste of the coffee reminds me of the time I traipsed through the Guatemalan coffee plantation, high up in the mountains of Santiago Zamora, where a band of brave women were struggling to provide education for their children against the strong deterrence of many in their village. They were proud to show me the coffee beans growing on the bushes and the ripe harvested husks that, surprisingly, were a myriad of colours like glazed pottery after the first firing. The beans were ground on ancient stone and hot rainwater poured over the granules making an undrinkable bitter liquid that I surreptitiously poured into the bare earth floor when no one was looking.

A thin smear of melting mist trickles down the window. It is late July and as the sun breaks through the clouds, light streams off the rooftops onto the grey slates. The end of another summer term at school approaches and I recall that is two years since I travelled to Cuba. Time has a strange way of creeping up on you and tying you in a straight jacket of mundane routine, until ultimately, the straps break, and you wake up, like Rip van Winkle, to find that weeks and months have drifted into years, and the years have become trapped in a safety net, imprisoning you to a cosy armchair. Real travel demands part of yourself that you have to be prepared to give heedlessly. Travel is like the pouring of time through a sieve; some parts glide through the mesh easily, while other aspects pulp, clogging up the mechanics of the journey and interrupting the natural flow of events with breakdowns, delays and detours. I am uncertain whether I am capable of giving so much of myself again to the unknown as I have lost the confidence to take risks.

While standing in my kitchen watching the sun spill through the trees, I contemplate the journey back to India and question my ability to cope. Suddenly, a bright vision flashes onto my white kitchen wall undulating, like a strobe light flickering through a film of dust. It is diamond shaped with a circular pattern in the centre, shimmering with an ultraviolet intensity and gleaming with an amazing breathtaking luminescence. I examine the walls to trace a reflection of something caught in the early morning sunshine, but there is nothing. I am drawn into the centre of the glistening vision as the glowing, revolving cosmos swirls outwards towards another dimension. Then it dissolves leaving no trace of an unearthly space in the void of the blank wall. The flickering pattern reminds me of the mystical signs for Durga, which I first encountered on a pre-engagement visit to India with Will, my husband to be, when we visited his family home in West Bengal. It was Durga Puja, the time of great rejoicing and celebrations for the goddess.

I remember walking through the crowded bazaar in the heat of the evening with clashing cymbals and tinkling bells amidst the chanting throng, as swirling dancers dipped in and out of focus through a golden sea of flickering candles blazing over a multitude of garish statues. Fresh jasmine flowers perfumed the humid evening mingling with the smell of hot wax as festive faces danced through the flames of the wayside fires. A grimy film of coal dust from nearby mines fed by cooking fires, hung three feet off the ground in the atmosphere clinging like a cloudy, murky curtain. I was sucked into the moment; held spellbound by the festival and the magic of the exotic images that remain embedded in my memory.

Mulling over the strange apparition on my kitchen wall, I think of the time just after I married Will, when we returned from our honeymoon in India. I was sitting on the sofa in our small flat in London, sewing a design of Durga on my calico blouse. It was Saturday afternoon and Will, being a keen photographer, was clicking away with his new camera. A few weeks passed before he got the film developed, and we were both shocked by the results. He had taken several photos of me sitting sewing, but neither of us had been aware of the strange light that crossed my chest where the design of Durga rested, or the amazing apparition of the goddess emblazoned in a golden light on the wall above my head, which was an exact replica of the one I was sewing. I had no idea at the time that the goddess was an omen of things to come and further adventures in India.

I walk into the garden where echoes from the past shadow the once carefully tended rockery. Weeds invade the roses. The recent failure of my third marriage saps my enthusiasm to tackle the overgrowth and with no spare money to buy seasonal plants, the garden lies forlorn. Again I face worries about finances and stress about being alone. I miss my little dog running in the grass and his happy face. To replace the emptiness, I have bought a little cat from the R.S.P.C.A. rescue centre. She is a mixture of Siamese and Tonkinese, an Oriental blend, creating a minx of a cat. I first saw Sheba when I went to visit the centre where my daughter was a volunteer dog walker and spied her climbing up her cage crying out to me with her electric green eyes and her sleek grey/blue fur glinting in the afternoon sunlight. I fell in love with her, but the notice on her cage gave a warning. She had belonged to an old woman who died just after she had bought her and a few people had taken her in, but she was too wild to adjust to family life. She had been given to a businessman, but he sent her back as she seemed untamable, biting and scratching at every opportunity. I felt sorry for her and was willing to take a risk.

I was nervous when I collected her as I was aware of her wild nature, and two young female assistants had to throw a cover over her to bundle her into the carrying cage. In my kitchen, I put down the carrier gingerly and arranged some food in a bowl and carefully opened the bars. At first she was very wary of me, but she soon realised she had the run of the place and shot out like a bat out of hell scurrying everywhere. I delighted at her newfound freedom as she went crazy bounding up and down the stairs, darting around every corner and investigating secret dark places. Slowly she has learnt to accommodate me, only occasionally lashing out. One morning when I was just waking, I felt her creep up the sheets to look at me. I was nervous to see what she would do, so I kept my eyes closed and felt a soft paw gently tap my hand. There were no claws, no sharp needle teeth, just a soft nudge. She had accepted me and I was filled with glowing warmth.

She plays in the bright sunlight, pouncing at shadows in the grass. I worry about what she might lay at my feet. She brings into the house dead and half-dead mice, as well as dead baby rats and ducklings; but I accept her nature and I am prepared to live with it. I know that while I am away my youngest daughter will take good care of her and help to tame her. As she springs into action, she is a tigress hunting prey and her careful poise midair is the powerful stalk of the Bengal tiger. Soon I will be back on Tiger Hill in the Nilgiris in search of my past. It is forty years since my first visit, and time has forged new pathways in many different directions. I wonder if my past will meet the present amicably or will it stir up all kinds of unresolved emotions. I am excited about the adventure ahead but there is also a lingering unidentifiable melancholy, which coils its tentacles around my memories where something lurks, hiding in the recesses: something that is buried waits to be resurrected and I am apprehensive.

One week later, I arrange to stay with my son for the weekend in London to organise our visas for the trip. Sitting in his lovely garden under the night sky, sipping velvety red wine we discuss our plans. Branden outlines our circular tour around Tamil Nadu, pointing out amazing places where we will stay, giving us opportunities to inspect schools. We will fly directly to Chennai from Heathrow. The new name, Chennai, is bland, bereft of the sights, sounds, smells and colours of old Madras, which was my very first taste of India. I was twenty years old when I flew there with my boyfriend, William, whose family on both sides had been stalwarts of the British Raj. Will's grandfather, on his mother's side, had helped to build the railways and had his own train with a single carriage in which he travelled up and down the countryside inspecting the lines. His grandparents on his father's side had been Indigo planters, hailing from Ireland and had connections with the well-known Irish whiskey family.

His father, Jeremy, had been an officer in the Indian police and had friends everywhere, so that when we first arrived in Madras we were taken to his friend's house in the suburbs where I tasted garlic bread for the very first time. I had lived all my life in rural England, brought up by country folk with simple tastes and had never eaten garlic before. The transition from a peaceful, tiny village to the brutal brashness and mayhem of the centre of Madras was overwhelming. Chaos reigned. Bicycle horns hooted, cars incessantly beeped, rickshaws screeched their squeaky hooters and horse-drawn carriage bells clanged impatiently, bombarding the stifled air. The intolerable boiling temperature cloyed my mouth and sucked out my energy like a hungry dog licking marrowbone jelly from a lamb bone. My clothes hung limp and stuck to my body. I had never known such intrusive heat, like oppressive leaden irons. It suffocated the air with the stench of unwashed bodies, stale sweat, untreated sewage and dank water in drains. The breeze, when it came, was fiery with spices, lingering with the smell of garam masala, which never died, only faded in the hot night air to be resurrected with added pungency early the next morning.

Everything was different. My secluded life in a farming village had not prepared me for the shocking living conditions—beggars on the streets, naked, diseased children and bodies slumped in gutters decaying and dying in worthless heaps, while cows roamed in and out of the pandemonium at will and were considered more precious than human life. On my first visit I was shocked by these sights and more—little children drinking from dirty puddles in the road, people born with monstrous deformities left to fend for themselves and children who had been deliberately maimed and scarred in order to earn money begging. I was not used to being attacked by hordes of children clambering for money. I was not used to the staring crowds. I was not used to having servants. I was not used to insects and mosquitoes and the drumming of the crickets. For twenty years of my life I had grown to know my world and had been living in it comfortably, but travelling to a different continent where I knew nothing and felt inadequate to face everything, my world had been turned upside down. It had been the greatest challenge I could ever imagine; would India challenge me again forty years on?

As the early morning sunlight spreads across the dappled sky back in my garden, I pause to watch the fish quivering, rising to the top of my pond in a very different setting from the exotic, tropical Indian estates where the jungle brush is never far away, forever stealing into the cultivated soil, demanding to take back the land in one gulp. I was young when India cast its spell over me and a whole lifetime has drifted by, like a sailboat on an open sea, day in and day out riding out storms, surging forwards when the wind is good, slumping into days of lethargy when there is no driving force and forging on through the foamy brine, until finally time has dictated the place to drop anchor. Once I was young and fresh to the world and I thought I had forever, but then one morning recently, I realised the path forwards fearfully, was only a step behind.

Forty years after my first visit, I wonder how things have changed and what I will find so different. It is like attending a school reunion; it can be foolish to think that you will relate to people who have metamorphosed into strangers with personalities so far removed from the ones that excited, inspired and amused you way back then. I did not want to be disappointed and shatter the magic of my memories.

Remembering the past made me nervous; there were aspects that were uncomfortable to recall. In the quiet of my garden as I watch the fish dart back under the rocks, the early morning sunshine fades and a gentle breeze stirs the roses. I wonder if there are roses blooming in Great Granny's garden in India. She was not my grandmother, but Will's. I recall my first meeting with her. I had heard she was an amazing woman with incredible healing power and that people wrote to her from all over the world to procure "absent healing" to cure not only themselves but animals. I was shocked, given her Victorian proclivities, to hear that she had once healed a stripper's snake. She and her sister had been sent away to boarding schools in England when they were very young and had returned to Simla in their late teens, where their parents enjoyed an extremely privileged lifestyle. They were close friends with the British Consulate and were treated like royalty and so it was imperative that I made a good impression.

My first ride up the mountain to her home in the hills was terrifying. Will and I innocently hired the first taxi we could find from Coimbatore at a cheap price, not questioning the driver's skill, being naively unaware that many drivers had never passed any tests or had any driving lessons. Along the sandy, dusty roads unevenly carved through makeshift shops, the highway was more like a fairground racetrack than a high street. Our little man scraped the gears into action, carving his way precariously through tiny spaces in between the traffic, regardless of what was in front. Will and I were petrified sitting bolt upright, unable to enjoy the ride. I tried not to look ahead, but to my disgust, the scene in the streets of men coughing and spitting up red phlegm on the side of the road made me feel sick, as I thought it was blood. Will assured me, however, that it was only the juice from beetle nut, which everyone copiously chewed and spat out onto the sandy road.

The dashboard was strewn with religious icons, beads, family photos and incense sticks burning a slow coiling smoke screen over the windscreen. Fresh garlands of jasmine flowers rocked and swayed as we swerved through bicycle taxis, rickshaws, horse-drawn carriages, motorbikes, cars and jostling crowds. We closed our eyes as we whizzed blindly around corners and edged through narrow indents in the potholed road. Eventually we left the torrid heat of the plains in a cloud of dust and began our ascent up the mountain, where the trees on the steep ledges created a heavenly canopy of shade. The sun sought to beat streaming shafts through the branches, but the foliage was too thick for penetration and gave protection against the continual glare. The road in places was not wide enough to take a two-way traffic stream, but our driver ploughed on regardless, racing around corners as though he owned the right of way. All Will and I could do was to close our eyes and trust that nothing was coming the other way. Several times when another vehicle fought for road space, our foolhardy driver took the law into his own hands and forced his way through. Will and I were parched from the heat, and the tension from the journey panicked us more than we dared to admit. Our backs stuck to the leather seats in a glued lather, so that by the time we eventually arrived at Granny's house, I knew I looked dreadful.

I appeared on her front porch, along with her beloved grandson, with my long hair dishevelled, my eye makeup smudged and my face dirty from an impromptu scramble amongst rocks and a waterfall, which Will had instigated to alleviate the tension of the drive. Granny was not amused and to make matters worse, I didn't arrive with bundles of bags and suitcases, just a scrappy rucksack. Disdainfully she showed us inside. My sixties, hippy style blouse and my tight jeans did not impress her. I was a new breed of young woman, the likes of which she did not approve worst of all, I was her grandson's girlfriend and she had hoped for someone like Princess Anne.

Will was given his mother's bedroom and his grandfather's dressing room. I was shown to Will's childhood bedroom. I was not used to the high, Indian style, corrugated tin roofs like the ones in the cow sheds at home; nor the strange bathroom with a square, concrete corner sectioned off with gullies cut out to take the excess water, like a cattle dip back on the farm, complete with steel buckets turned upside down and carbolic soap perched on the sink. Windows in the high roof shed light from above and I stifled a scream when I spied a wide-eyed, hairy face staring down at me as I went to the toilet. The monkey seemed to jeer as I hurriedly washed my hands. I had only ever seen monkeys behind bars in zoos and I was nervous being prey to the monkey's curiosity. Shaken, I retreated into Will's room to sit on the lumpy bed and wait. I was cut off from the main house and tinges of homesickness and loneliness began to taint my self-confidence. I knew Granny didn't like me and made her feelings known to Will, so that he kept his distance and offered no comfort or support. I had hoped he would visit my room to reassure me all was well, but the house remained still. After the trials of a two-day journey from England to Coonoor, to sit dejectedly listening to an antique clock echoing monotonously around unfamiliar whitewashed walls was hell.

The house was a strange amalgam of English and Indian cultures, steeped in the Victorian era of Granny's childhood with all her old-fashioned ideas and principles cemented into the fabric of a little piece of India. The grounds replicated a quintessential English cottage garden set under the haze of the atmospherically charged Nilgiris sky. Many British people had settled in the Nilgiris because the climate and the beautiful mountains reminded them of the familiar English Lake District, but with its tigers, wild dogs, dingoes and bison claiming lives, it was far from homelike. Time dragged wearily through the afternoon, and I was afraid to leave my room. I suppose they thought I was resting, but I desperately wanted company. Eventually when we sat down to eat in the dark dining room with its highly polished furniture and glass cabinets laden with shiny silverware, which were presents from the deceased King of England and his Consulate in India, I was lost in the grandeur of the moment. I had never been taught aristocratic table manners or learnt what, when and how to use certain pieces of cutlery for specific dishes. My background was that of a working class family who rarely sat down to more than two courses at meal times and where one knife, fork and spoon were quite adequate for one person at one sitting!

I sat opposite Granny like a naughty child. With her piercing eyes scrutinizing my every move; I felt deflated. I had no fine dress to bedazzle her or impress Will, just my basic tee shirts, one evening dress, which was really a nightdress that my music teacher had bought me as a farewell gift, and a couple of short miniskirts, which were unsuitable for the Indian culture, of which I was ignorant. I watched Will and his grandmother and copied them. I wanted to hide my broken, dirty nails as Granny's were beautifully manicured and delicately polished in pale pink varnish. Her hands were long, thin and elegant. Her make-up was immaculate with only a hint of powder and blusher and a thin line of rose-pink lipstick. Her complexion was flawless. Her glossy silver hair was immaculately tucked in a neat bun at the back of her upright neck, and her forget-me-not blue blouse matched her striking eyes.

I was in awe of Granny's quick mind and sharp intelligence. Strange as it may seem, I had never known such a clever old lady. All the members of my family had never been educated beyond the basics of reading and writing. I was the first person in my family to have higher education and to be granted a university place. My great-grandfather had been the village poacher and to feed his fourteen children, had been forced to catch sparrows in the garden for my great grandmother to make into pies. My grandparents were ordinary country folk and my parent's working class, but most of the family did play the piano, dance and sing, as it was a traditional way of making their own entertainment and that "performing world" influenced my life.

Will had explained that whenever Granny travelled, she had a servant on hand to tidy her hair, clean her shoes, arrange her clothes and provide sustenance whenever necessary. Granny never appeared anywhere without pristine preparation. She never came out of her dressing room before eleven o'clock in the morning unless her maid servant, Mary, had done her nails, brushed her hair one hundred and fourteen times and served her breakfast in private. I listened in awe of her talking about the stock exchange and the price of shares and how to manage financial matters. I admired her and wished I could emulate her easy, stylish grace. I had never experienced an old person with such worldly knowledge. None of the old people in my village knew anything about stocks and shares; their world evolved around the weather, local news and gossip. When I first went to college, my grandmother had to pluck up courage to go to the post office and use a public phone to contact me, which had been a terrifying experience for her, as it was a newfangled contraption brought into the village from the outside world. When I next visited her, she said, "It was very confusing picking up the telephone thing. I managed to get my money in the slot and I heard a buzzing, but you didn't answer and I didn't even hear your dog barking!" I smiled stifling a laugh. My grandfather had been a navigator in the First World War flying in tiny planes, which were no more than thin biscuit tins held together by glue and prayers. He had very little worldwide experience, blaming the bad weather on "all the space ships flying around disturbing the sky"; and he would say to me, "You know, those scientists are clever—whenever they find a new planet they always know its name!"

My background had been far from privileged and I was ignorant of the aristocratic world. My embarrassment heightened when certain dishes were placed before me and I had no idea how to eat the strange concoctions; such as whether to leave the vegetable skins on the vegetables or eat the seeds of the fruit or take them out. Will had not prepared me for such a trial and Granny left her seat to show me how to dress an avocado pear, how to tackle a custard apple and how to eat lady's fingers. I was inadequately prepared to fit in with their life-style and saw Will's humiliation at my ignorance. To make matters worse, I inadvertently flung Granny the worst insult I could ever muster. I had wanted to compliment her and told her that her complexion was like that of a "china doll," to which she immediately took umbrage. Apparently it was rude of me to address her in such a familiar way as it was considered impertinent; furthermore, the idea of being compared to a doll was grossly unacceptable. I had dug myself into a ditch and I had no idea how to climb out and no matter what I did or said, there was nothing I could say to retract my flippant flattery.

After dinner the oppressive tranquillity of the hills hung like a heavy curtain, imprisoning us all in an embarrassed silence. There was nothing to do. Granny did not allow alcohol in the house so we couldn't even relax with a drink. We sat on the veranda and listened to the world service on the crackly radio. Several times the electricity failed and we had to resort to candles. By eight thirty it was time to get ready for bed. Both Will and I were sent to our separate rooms at far ends of the house. My first night alone in my room was a nightmare. I fell on the unfamiliar bed and cried. I had made a fool of myself. I was afraid to go into the bathroom in case there was a monkey glaring at me, or worse, large spiders or insects waiting to pounce. As I lay on my stomach, the exotic night sounds drowned out the stillness. At first I thought someone was practising the Spanish castanets outside my window. The strong rhythm and loud clicking made me sit up and listen. Dancing was my nature and the call of the tempo focussed my mind on creating steps to match the pulse. I soon realised that the sound was a night creature and my imagination went into overdrive conjuring up an army of insects attacking. I jumped into bed to hide. I was afraid to turn out the light, but the electricity failed and I was plunged into darkness. Alone in the strange room with the night dissonance beating a racket outside my window, I was homesick and wanted to go back to England where I knew the rules and where I understood the people.

As I peeped from under the covers, something glittering caught my attention. I sat up to gaze at a floating ruby jewel dancing at the end of my bed. I had never seen such a beautiful glowing ember. It fizzed in the dark glistening in a golden halo and lighting up the night with fiery magic. Will had spoken about fireflies, but I had never imagined them to be so enchanting. I watched in wonderment as the single creature flew around my room switching its firework display on and off until it disappeared completely and I was left again in the stark blackness. The exquisite magic reminded me of an incident that occurred when I was about six years old. I had been upset and afraid of strange energies in my room. Too disturbed to sleep, I had sat up watching the twilight fade, fearful of what might emerge when suddenly I heard a beautiful haunting tune played on a reed pipe. Its unearthly melody soothed me to sleep. I tried to recall the eerie sound in the hope that I might be lulled into slumber, but I was terrified of things lurking and of mosquitoes waiting to bite and creatures on their nocturnal prowl for food. I hardly slept and only drifted to sleep as the first rays of dawn streaked through the moth-eaten curtains.

Eventually I got up to face the trials of the farmyard bathroom and breakfast. A servant had tidied up my wash things and left the window open. I searched for my toothpaste and was horrified to spy a monkey grimacing at me from the roof window with my toothpaste in his hands, lustily sucking out the peppermint paste. I hastily closed the window in case it jumped in. As Granny never appeared in the morning until she was perfectly coiffed, manicured and made up, Will and I had breakfast alone together in the grand dining room. Dickie introduced himself as our bearer in charge of our breakfast. He was a delightful little man with bright shining eyes lighting up his careworn dark face.

"I bring you special chili scrambled egg," he chuckled.

It was hard not to laugh when he appeared again balancing two large plates of bright yellow scrambled eggs with a little green chilli standing to attention like a phallus in the middle. Will spluttered over his coffee and I turned away, thanking Dickie.

"Oh missy Sahib, I very much hope you like it. Sahib Sir like it so much. You know one day when he was alive he nearly took me to England, on big boat. I had papers and all, and we went to Bombay where there are many big ships, but Sahib did not tell me about boat and open railings and I fell off the side into the big dirty water. Oh Missy Sahib, I got very ill from the water you see and never went to England. Oh yes, yes, yes, I tell you it was very big shame!"

His sorry story was so comical that I nearly choked on the eggs.

"I like you like my food, Missy Sahib. If you are too warm, I can put on electric fanny!"

Will and I nearly exploded with laughter but managed not to look at each other until he was back in the kitchen. Dickie's lighthearted banter set us in a good mood for the day, and by the time Granny appeared from her morning toilet we were smiling.

Day by day Granny was patient with me, getting to know and understand me, entrusting my skills with "little labours of love" as she called them, like mending holes in Will's jacket and sewing on buttons, all the kind of women's duties that she considered wifely. As I sat sewing under her watchful gaze, she talked to me about her life and healing. Slowly her attitude towards me mellowed, especially when I played the guitar for dinner parties and was asked to give a lecture at the hill station university on the Psychology, Sociology and Philosophy of Drama Teaching in Education. I practised my speech on her and she seemed pleased with the results. I had learnt to say my opening sentence in Hindi but when I delivered it, I was so nervous that it came out backwards, much to everyone's surprise and amusement.

I was the honoured guest at lunch that day in the university and was invited to approach the buffet, which was set out on a long trestle table. After I had taken a token sample of everything, a hushed silence descended and a quiet tittering arose from the women gathered in the hall. I plucked up the courage to approach one of them asking tentatively, "Have I done something wrong?"

The woman looked away shyly smiling and replied, "Yes, you have put your pudding on the same plate as your main course!"

I laughed and we all laughed together, alleviating the tension. I explained that quite often we put fruit together with our curry, but they smiled wryly and pretended not to notice my stupid mistake.

Sundays were always a source of embarrassment as I was not allowed to wear trousers or jeans, and the only dress I had was a mini dress, which was considered by Granny to be brash and common. She made me cover my legs with a shawl when we went to Church, and I felt uncomfortable and silly. Back in the confines of our garden I was allowed to walk freely, but only under the shade of an umbrella, as it was considered a sin to become sun-blushed. I had been used to running around on a farm jumping in haystacks and milking goats. I never dared tell Granny this, as she would have thought me a heathen and as it was, she was training me to "eat like a Christian" whatever that entailed!

Despite our differences, however, I grew to love her and by the end of my first visit, I think she had also grown to accept me and love me too. Eventually my first visit ended and as I stood on her doorstep looking deeply into her sea-blue eyes, we were both sad. I felt insecure leaving her and the place I had accepted as my surrogate home. I knew she had unwittingly accepted me as her granddaughter-to-be and I was grateful for that. The journey we were about to face was harsh; it entailed travelling three days non-stop on a train. Just as I turned to leave, she put her arm around my shoulder and said,

"Now remember, dear, if ever you need me, I'll hear you whether I'm asleep or awake! Just call me and I will be there."

I marvelled at her words and repeated them constantly in my head as I watched the familiar eucalyptus trees fade in the distance and the Blue Mountains dissolve behind me as the driver sped out through the forests and down the winding roads back to where the atmosphere grew hotter by the minute, plunging us back into the sticky humidity of the boiling heat of the plains.

In Coimbatore, Will and I boarded a train to Calcutta, but as students we could not afford the best seats and so travelled with what he called the "unwashed." I thought how Granny would be shocked if she knew, as she once had her own carriage and servants to tend to her every need whilst travelling on the family train around the countryside. All Will and I had was a dirty, tiny bit of the seat in the carriage that we had booked just for us and I was shocked when we were forced to share it with unwashed strangers, who lay under the seats, and crouched by our feet, and lay in the luggage rack. Will explained, everyone took it for granted that when you travelled third class, it was a free for all. Men jumped in through the windows until our carriage was ceiling high with bodies and some even hung off the windows. I was shocked by the intrusion, but kept rigidly still trying to avoid the gaze of men with curious eyes. I understood why Will's mother always travelled with a small gun tucked in her handbag.

Gradually as the train sped through the jungle passing pockets of villages, the number of bodies in our carriage dwindled until there were just four, Will and I and two men who were office *wallas* dressed in the loose white uniform of pen-pushers, complete with black rimmed glasses and bundles of paper. When we stopped in stations, we were attacked by a tirade of beggars and children selling meagre snacks with the call of "*Chai, walla, chai, Beechams,* Sahib, *kergolis*!" ringing from every doorway. Will laughed as he translated the cries as: "Tea, tea, Beecham's balls for the white men,"- meaning medicines and pills. A multitude of small hands poked through the bars into the carriage begging for money. One little boy shouted he would get me a frothy coffee and I agreed. A few minutes later he appeared with a foaming plastic cup. I paid him, but the moment he handed it to me through the bars he ran away. I took a sip and spat it out. The froth was soap!

Needing to go to the lavatory, I pushed, pulled and stepped over bodies in the corridors before finding the door hidden in a corner surrounded by a group of men who were sitting on the floor gambling and rolling dice along the swaying, uneven boards. They let me pass and as I opened the door, I nearly fell backwards. The stench was insufferable. There was only a hole in the middle of the dirty wooden boards where the tracks rolled past. I thought at first someone had stolen the lavatory and looked around hoping to find it, but there was only an open fissure juddering from side to side as the train sped along. Any accurate aim would be virtually impossible and so the closet was besmirched in urine and excrement which had piled up in heaps over the floor and walls. Crouching was out of the question as there was nothing to hold on to. I had no alternative but to relieve myself watching my urine trail in rivulets over the boards along with everyone else's! There was no paper, only a tap and a battered steel jug. Hurriedly, I plunged my hands into the rusty water and exited quickly. My open-toe sandals were embarrassingly wet as were my legs and trousers. I tried to step carefully over the men, but the swerving movement of the train in motion made it impossible and I ended up falling on top of them. When I returned to the carriage, I burst into tears. I couldn't imagine travelling two more nights and three days in that unbearable condition.

As the train rolled on, I began to feel sick, not just physically but mentally disoriented. I had entered a world of horrendous sights, the likes of which I had never imagined. People were living in unendurable poverty, while I had experienced a way of life that they could never own. I struggled to come to terms with the duality of India and her caste system. When we stopped in another station, I avoided the cries and pleas of the children and hid behind a newspaper. It was late afternoon and Will had ordered us a meal. A bearer entered our carriage beautifully dressed in an impressive uniform complete with red and gold turban. His old, rugged face beamed a toothless grin as he handed each of us a steel tray which he meticulously cleaned with his tea towel. Standing back ceremoniously, he ordered his minion to slosh dollops of rice, *dahl*, mutton curry and tiny splodges of pickles onto our trays. I looked at Will in disgust, but he was used to the procedure. I asked for cutlery, but Will laughed saying, "You eat with your fingers like this, with your right hand, and don't get the food beyond your knuckles!"

I was astounded. I watched the bearer walk back onto the platform in his fine regalia and was horrified to see him take the same tea towel, with which he had wiped down my tray, and lay it out carefully on the dirty floor to sit on. I wanted to vomit. Will was already tucking into his meal with great gusto and I stared at mine disdainfully. I felt guilty that many starving children were crying out for food and I couldn't bring myself to eat because of the thought of the filth. I tried to put a little rice into my mouth, but I gagged.

Will offered to eat mine and I was relieved. At the next station the empty trays were collected, and I ordered an orange Fanta knowing that no one could have tampered with it. As the evening drifted into night, the heat did not subside. I watched the two office *wallas* in the carriage open out the seat into beds and close their eyes on the world. Will read his book, and I gazed at the night fires burning in the villages and waved back to a goatherd boy. Just as I turned back into the carriage, I caught a glimpse of something creeping out of my seat. A huge cockroach with its brown, shiny back nonchalantly wriggled its antennae at me and slipped out of its day lair into the bright lights. I stifled a scream and nudged Will to do something about it but by the time he leaped up, the creature had sidled down the back of the seat. A trickle of fear rolled down my back. I was terrified of creepy crawlies and couldn't lie down on the seat to sleep in case the cockroach came out to creep across my sleeping body.

During the night, I developed a fever. Ranting and raving as the train trundled on with the rhythm beneath me pounding out the miles, Will and two pairs of strange hands tried to pour rusty water down my throat. Someone came and a sharp pain in my arm made me sleep. In the drowsy dawn I called to Granny. I asked for help to make me better, sending a myriad of befuddled religious questions through the night to disturb her sleep. Through my delirium I heard Granny answer, healing me with her soft power. In the bright morning light, I noted that the two office *wallas* had departed and I sat up declaring I was well. I told Will that I was sure Granny had helped me, but I thought that it was just a dream. Somehow I managed to cope with the rigours of the rest of the journey, so that when we finally arrived in Calcutta and was met by Will's mother waiting for us on the platform, I was relieved beyond measure. She was friendly and chatty and held out a letter for me to see. She said: "I received this letter from my mother this morning enquiring if you were well, as you asked for her help on the train. She also wondered if she managed to answer all your questions."

    I was dumbfounded. I believed in telepathy but was always shocked when the evidence was real. The letter was concrete proof that telepathic communication had happened between Granny and me and that she had definitely helped to heal my sickness giving me strength to face the challenges of my situation and the tragic events that lay in wait.

CHAPTER 2

Ghost

Granny's daughter, Prudence, was not surprised in the slightest by the amazing letter her mother had written. Granny just wanted to know if I was better. Prudence couldn't journey with us to her home in West Bengal as she had shopping to attend to in Calcutta and would catch up with us later. Will's father, Jeremy, was going to meet us along the Grand Trunk Road, so Rashid, their trusty driver, was assigned to take us to the meeting place.

The drive from Calcutta through West Bengal was very different from the serenity of the hill station. We passed endless rice fields with children and people of all ages working long hours with their feet planted in a bed of water, digging in new rice shoots. We warily circumnavigated water buffalo with horns painted green and red, trudging along the highway pulling carts. Farther along we passed villagers carrying bundles of wood on their heads and women carrying water pots on their shoulders and some balancing large pots of vegetables on their heads. Driving through the villages we saw tanks, into which everyone performed their daily ablutions, washed their clothes, cleaned their teeth and drank the water. A different pulse of life throbbed within the plains as people toiled in the humid heat struggling to survive.

Along the Grand Trunk Road convoys of brightly coloured trucks lined the way with ornate writing and little sayings painted on the back of each vehicle like "okay," "ta ta for now," "a stitch in time saves ninety" or "Bata, there is no anything money can't buy." Eventually we stopped at a high-class "jungalow," a bungalow in the jungle set aside for privileged visitors. We parked under a huge tree away from the glare of the midday sun and found Jeremy waiting for us. He was a lovely, friendly, handsome man of fifty-seven years of age. He was one of nature's gentlemen and always put others before himself. He was witty and intelligent, having taught himself to speak, read and write five different Indian languages. He had been in the Indian police and fought in many riots trying to keep the peace through difficult times. He had given up the police force to work for Andrew Yule Company in the coalfields in West Bengal. Through the brush scrub we made ourselves comfortable in the garden and Jeremy unpacked several containers of food and served us hot coffee from a thermos flask. He was easy to talk to and made me feel welcome and had a wonderful sense of humour.

I sat in the back of the car with him on our way to the house, watching the world slip by with the windows wide open, tasting a film of dry, dusty earth caking my lips. Jeremy delighted at my reaction to the wild countryside as he pointed out typical tiger landscape and elephants working in the fields. I was agog at the way the elephants picked up heavy tree trunks with one fell swoop, placing them gently on the ground as though they were matchsticks. Vultures perched by the side of the road. I had never seen such disgusting creatures. They repulsed me with their scrawny, bloodstained necks and their beady eyes, watching, waiting for death to deliver their next meal. The smell of West Bengal was different to the eucalyptus and pine freshness of the mountains as the air was thick with soot from the coal mines and with earthiness from the paddy fields mingling with overtones of cooking spices. For some reason our conversation strayed to philosophical themes and I heard myself saying from afar, as though I were being used by an outside energy, " When we have achieved our greatest vibration in a lifetime, like a taut violin string, which cannot be pulled farther, we break free and leave our earthly home." Jeremy understood the message beyond my comprehension. I had no idea why I had chosen those words, but I know I was guided to pass on a message to him, for death was already tracking his shadow.

Will's parents' bungalow was surrounded by paddy fields and jungle. Their garden was tamed and tended by a small workforce of gardeners who kept the jungle at bay so that the family could enjoy exotic flowers, fruit and vegetables. Their Siamese cats helped to keep down the snakes, although when Will was a baby, his Iah found a poisonous viper curled up at the bottom of his cot and had to fetch one of the snake charmers to remove it. The long veranda had "chicks" (blinds made from reed matting) protecting every open window from the glare of the sun and the battering of the monsoon rain. Geckos scampered out of sight as we entered and I shuddered at the thought of them running wild; I had only ever seen them behind glass cases in zoos.

Inside, the living room was decorated in the fifties style, complete with a large square radio on a stand, a neat high-backed sofa daintily decorated with antimacassars and a couple of staunch matching easy chairs. Beyond was a large, dark mahogany, highly polished grand piano and a dining table complete with antique silverware handed down through the family from King George. All the floors were white marble enabling effective and easy cleaning, as all the doors to the bedrooms and bathrooms lead off the one living space and Will delighted in recounting how, when he was young, he used to slide naked on his bottom from one end of the house to the other on a soapy trail of suds.

I was shown to Will's old room, and he was given his parent's dressing room with a makeshift bed. Something twitched behind the painting on the wall just behind the bed. A gecko darted across the wall and up the ceiling with its scaly dinosaur tail swishing. I stifled a scream and told myself I had to get used to it or die! My room was situated to the left of the main room through a single door, and I felt safer if I opened it so that I could see the rest of the house; but at that moment something furry ran in from outside and hid under the sofa. I screamed. Will laughed; "It's only a mongoose, you silly fright-bear!"

A mongoose, geckos—I was a gibbering wreck fighting my phobias of anything rat-like, or crawly. Had I known what was in store I might have fled? At that moment Prudence arrived in a flurry amidst boxes and large bags towed by servants. She waved as she disappeared into her bedroom shouting, "Dinner at seven." I decided to wear my only long dress, as I knew no one would know it was really a nylon nightdress cut in Regency, under the bust, style, in fawn and burgundy. I scraped my hair up on top of my head not realizing that it was a male Sikh style; Will's father found it odd but didn't say anything, though his eyes betrayed his thoughts.

When we all sat at the grand table to eat, the air was heavy and claustrophobic. The monsoon humidity was overpowering and my nylon dress was not the best material to wear in that climate. Sweat poured in tiny rivulets down my back and I tried to ignore the sweat beading on my forehead. Just as we were about to start our soup, a gecko ran across the ceiling. I nearly choked. It paused in the centre above the table uncurling its coiled grey tongue ready to catch a fly and as it shot out, it shed its dead skin tail in the middle of the large silver tureen splattering splodges of vegetable soup over the white tablecloth. Everyone laughed, but I was horrified. I forced myself to remain calm as a servant, Sathu, rushed forward and removed the offending sight. As I looked up, geckoes were watching from vantage points all over the walls, sticking out their curly tongues ready to whiplash flies and insects in mid flight. No one else was panicking. To them it was perfectly normal. Inside I was panicking in and out of a nightmare and was on the verge of rising up out of my seat and screaming hysterically, but I made myself stay still and cope with the situation.

The evening passed with polite conversation but Will and I were very tired after our long journey and bid his parents goodnight, departing in opposite directions of the house. I had resigned myself to Will's distance and his formal aloofness around his family. I felt detached and remote from all that I had known and resolved to carve a new existence for myself in a different world and learn to adapt and win through the challenges. As I walked into the bedroom and closed the door, fear flooded my mind and fired my imagination with monster insect images waiting to pounce. I stood rooted to the spot afraid to move in case something ran at me, or flew at me or scampered at my feet. I had been told to store my shoes upside down and to shake them out before putting them on in case a scorpion was hiding inside. I had never considered facing a live scorpion, or finding one hidden in my shoe. After a few minutes of standing still, I plucked up the courage to move to the bed, telling myself that I was not going to be murdered by a gecko and that it was probably more afraid of me than I of it.

A cough outside my window made me start. I had forgotten that an armed guard was keeping watch outside my room. He was a small, fat man, who wore his uniform of red and gold with great pride but had no training with guns and often held his rifle upside down or leaned on it like a walking stick. Will laughed when he told me that the little man had nearly shot off his own foot when he was asked to stand to attention. Apparently he was a decoy to scare away intruders, especially a marauding, renegade political group, the Naxolites, who were rioting in the region. They had chopped off the British governor's head and sent it to his wife in a basket, so Will's family was cautious, in case the rebel group targeted them.

I didn't dare take off my sandals as I noticed big black ants creeping in by the bathroom. At home I would have stamped on them, but there were too many and I was trying to adopt a new policy of adaptation rather than annihilation. Inside I was shaking with terror as I tried to cope with my silly phobia. I switched on the bathroom light. Giant cockroaches with brown armored backs and twirling feelers were swarming up the bath. In and around the lavatory insects buzzed and hid behind the pipes. The sink had black patches of insects feeding around the plughole. I stamped my feet and made low howling noises in the hope that it might frighten them as I hitched up my dress and perched over the toilet seat, fearful to sit down in case something bit my bottom. I looked away from the sink as I washed my hands. Stomping back to the bedroom, I noticed that more black ants had marched in and claimed further territory. The opposite corner housed another type of brown ant that had set up camp in the nocturnal fight for territory. No one had explained to me that at night two species of ant would invade the white marble floor in a black and brown undulating carpet fighting for territory through the night until dawn.

In bed, a queasy, uneasy, itching sensation began to creep up my naked body. Under a single sheet, my skin was wet, lathered with hot sweat from the monsoon heat, and cold with unimaginable night terror. I had become accustomed to the sounds, so the constant din did not scare me but in the dark under the mosquito net, tiny burning sensations over my body began to turn into a fierce itching. I tried to tell myself that I was imagining insects crawling all over my body and biting me. I imagined that my bed was an infested nest of crawly creatures. I tried to close my eyes, but the burning increased. I was afraid to reach my hand out through the mosquito net to turn on the light, but I forced myself to do it. In the beaming lamp light I saw little red ants scampering under my pillow, over the sheets and over my body. My bed was a nest of little red ants. My body was covered in disgusting red insects. I swung my legs over the side of the bed, horrified to see that the once white marble floor was aquiver with a mass of undulating black and brown ants swarming over each other and masses of dead ants lying on their backs. There was nowhere for me to tread except onto the crawling bodies.

I rushed to the bathroom to find the same riotous mayhem of the insect world fighting out their nightly battle. I had to wash off the ants and spray myself with cold water from the shower tap, so with half closed eyes I performed the task in a frenzied dance. When I returned to the bedroom I saw with utter horror, an army of red ants marching in from the top of the high tin roof, following each other nose to tail along the floor and up into my bed. I screamed for help. The guard outside my door, who was snoring, poked his tired head through the chick blinds, and Will came rushing in wearing his loon pyjamas. When he saw my distress and the ants, he too was shocked and took me back to the sitting room. Apparently that morning my mattress had been aired on the veranda and the ants had nested inside it. My first night in West Bengal had been a baptism of fire, the red ant kind, with a fiery bite that I would never forget.

We had arrived in West Bengal on a Thursday. Friday was spent looking around the area with a wonderful friend of the family, Major Stiffle, who drove us in his Land Rover and took immense time and trouble to entertain us. He was an Anglo-Indian with impeccable manners and a lovely smile. Friday evening we all went out to dinner and I wore my nightdress again, only with my hair down trailing across my shoulders, not Sikh style, much to Jeremy's relief. By Saturday evening Jeremy was dead. I had known him for such a short time, but he made a tremendous impression on me and on everyone else who knew him.

After we returned on Friday evening from the dinner, he had a heart attack brought on by a thrombosis in his left leg. He was rushed to hospital in the early hours of Friday morning. When I woke from another fitful night, having slept on a new mattress and not been eaten alive by red ants, I stepped into a different household. There was no one around. Will had gone. Sadhu met me on the veranda explaining he had laid a place for one at a small table overlooking the garden. "Please, little missy sahib, I serve your breakfast here. There is sad news. Sahib Sir is in hospital. Mem Sahib and Master Sahib are with him."

I nodded and sat down. My loneliness returned in waves. I was an intruder into a close family affair. I was sorry for Will as he hadn't seen his father for nearly seven years, and to be reunited with him for one day before he was rushed to hospital was terrible. Sadhu could not give me any more information, and I wondered what I should do. As an outsider I felt guilty for being there. I picked at the breakfast that was beautifully cooked and served, but I had lost my appetite. Suddenly Major Stiffle appeared and walked up the veranda steps. He took coffee with me, trying to hide his deep sorrow for his best friend behind polite conversation and forced smiles. He offered to take me for a ride to the bazaar and I gratefully accepted.

The bazaar in Asonsol was unlike anything I had ever experienced. It was a raw market with sounds and smells idiosyncratic to itself with its Eastern exoticism and Aladdin's cave treasures. Before we reached the bazaar a multitude of voices rising and falling in a haggling pitch, screeched across the dusty road with the clashing of *puja* cymbals and popular Hindi songs played on a worn out p.a. system, which pounded across the sun-bleached walls. In the middle of the market women sat on hand-woven mats selling spices of all different hues laid out in amazing designs. Similarly flowers and petals were displayed in intricate patterns on the bare earth, as were vegetables and chillies of every description exhibited like works of art. Bangles and beads, sparkly trinkets glittered in the afternoon sunlight. Holy men sat in tiny stalls, half-naked with their matted hair and shiny skin covered in layers of red and yellow paint. Incense burnt freely from brass pots and low humming prayers reverberated through the dense humidity. The Major insisted on buying me six sterling silver bangles, and I was overwhelmed by his generosity and kindness.

As we strolled in the baking heat, the Major told me about Jeremy and how the people loved him. He had the common touch and never turned away the needy from his door. I thought of him lying in hospital and my words to him, "When we have achieved our greatest vibration in a lifetime, like a taut violin string, which cannot be pulled farther, we break free and leave our earthly home." I knew he had achieved his life's work, and it was time for him to move on.

In the early evening I dined alone on the veranda, jangling my beautiful silver bracelets in the quiet of the house. Only the servants moved around softly. As the night quickly descended, I was afraid to sit outside, so I placed a chair half in and half out of the sitting room facing the drive so that I could see immediately if anyone appeared. I had dressed for dinner in my only long nightdress and sat like a princess waiting for the royal court to arrive. Suddenly there was a light, scuttling noise in the bushes. A plant near the door rustled. I froze. A massive hairy black spider the size of a large hand, hopped into the leaves with bulbous emerald, glowing eyes glowering in the dark. I froze imagining it jumping out and biting me with its fanged teeth. I wanted to run, but my legs were numb. My arms dangled aimlessly by my side. In my mind, I urged myself to get up, but I was glued to the green orbs flashing in the bush. Terror held me captive to the spot. I daren't close my eyes. Just when I thought my heart would pound through my chest, the armed guard appeared in his rotund, wobbly manner with his rifle upside down dangling by his side and his wide, fat face beaming. He politely addressed me and took up his post by the door by which time the spider had disappeared.

I ambled inside feeling helpless and hopelessly ill equipped to be of any use to anyone at such a serious time. The only thing I could do was to play the piano and fill the house with beautiful music, offering my good intentions into the cosmos to help Jeremy fly from his body through the vibration of harmony, back to where he truly belonged. The first few notes of Debussy's *Claire de Lune* reverberated with pure tones through the house and out into the stars. I could feel and see through my fingers the strings of energy pouring forth into the closed night, lifting the sound high above the world to a sphere beyond, in preparation for Jeremy's spiritual flight.

Just as I played the last chord, I heard someone on the porch. I closed the lid of the piano and went expectantly to see who had arrived. As I stood in the doorway a gushing, rushing wind stirred the bushes and whirled around the veranda. Instantly I knew it was Jeremy. He had returned in spirit to the house. I watched as his energy passed through me into the sitting room where it fizzed and bubbled, twirling like a tornado in a peaceful cornfield. His presence burned for a few moments, like the flame in a fanned candle then faded, leaving an empty pause in the atmosphere.

A few moments later, Will and his mother arrived in the car. They were drained of emotion. They had stayed by Jeremy's bed until he died. That night Will slept in his father's bed near his mother, and I slept in Will's bed in the dressing room, as we all needed to be together. The sudden shock of Jeremy's death had left us all deeply marooned on a strange island of bewilderment and we hadn't the energy to paddle our way back to normality.

The next morning was spent in funeral preparations. Prudence asked me to make a wreath to place on top of the coffin. I wandered around the garden serenely amidst a muffled kafuffle of servant activity. I made a beautiful wreath from varieties of green leaves and foliage with delicate white, star-shaped flowers intertwined in a circle of white daisies. The beginning of the first heavy rain had begun, and the pre-monsoon pressure was oppressive. I took a dry biscuit out of the tin and within seconds it was a mushy mess. I could not believe the humidity. The rain didn't stop but beat continually on the high tin roof, reverberating like rice grain pellets hurled at a glass window. By mid afternoon when the hearse arrived bearing Jeremy's body in a solid oak coffin, the rain had stopped and the sun blasted heat waves along our slow path to the cemetery as curling steam seeped through the rough earth. My stomach was nervously knotted and I hid my tearful eyes behind my sunglasses. Hundreds of people lined the way and watched respectfully as we passed, throwing flowers at the car. The monsoon rain that morning had turned the dry, rich, red earth into mud fields. Splodges of thick grunge flew up into people's faces and splashed their clothes as our car forged its way through the slop.

When we arrived at the cemetery, the car had difficulty in pushing through the mud, so people helped to push it up the slight incline to where Jeremy was to be buried. Flocks of people stood in a hushed, moving silence. Jeremy had been greatly loved and respected, and it was humbling to witness their devotion. When we got out of the car, the mud slopped and slipped over our shoes and seeped into my white trousers. The coffin bearers had great difficulty in walking a straight line through the quagmire, and many men rushed forwards to balance the heavy wooden box on their shoulders. As the coffin bearers slipped forwards towards the open grave, one poor man slid and fell into it and had to be helped out before the service could begin. I knew Jeremy would be laughing at the high jinx the rain had caused, and in truth it helped to lighten the seriousness of the moment. I glanced at Will and we both found it difficult to stifle our laughter. It was so amusing watching the man disappear down into the muddy grave, attempting to scrape his way back with dignity. However hard he tried, his predicament made him a clown in the minds of everyone gathered. Somehow the incident made light of the sheer horror of the situation. After the service by the graveside, we trudged our way back to the car and were surprisingly light hearted, as the whole ceremony had been one long farce with mud pies slopped on the top of the coffin instead of wads of earth.

Visitors came and went from the house, pouring out their commiserations until we were finally left alone to take stock of the situation and come to terms with Jeremy's death. The next day Major Stiffle arranged to drive us to nearby Jain temples where Jeremy had spent much of his spare time. We drove in the Major's bumpy Land Rover through brush jungle and high plains of pampas grass delicately dusting the skyline with feathery fronds. Jerkily we made our way over outcrops of rocks heading towards tiny golden pimples glinting high above the mountains in the distance. We scrambled through bamboo groves arching as high as cathedral spires until the golden peaks were directly above us. We clambered onto a stony, uneven winding road snaking up into the mountains to a small village where the first of the golden temples was situated.

On our arrival small children swamped us cheering and touching our arms and a few adults watched from a distance as a crazy dog went berserk growling, howling and barking, backing away from an invisible energy shadowing us. The Major looked perplexed saying that the dog's behaviour was unusual as the dogs there were always friendly. Another dog shot out from nowhere grizzling at an unseen presence. The adults watching attempted to calm the dogs but were unsuccessful. Then something happened that made their wiry hair stand on end in fright, and they cowered away into the shadows hiding from the imperceptible energy.

"It's like they've seen a ghost," stated the Major puzzled by their behaviour.

As we climbed the antediluvian steps up into the temple courtyard, I quickly glanced behind and thought I saw Jeremy following us. I blinked the thought away. Inside the primeval temple a priest sat cross-legged and half-naked with his closed eyes cast heavenwards, while small circles of incense curled around him. As we strayed in and out of the small shrines, I was certain that I kept seeing glimpses of Jeremy. Shafts of sunlight streaked in through broken bricks in the ancient walls, casting beams of golden light effervescently dancing with specks of dust flickering in the haze. Through one of the beams I saw him again. Through the glinting spotlight he smiled at me; it was as though the power of the sun gave him form in a game of hide and seek. Just as we were retreating down the steps, I saw him pause and look back at me and smile again. I knew he was with us and as we walked back to the car, the dogs hid and I understood. They had seen Jeremy with us and reacted to the spectre, having known him previously in his human form.

Back in the house in the bedroom I lay on the bed gazing up at the ceiling where the red ants had marched. There was no sign of the creatures. Will came in and sat on the end of the bed smoking a cigarette. I told him about seeing his father and he was pleased, relieved to know that he was happy and that I had seen him. We discussed the dogs' reaction understanding the Major's comment about their "seeing a ghost." Staring up into beyond, I said, "One day I will write all this. One day I will tell this story."

In the warmth and knowledge of the present, I look back on that time and understand the moment of infinity that moulded the memory, which is and was as mysterious then as it is now.

Once India has crept into your bones, into your blood, into your mind, into your heart, she never leaves your side and Jeremy's death forced Will and me to take a different path from the one we had originally planned. Will decided to help his mother adjust to her new life alone, while an emergency telegram from the principal of my college ordered me back to England to take up the single place offered for a B.Ed. in Drama degree. It was a great achievement and I had to take it. I had no idea that my decision would lead me into an unbelievable adventure in Moscow, but I cannot retrace my Indian pathway without recalling Pear Tree Cottage events, which were horrendously unbelievable.

    William and I eventually married but didn't live together as he was studying at York University and I was studying in London. Months later we returned to India where we spent our honeymoon, knowing that after a brief respite we had to go back to the drudgery of life in London. Another year slipped by and I became pregnant. Will wanted to return to York to study for an M.A. so we decided to sell our small flat in London and live in rural Yorkshire. At the turn of the New Year we spent a few weekends chasing houses, but nothing inspired us. Nearing Easter we had sold our flat and so it was imperative to find a house in Yorkshire, as the baby was due in October and we needed to prepare our nest for her arrival. Just when we had given up hope of finding our dream house, we came across it purely by chance.

    It was a Sunday afternoon and we were driving back to London in a halo of spring sunshine. Speeding in our little, custard yellow, lotus sports car, I spied a "For Sale" sign. It seemed to jump out from nowhere and I shouted to Will to stop and back track down a little lane until we came to a beautiful old-fashioned village green, the kind where Maypole dancing, village fairs, high days and holidays were quaintly celebrated. Two eighteenth century farm cottages had been built into one and painted white. The name Pear Tree Cottage was engraved in a gnarled piece of wood by the large black door. We employed the shiny, brass, lion's head knocker enthusiastically in an attempt to enquire about the house. I gazed across the green at an old farmhouse in the far corner, overgrown with nettles and weeds, with crumbling, tumble-down sheds leaning at the side. On the far edge of the green was a square fronted old house, grey mottled with stippled concrete outer casing with a neat privet hedge in the shape of a droopy Mexican man's moustache. There was a modern house in the opposite corner and a bungalow next to Pear Tree Cottage hidden by trees and large bushes. An open dirt track to one side of the house lead to fields, and in the distance there was a railway line. At the time I did not question how I could have glimpsed the "For Sale" sign as we had been speeding on the open road far away from the house. We waited a few moments, but no one answered. We looked around to see if there was anyone who knew the occupants, but it was deserted. A rural, Sunday afternoon Yorkshire hush had descended, and no one moved or stirred; no curtains twitched and no children played on the green. The bright sunshine threw shadows over the lawn as I peeped over the old gate. A cat appeared from under the bushes and brushed her body against my legs. She was ginger, white and brown with black patches around her eyes. She seemed to want to lead me around to the back of the house. I followed her, much to Will's cautious calls, 'You can't go there. You can't do that—come back!" However, I didn't pay any heed. I was under a spell of intrigue and needed to satisfy my curiosity.

From the open farm track I stepped over stones and peered into the kitchen. The ceiling was the original thick, old oak beams and the units looked new, gleaming clean in candy blue. The cat meowed at a creaky gate overgrown with rambling rose briers so I pushed it open and stepped inside a beautiful cottage garden, lovingly tended, where an ancient pear tree stood in the middle of a massive lawn. I cheekily stared into the windows and gasped at the large open-grated fireplace, the kind I had always dreamed of owning. Will grew angry and impatient, fearing the owners would come back and catch me. The cat did a little dance in between my legs and seemed pleased to accompany us on our tour of the house. As I rushed back to the car, she disappeared.

"We have to have it!" I gasped.

"It might be sold—you never know!"

"No, we're going to get it!" I was absolutely sure that the house would be ours. I had no idea what I was walking into; I only knew that more than anything after living a student, Bedouin existence, I wanted to settle down there.

During the long drive back home thoughts of Pear Tree Cottage swamped my mind. Its charm and its position snuggled in the centre of a rural village, delighted me; I wanted it more than anything and paid no heed to the warning bells urging me to question how I managed to spot the "For Sale" sign so far away from the property. Owning the house became a driving obsession during the ensuing weeks. Someone was already in the process of buying it, but I still clung to the possibility that their offer would fall through. Three weeks later it did. Will and I raced up the M1 to go and view the cottage with a definite offer to buy. As we approached the tiny village in a grey mist, the rain drizzled, shrouding the house in a dreary mantle that was far from the sunny welcome of our first sighting. As we drove up to the village green, the cottage had a lonely, forlorn look that made me want it all the more.

Mr. Shyers opened the door and greeted us with a warm welcome. The hallway was most unusual with a high stairway bending around a circular wall, which was once a hay barn. As we walked into the oak beamed sitting room, a blazing log fire crackled from the medieval style open grate and horse brasses shone reflecting the dancing flames, lighting up the gloomy day. Mrs. Shyers was a delightful, Women's Institute kind of woman who knew everyone's business and was always very helpful to everyone in the village. She explained that the house was originally two farm cottages, built in 1860, but had been converted into one cottage at the turn of the century by an eccentric gentleman adventurer who had brought delicate, antique tiles from China to decorate the bathroom. Impressed by that gem of information, we followed them into the dining room. All the wooden framed doorways were small, and Will had to bend to go under, but being small I didn't have that difficulty. As I sailed through, I spied a wooden cross nailed over the arch of the door and noted it with interest thinking that perhaps the couple were Catholics. Unprompted, Mr. Shyers answered that question in his formal lawyer's voice: "We love the house, of course, and don't want to move; it's just that we need to downsize as our family has fled the nest, so to speak. The only thing we haven't liked is the noise of the church bells at nine o'clock sharp on a Sunday morning. You see we're not religious."

If they weren't religious, then why did they have a crucifix? The dining room was charming with the same old oak beams and quaint windows framed by English roses. The sight of the crucifix lodged above the dining room door troubled me, but a shaft of bright sunlight gloriously broke through the grey clouds filling the dining room with a golden glow. Mrs. Shyers opened the French windows flooding the small room with a fresh earthy smell from the morning rain. I followed her into a picturesque rose walk that had slipped my notice on my first sneak preview. It was delightful, encapsulating the essence of a genuine country cottage. With a comprehensive tour of the garden complete, we returned indoors to view the kitchen. Mrs. Shyers was proud to show off all her new labour saving devices and the space saving cupboards. After my primitive kitchenette in the flat, it was a palace.

The light from the conservatory flowed into the kitchen spotlighting a brass crucifix. Mr. Shyers saw me gazing at it and snappily said, "Oh the house is full of those! We inherited them from the previous owners. I believe there's one in every room. They must have been devout Catholics, you know. Mary and I never bothered—can't see the point of them myself; still, each to his or her own as they say!"

I smiled and followed everyone up the round staircase.

"There's not a straight wall in this house," laughed Mrs. Shyers. Each bedroom was completely different in style and shape, and the bathroom was small but the scenes of the delicate Chinese ladies on the imported tiles were beautiful. I decided that one of the small bedrooms would make a perfect nursery and I began to plan the décor as Will and Mr. Shyers gave their gentleman's word and shook hands on an agreement. Three months later the house was ours.

On the night before our great trek north, I pondered the crucifixes stationed above the doors in all the rooms and wondered whether I should remove them. I asked Will what he thought.

"Oh, just keep 'em where they are; they've obviously been there for a long time. Anyway, you never know- there might be a ghost!"

CHAPTER 3

Chennai to Pondecherry— Lost Paradise

The night before Branden and I were to embark on our amazing journey back to India, I sat in his garden musing on the very first time I had flown in a jumbo jet with Will to meet his family. As students we couldn't afford luxury and Will had insisted that we travel light with just a back pack, so my plans for taking any items of indulgence were squashed. I was both anxious and excited about the trip as I had never been on a long flight and on the night prior to our departure we stayed in Cambridge at his aunt and uncle's futuristic house built mostly in wood and glass. His Uncle Chris was a lecturer in Art at the Royal College of Art and had built an impressive modern house that reflected natural light. The design was incredible so that from any angle you could see outside and feel part of the forest. I was given the small room on the ground floor that had a large, dark wooden cupboard across one wall and a large window opposite. That night in the wooden and glass house, it was difficult to rest as I was so nervous but after I eventually drifted to sleep, I woke up in a panic. Somehow I had walked into the coffin-like, dark wooden cupboard. In the black enclosure I was blind. I couldn't find the door. I couldn't feel my way through the winter coats and clothes hanging in the depth of the closet.

My breath was drying up and my heart was pounding abnormally. I panicked. I was suffocating, unable to break free. Suddenly an awful awareness dawned. My body was missing! I was standing there without hands or feet or head or trunk; they were still lying in bed while I had wandered out in spirit and couldn't remember how to return. I knew if I didn't get back quickly, I would die.

I tried to walk through the door, but I hadn't the energy to manipulate material matter. With one, huge, concentrated effort, I willed myself back. I flew into my convulsing body managing to steady my heart and calm my pulse. My body was bathed in a cold sweat. I was so relieved not to have died, as I would have hated to miss my journey to India. I laughed at the memory. I was only a young student and if I had known at the time all the unimaginable, unbelievable, mysterious things that would happen to me on my life's journey, I would have considered a mere out-of-body experience quite tame.

I looked up at the night sky knowing that the next night Branden and I would be flying to India. Forty years on from my first visit I wondered what I had learnt along the rocky path of life's surprises. I had learnt that desire drives the journey and that thirst for knowledge sustains the driver when the road is bleak and empty. I reflected that the smallest detours on the road can alter the journey drastically; just one unscheduled turn and north can become south in one swift manoeuvre. The smallest detours from yourself can lead you astray from who you are and who you want to be. Perhaps one thing I have learnt is that just when you think you know where you are and think that you have arrived, life gives you a little kick and you're back on the road again where nowhere is somewhere and somewhere is never too far away from anywhere, except that it keeps changing direction.

On the journey the next day I wasn't afraid because Branden was with me. I had spent a lifetime travelling, yet a two-year gap, locked in a stifling marriage, cost me my inner confidence. Disillusion had hacked into the self-assurance file in my brain and stolen my self-esteem. I had allowed thoughts of self-respect to drift and sift into limbo. I had lost my words, which shaped my journey's map, and I longed to be reacquainted with old ones, new ones, forgotten ones—words false or real, words stealing a heart or killing love in one fell swoop. I ached for words to heal a broken heart or a strangled thought. I needed my words to fill a gap where there was nothing left when emotion had dried up. I thought I knew words. I thought I had experience of a whole gamut of them; but sometimes when you have nailed words and pounded them into sense, one leaks away and falls off the edge of the page dripping onto your jumper. I thought I could weigh up the worth of words and deal out sentences to affect meaning but insecurity had hidden them, and I had to find new words on the return journey to myself. India, I knew, would help me to find some answers.

Excitedly, we rose in the early morning and were driven to Heathrow Airport. Everything was different with modern technology and computers to check you in to help choose your seat and to welcome you to the flight. I was relieved to have Branden to cope with all of that. On a journey nothing is ever at your will or command or pace, as everything happens outside your control; it is necessary the moment you step out of your routine, to accept what is thrown your way and be patient, trusting that all will be fine. A journey has a double layer—the tough outer skin, which is planned, and the inner thin, unknown skin, where destiny takes the reins and only she knows where the traveller will be lead and where the unscheduled delays are scheduled. Only she has access to the stops, the minutes stolen, the seconds gained, the ticking of the clock when time is choked. Like on life's journey the outer casing of our body claims one thing while the inner landscape of the mind discovers another.

We set off on a Monday leaving Heathrow in the early afternoon, and with a nine hour flight we arrived in Chennai at five o'clock in the early hours of the same Monday morning. Strange to travel backwards and relive the identical time span in a different zone. Time never is what we think it is and although we wrap ourselves in a mantle of programmed routine, it is possible to slip through the barriers to find ourselves in a different dimension, as I did once in Crete, when I was hurled back through time to share a little girl's life in her last moments when she was murdered by her stepmother. To slip in or out of time is nothing new to the ancients as they were close to the "out-of–time sphere" from where we all begin. When we place ourselves on earth, we surrender our freedom to the man-made clock that binds us in a false daily ritual. My daughter recalls travelling across certain states in America, where it remained six o'clock for three hours as she travelled across different states. Experiencing time standing still in that way makes a mockery of the limitations we place upon ourselves regarding our life span and age restrictions.

When we alighted into the heat of the Indian morning, we were tired and had a tedious wait for our luggage, which was late, but eventually arrived chugging its way around the carousel squashed amongst boxes and over-packed bulging bags. When I took my case, the handle had been broken making the wheeling of it difficult but I managed by walking with a bent back. As we ambled out into the new morning, rows upon rows of familiar Ambassador Taxis beamed a welcome like long lost friends and the hot earth smiled. The smell of India was unleashed from my box of memories. I was alive. I was back!

Branden had arranged for us to stay in an amazing hotel for one night to treat ourselves to a little luxury before embarking on the core journey. The Radisson oozed sensual decadence of an epoch of elegance and passion. As our taxi swung into the magnificent, palatial grounds, we were given a stately welcome and our luggage was politely searched before entering the imperial lobby. It was splendid in every aspect and we were given royal attendance, being served a refreshing fruit cup before shown to our room. My son ordered *masaala dosa* for breakfast, but I couldn't understand how he could eat such a spicy dish first thing in the morning. The bathroom was incredible, providing every luxurious pampering lotion and potion you could possibly desire, along with a soft, thick, white, towelling dressing gown and an ironing station inside the heavy mahogany wardrobe. Biscuits in cookie jars were tantalizingly placed by the window, but not just any cookies—there was choice on the menu ranging from chocolate chip, coffee and walnut surprise. Fresh fruit was displayed just in case you favoured a healthy snack, together with bottles of water, tea and coffee and a fridge full of goodies. It was the quintessential heavenly hotel.

Out in the courtyard the chipmunks darted amongst the trees and exotic birds raucously cawed as we sat in the shade watching the light glinting over the swimming pool. The jungle outside surreptitiously attempted to creep over the high wall. The dense overgrowth was never far away, always creeping, seeping into the brickwork, and forcing an entrance through the tiniest cracks. It was still early morning, but the intensity of the heat began to rise stifling my energy. As there was no one around, Branden and I enjoyed the luxury of swimming in peace to cool down. Afterwards we took a *phut phut dogem* car (a motorised rickshaw) down to view the sea. The midday heat was fiercer than I remembered and as we stepped into the little cabin, I realized how vulnerable we were in an open tin can racing against the tide of all manner of motorised vehicles. I was terrified as we rolled in and out, between and around, and almost under the jam-packed traffic. The huge holes in the road made the journey almost unbearable with my hip replacement still sore, the banging and jolting were torture, especially as the road was crammed with hundreds of *phut phuts* exuding petrol fumes, plus scooters, motorbikes, cars and cabs all vying for tyre space.

Chennai was different from the old Madras I had known, being more commercialised with office blocks and modern buildings cramped into tiny spaces. There were no horse drawn carts or hand-held rickshaws any more, only bicycle and motorised ones. Our driver veered so close to lorries and racing taxi cabs that I had to close my eyes. I was astounded how the ladies sat demurely and calmly on the back of scooters, folding themselves into a side saddle position with their saris trailing behind like fresh sails in a yachting race. As the scooters pounded in and out of the dusty holes, the women remained motionless like heroines in a Bollywood spectacular gliding through the traffic with serene smiles and shy glances amidst the overwhelming petrol fumes. Branden suggested that we walk along the front, but the sand scorched my feet through my sandals. The sizzling heat was debilitating and Branden bravely stopped near a stall for a sugar cane drink. I say bravely because during my time in India I was never allowed to drink, eat or accept anything in the street for fear of catching a terrible disease like cholera, typhoid or dysentery. A rusty, squeaky machine pulped the long, ragged, straw-like, raw sugar cane stems through an ancient mangle and the juice sluiced down into a bucket below. As the sweet liquid was poured into a cup, I shuddered. I couldn't watch him drink it and prayed that he wouldn't catch anything. He assured me that on his travels around India he ate and drank everything locally, whereas Granny had always forbidden any contact with the community, not even in the bazaar. I realized that the gap between my British Raj background and my son's experience of India was immense.

Our little *phut phut* driver met us by the stalls, and I wrapped a shawl around my hip to cushion the blows of the bumps and scrapes of the ride. The noise and the fumes were unbearable, so I tied another scarf around my head, eyes and mouth. Branden ignored my eccentricity; but when I fell asleep through the din and hullabaloo of the main city traffic, he was astonished.

"Mum, how could you do that?" he laughed.

I had found the heat and the onslaught of the pandemonium too much, so I had taken myself to a calmer place and slept through it remembering another time when sleep rescued me from fear beyond measure, when a new phase in my life, which should have been joyful, turned into a hideous nightmare.

Having bought Pear Tree Cottage, I was ecstatic and couldn't wait for the great trek north from our poky little London flat. At the onset the task of packing seemed easy but as each day passed, the congeries of books and crates of paraphernalia turned the flat into an obstacle course, which was difficult to manoeuvre with a heavily pregnant tummy. To exacerbate matters, the country was suffocating in a heat wave that had reached disaster level: it was the hottest June on record for twenty years. It was hard to bear the heat as the skin across my tummy stretched like a singing drum and ached in the hot weather. Furthermore, my morning sickness was all day sickness, and the baby intermittently suffered from hiccups that gave me indigestion.

On the day of our move we had arranged for me to go to the midlands by train with my little Shih Tzu dog, Chinda, where I would be met by my parents, who would drive me to the house. Will and our friend Dan would drive a hired van with all our belongings to Yorkshire, and we would all meet up at the cottage. My father, as a housewarming present, had hired a friend of his to decorate the whole house so that it was lovely, clean and fresh, ready for our new start and the birth of my baby. As I proudly opened the front door, I was delighted at the transformation of the hall, as the round wall had been decorated with green and gold, heavily embossed wallpaper, which suited the character of the house. Everywhere was painted brilliant white that accentuated the old dark beams and the sun soaked the cottage with a warm Yorkshire welcome. My parents didn't stay long as they had to get back, and I felt a strange pang of emptiness as the car sauntered out of sight, but as I stood in my beautiful cottage garden with Chinda running in and out of the colourful borders, a sense of achievement drove away my fleeting panic.

As I wandered around the large lawn peering at all the beautiful flowers, worrying how I was going to keep them watered in the drought, I remembered the first time I saw the cottage. We were whizzing past the countryside in Will's bright, shiny yellow sports car when the sign appeared from nowhere. As I stood imbibing the balmy light scent of the honeysuckle framing the gate, the thought of the house sign appearing suddenly from nowhere struck a disharmonious chord. The 'For Sale' sign had definitely appeared, yet from our position on the road it was a physical impossibility. The house was nowhere near the main road and I had impetuously called out to Will to change direction. When we found it, I immediately fell in love with the cottage and a strange obsession to own it invaded my energy so that nothing deterred me from my quest to get it. Ownership became my driving force and yet, standing in the garden, instead of being elated, I felt that something wasn't right; something was clawing at my certainty and jangling my nerves.

Chinda barked at my feet wanting to play and check out her newly found freedom of being able to wander in and out of the house, but I was tired shrugging off any further dark thoughts lurking in the hidden recesses of my mind. I hovered near the profuse lavender bushes, waving my hands over the oily perfume and making a note to give little lavender bags as Christmas presents. I shivered. The sky was turning lilac and the sun was slowly sinking behind the conifer trees. A damp chill moistened the parched grass, which Chinda began to lick as she was thirsty. I was comforted at least in the thought that Will would be bringing her bowl and everything we needed, including a takeaway meal and a bottle of Champagne. Apart from being hungry, I began to feel uneasy. As the shadows lengthened across the lawn, drawing dark streaks towards the garage, I felt my baby kick, so I rubbed my distended tummy wondering what she would look like. Intuitively I knew she was a girl and I already had a name for her, Sarena. I could imagine her playing by the old pear tree, swinging happily on the old swing and filling the garden with her laughter. The thought of her reinstalled a good mood and I resigned to wait patiently; after all, Will promised he would soon arrive and we would have a party.

I wandered back inside the house in case Will phoned. The quiet was overpowering. Was I imagining someone watching me? I told myself I had been a townie for far too long and that I had to adjust to the quiet of the countryside. The silence was heavy and intensely invasive, holding me captive inside a cocoon of waiting, waiting, waiting for Will, waiting for another human being to shatter the barricade of stillness. The deadly peace was suffocating and I needed to escape back into the garden for air. As the sun was finally taking her last curtain call, I realized the night was quickly descending and I had nothing to wrap around me except a thin cardigan. I kept my thoughts focussed on Will's arrival and how we would all enjoy our housewarming celebration. Chinda began to whine in hunger but as it was Sunday, there were no shops open in the village. I wandered back inside as the mosquitoes were just beginning to hover. I closed the conservatory door and the clang echoed freakily around the empty house. I regretted shutting out the fresh scents of the garden as a prickle of panic quivered down my back. I was totally alone.

I was used to my busy life in London and being able to pick up the phone to speak to a friend but I didn't know anyone in the village, and I didn't want to admit to my friends in London, that I was already missing them. I walked inside the kitchen in the dark. Night crept in quickly. I turned on the light viewing my reflection in the window before waddling through the downstairs rooms turning on all the lights, becoming sharply aware that there were no curtains. I was, in effect, inside a goldfish bowl, on display for everyone to see. The soft pad of my feet on the carpets resounded through the hollowness. The air thinned and I struggled to breathe. I was vulnerable to something I couldn't see and was defensive against an invisible energy. I jumped at my own shadow on the wall and flinched at my reflection in the windows. Out of the corner of my eye I glimpsed a crucifix; its simple form screamed a warning as Will's words returned, "Perhaps there's a ghost?"

Chinda followed close at my heels, her tail half drooped; she too was afraid. I told myself that I was being silly and that if I investigated the whole house to make sure there was no one hiding in a corner, I would feel better. Inside the hall the walls enclosed me in a strange capsule of timelessness. Each stair creaked as I ascended echoing in the heavy emptiness. Sweat dripped down my back and face. My heart raced as my baby gave another kick. I held my stomach, needing to protect my unborn child, clenching my fists as I fought the rising panic. Before I reached the top of the stairs, the phone rang in the kitchen and I turned back quickly in case it was Will. It was wonderful to hear his voice linking me to the outside world.

"Hello, Love! Look I've had one hell of a time with this damned van. It broke down twice on the motorway and it's finally clapped out on the M1. We're in a service station waiting

for the break down truck. I can't say when we'll arrive but . . .";
the pips raced and Will was lost.

"Wait! Wait!" I cried.

The eerie silence coiled around me like a snake waiting to strike. I was afraid to turn around as the energy lurked. It was feeding on my rising fear, which crackled inside like a desert fire spreading up from my legs and through my body. I was trapped near the telephone unable to move. The thing was drawing closer and in terror I realized it wanted my baby. Like a tigress protecting her young, I pounced into action and picked up Chinda, striding ungainly into the sitting room, boldly marching through the shadowy darkness. With Chinda still clutched to my chest, I inched myself down the back of the radiator to prop myself up on the floor. I could feel her little heart pounding in time with mine. I was not going to allow anyone or anything to harm my baby. I remembered what Granny in India had taught me to say whenever I was afraid, "I am a perfect child of the universe; nothing and no one can harm me!" I repeated the mantra again and again, feeling the spectre hovering high above me but not able to touch me. "I am a perfect child of the universe, nothing and no one can harm me!" I persisted in my task, gaining power to send it away until I fell into an exhausted sleep. I must have slept with my little dog on my lap for over an hour. When I woke, the thing was not near me but it was still watching.

I spoke deliberately, loudly to Chinda, hearing my words echo as though through an empty shell, saying that we would go to bed. As I hitched myself up off the ground, I knew it was close again, ready once more to resume its stalking. I turned off the sitting room light and walked into the kitchen. Two long strip lights glared in the heavy blackness. I had left the hall light on in case Will arrived, so I was not afraid to turn off the kitchen lights and walk into the hallway. The switch registered a loud resounding click as I flicked the switch and closed the door behind me. I took two steps forwards before a resounding click echoed in the dark and the lights flashed on again. Momentarily my heart missed a beat. I knew I had turned off the lights. I had registered the sound in my mind and acknowledged the lights going out, yet somehow when my back was turned, they clicked themselves on. The switch was heavy and needed pressure to flick it, so I knew that it couldn't just turn itself on without physical force. I made myself go back. The double strip lights blazed triumphantly reflecting my terror in the windows. Whatever or whoever was playing silly games was enjoying my fear. With seething resolve, I petulantly turned off the lights and stood for a second in the dark. Yes, they were off! The lights were definitely off. I banged the door shut. I took two steps forwards and the loud click echoed as the lights were turned on again. I began to shiver. Quaking, I dared myself to go back in. The lights jeered a welcome, mocking me with bright intensity as the yellow glare dared me to respond. I quickly turned off the lights again and hurried into the hall pounding up the stairs as fast as I could waddle with Chinda close at my heels. When I reached the top, I heard the dreaded loud click: I knew the lights were on again, but I dared not go down.

I hurried into the empty bedroom and locked the door. I turned on the light but the blackness outside echoed my bleak, lonely terror. I plucked up the courage to turn off the light and stood by the window. The moon was hiding behind the clouds but a stray, silver beam danced across the lawn. The wind picked up and began to howl in a deep low tone as it bounced through the conifers and rattled the old window frames. There was nothing to lie down on, nothing to curl under. The floor was hard and it was uncomfortable with my heavy stomach to lie on my side. I wanted to cry in desperation, but tears were lost. I had yearned to move into my dream cottage but it had turned out to be a nightmare, and I had to face the long night alone with my little dog curled up against my chest. I recited the mantra as I dipped in and out of sleep with horrific sounds clanging through the house like a battlefield at the height of a skirmish with swords clashing steel on steel. The radiators banged, retracting in the cold, but I had not used the central heating, so I didn't understand why they were making such a din. Throughout the night the house protested at my presence and by the first early rays of dawn, I managed a little sleep. Had I known what terror lay in wait I would have left immediately run into the night to escape the evil presence.

Back at the hotel in Chennai, I left the memory behind and concentrated on enjoying the moment. Branden and I had a fantastic, free, foot massage, which was calming and soothing, making us feel both tranquil and energised for the next day's taxi ride to Pondecherry. That evening we dined in the restaurant, which was offering a buffet of local dishes. The gentle blending of spices and herbs was tantalising and the food salubrious with tingling chillies bursting through delicate flavours. At the end of the evening we were tired and slept until early next morning when we packed to make ready for the next stage of our journey. Branden, as always, was amazingly adept at organising everything and haggled to get the best price for a driver to take us to Pondecherry. I was looking forward to wandering through Pondecherry as I had read about its interesting architecture and beautiful coastline, earning it the title of the "French Riveria of the East" with its winding coastal roads and interesting streets influenced by the French from the time of occupation. Our next stop was in an eco village, Dune, in Elephant Valley. Branden thought it would give us a completely different experience of the area and a chance to see the coastline where the tsunami had tragically taken many lives.

As we drove along the main road with the impenetrable early morning traffic condensing into five lanes rather than two, the fumes and the noise were almost unbearable. This time my inner landscape was painted with a myriad of life experiences and so I was not shocked to see people living in shaky tin huts next to disgusting medieval open gullies clogged with sewage and decaying rubbish or to see red and green horned cows defecating in the road, while thin dogs fought each other for scraps of food. I didn't flinch to witness people living in straw mud huts, which were a foot under water after the monsoon deluge or to watch them slosh their way through the refuse in their bare feet with the nauseating smell of daily living seeping into the early morning. Surprisingly I didn't see as many beggars on the main roads, whereas on my earlier trip the throng of starving people and the sight of their hands forever outstretched begging, shocked me. Previously I had been appalled to see people squatting side by side in the open road busy with their morning ablutions with no paper or water to wash their hands or clean themselves. This time I saw the scene differently. Previously I had been surprised to see people breaking branches off trees to use as toothbrushes to clean their teeth, and I accepted all without prior judgement or with Western eyes.

Our driver took huge risks and drove towards an oncoming bus, swerving at the last moment. Branden and I exchanged worried glances but didn't say anything as the driver continued to barge his way through barriers, bluffing his way forwards. We passed a small school where the children were having their lessons sitting outside in rows while in an adjacent yard older pupils, dressed in navy, were uniformly assembled. It was refreshing to see even from the very young, a healthy attitude towards discipline and a genuine interest in learning. As we drove on weaving in and out of the endless battlefield of traffic, the brick buildings dwindled into small dwellings with straw matting walls and thatched banana leaf roofs. Some people on the roadside had only black plastic bags and sheeting to keep out the rain. The same resigned look of acceptance of fate was inscribed over the faces of the old men sitting watching life pass them by, with their begging pots leaning against their gnarled legs.

We drove onwards towards the coastline with the Bay of Bengal stretching hazily towards the glassy horizon and we passed a young goatherd with a handful of goats nuzzling sparse bushes. He waved heartily at Branden, who smiled and returned the greeting. The beaches were empty as the spray from the playful waves washed the shore. Seeing the sea in its light-hearted and bouncy mood, I couldn't imagine the terror of the onslaught of the tsunami. The little shrines to the lost ones, which were scattered along the coastline garlanded with fresh flowers, were, however, a solemn reminder. The people did not forget—could not forget that terrible day. The breath of the sea, the call of the wind, the nudge of time with its decades of death, and the dying call, like a remembered soft lullaby drifting on the wind, will always remind people of their lost loved ones.

Our driver sped along the less crowded roads, picking a spot on his face, not heeding the beautiful temples that splashed the countryside with colourful signs and symbols. Colour was all the poor people had to give the gods, and their profuse artwork lit up the roadsides with a cornucopia of brilliance. We passed fishermen using ancient fishing nets applying skills that had been passed down to them from their forebears. Different types of palm trees stood to attention in the flat fields and yellow butterflies hovered over quivering grasses like tiny flying buttercups. The driver stopped momentarily to relieve himself by a clump of trees and then proceeded to pick his nose as we scurried along the bumpy highway.

A little, lost black goat strayed onto the road and our driver, on his mobile, only just missed it. Salt marshes lay fallow along the way as the jungle sneaked into cracks and crevices in the roads. We passed new building sites where women balanced red bricks on their heads as they walked up and down ladders, while men looked on and directed the operation. Folding light bounced off the dense trees cascading into deep shadows where a purple palace pounced incongruously out of the forest. Farther along, a red palace, and then a yellow one haled a modern welcome as each new building bombarded the jungle with brash colours which would quickly fade in the deluge of the monsoon rain. We did not hire a taxi with air conditioning, as neither Branden nor I like it, so all the windows blasted hot air into our faces. I tied my scarf around my head and face appearing like a Bedouin woman fortressed against a sand storm, mystifying young children who stared at the passing strangers.

After hours of driving, we suddenly turned down a rough track. An old wooden sign pointed to Dune, an eco village initially formed for artists, musicians, designers, creative technologists and writers. Paved along the tiny trail were mud huts and rush mat dwellings belonging to the workers. Arriving at the compound, the guards opened the palm gates and friendly attendants handed us sweet hibiscus drinks. The heat of the noonday sun burnt into the dry sand and we retreated under the colourful reception canopy while waiting to be taken to our garden apartment. We had only arrived in India early the previous day, yet it seemed we had been there for much longer. The heat quietly raged as we were driven to our garden room and our bags efficiently dispatched. We were relieved to escape the blazing rays in our little garden flat that consisted of a simple air-conditioned room designed in seascape colours with a basic bathroom. Our beds, dressed in pale blue and silver coverlets, were raised on a concrete platform set against an azure wall with an arrangement of shelves on either side of the dais decorated with unusual ornaments, including a Father Christmas, a Durga goddess and some little dolls. Above a dark blue wall a beautiful stained glass window poured red and white light onto the seascape floor, and long white net curtains fluttered in the gentle breeze through large French windows leading into our own private, bijou garden. The room was cool but when I stepped into the bathroom, the humid heat pounced stealing my breath. The concrete, turquoise bathroom was dark, and I was afraid of insects creeping in through the open grating. Pictures of Bollywood stars were arranged around the sink and lovely miniature bottles of shampoo and bath foam were displayed on a shelf near the basic shower.

Branden suggested that we take a walk around the compound. I found an umbrella to shade me from the intense glare of the baking sun. I realized, with a smile that it was a reflex reaction left over from Granny's insistence that I stay out of the glare. Workers in the garden stared as we ventured forth through the grass. We passed the unusual circular design of the open restaurant with picnic tables dotted around the central eating arena. We sauntered past different houses set apart in the scrub jungle, designed in various styles with apartments ranging from modern high-tech palaces to modest garden huts spread out around the compound. The eco village produced much of its own food with home grown fruit and vegetables and basic crops. Dairy products came from the lovely herd of cows retiring under the shade of straw matting open huts. Chickens and goats were kept in clean compounds and there was a wholesome feeling of a sturdy farming culture providing much of the community's needs.

The garden areas were beautifully tended with all kinds of strange and unusual sculptures formed out of ordinary every day materials, such as lovely lights made from different coloured plastic water pots folded one on top of another. Artists who stayed in the village left their individual marks on the landscape, and it was a delightful surprise to come across a statue or a sculpture in the middle of jungle over growth. Turning a corner a Cadillac car blazoned a hippy era psychedelic yellow and red "Lost Paradise" on the side in bold black letters. It reminded me of my trip to Cuba where I became fascinated by classic Cadillac cars. In the heat of the sun the bright red flames licking the side of the car shot out like yellow shooting sparks on a funeral pyre. The little eco village was a taste of heaven set apart from the rest of the world and in the surreal moment of seeing the car, I was taken back to my wild hippy days of dancing in Hyde Park and singing antiwar songs in my Earl's Court student flat. The car was left haphazardly in the dry dust next to an abandoned long, rusty pole and a small mound of rubbish was scattered near a heap of rich, terra cotta sand. The moment held a timeless melancholy-time is, time was, time has been and will be repeated- I mused, feeling time fuse into one second. I thought how different I was to the person I had been and have become and perhaps will become.

We walked on dragging our heels in the sizzling heat heading towards the sound of the sea pounding gently in the distance. The small roads were rough and stony winding in and out of rough patches of scrub jungle alongside tended gardens with flowers and vegetables dutifully set out in rows. Palms with long, thin, turquoise stems were planted in clusters growing afresh to replace the mass vegetation destroyed by the tsunami. Three women workers appeared from the garden wearing matching purple saris, smiling a shy greeting as we followed them towards the farm, where the smell of cow dung stung the air. As we passed the cow shed, the small Jersey herd turned their large brown eyes towards us. It was too hot to utter a sound, so they stared, changing position from one hoof to the other, shuffling in the dry earth.

When we returned from our walk past the "Lost Paradise" Cadillac, the forgotten world of yesterday meandered back as I remembered a Maharajah's palace of wonderful splendor and past glory where Will and I had been invited to stay. The Maharajah was great friends with Will's family and had been educated at Oxford. He had an impeccable English accent and beautiful aristocratic manners and his wife, the Maharani, was elegant and had once been a ravishing beauty. Their daughter, Sanita, was a troubled girl. She had everything money could buy but not happiness. She was a gifted artist and unaffectedly showed me her collection displayed in her own gallery. When we were alone, she hinted at being in love with someone her parents would never accept and I gleaned from her anguished eyes that she was suffering. Her body was thin and emaciated, and her lovely, long black hair was thinning. The palace was everything you could imagine an exotic paradise to be but Sanita was trapped in a prison, hewn out by social etiquette and eons of Indian family and religious tradition. Our meeting was brief, but the look in her eyes when we parted haunted me and I wished I had had the power to help her. Months later I heard of her untimely death. It was hinted that she committed suicide by throwing herself off her gallery balcony, but I knew she really died of a broken heart.

Years later in York I was taking tea at Yorkshire's famous Betty's Café when I spied a little Indian girl swinging her legs under the table cloth, carefully eating a bun. Her eyes, her face, and her demeanour were Sanita's. I thought what on earth is Sanita doing here in York? I smiled at the child and she smiled back. It was Sanita, and I knew she had returned to address her past life issues. Inwardly I wished her well as I left and although she had no recollection of me, she received the energy I sent her and she spontaneously returned it. Walking past the "Lost

Paradise" sign, I recalled her pain and hoped that she had finally found the happiness she craved, understanding only too well that being in Paradise is not always the answer to our desires and does not necessarily create the inward paradise we seek.

CHAPTER 4

Tsunamika

Our first evening in Dune was relaxing and while my son visited a nearby temple, I ventured to the meditation centre that nestled amongst the jungle bushes with a life-size, weatherworn statue of a male dancer balancing on one leg. Inside I followed a long walkway lined with stone pillars, which mysteriously lead to the elongated Yoga hall built in the lush jungle scrub. A large red and black tapestry of Buddha was mounted at the far end where a small lamp burnt. Set out on the red tiled floor were red and blue Yoga mats. The Yoga teacher welcomed me warmly shaking my hand as another person entered and all together we waited in silence before the lesson listening to the constant drone of night insects waking to own the evening. As we closed our eyes on the fading light, the bushes peered through the open pillars reminding us that the outside was only a breath away from the inside, like the inner landscape of our minds- all we had to do was relax and tap into the great wealth of our own inner worlds. An hour passed by in the tranquil setting and when we opened our eyes, it was a surprise to find that the night had stolen the last remnants of day and we were enclosed in jungle darkness.

In the hot night air, I was afraid to be bitten by mosquitoes and hurried to meet Branden outside the restaurant where we quickly took a table. He explained an unusual event. He was passing the workers' huts on his way back to Dune from his visit to the temple, when he saw a funeral procession. The tiny road was strewn with flowers as people gathered around the pyre where the body was laid. Just as the burning torches struck the dry wood, a shimmering figure rose out of the body and walked across Branden's path disappearing into the trees. I was not surprised at the apparition and neither was he. When I was a small child, I could smell death and knew when someone was going to die. In the process of growing up, however, my senses were dulled and I lost the ability to smell death, although my psychic intuition and other gifts sharpened. Death is not a fearful process; it is only the passage into elsewhere.

After our meal, which was of a satisfactory standard, we walked back to our garden apartment under the full moon haloed in a golden aura with the sound of the sea echoing across the high wall that safeguarded the eco village. I thought of a dance pupil who had visited the place with her boyfriend on that fated Christmas before the tsunami struck. She had phoned her mother on Christmas Eve and left a loving message. The next day both she and her boyfriend were killed and their bodies never recovered. All her mother has left of her daughter is her voice message. The sound of the sea mocked the moment. The mother's life was changed forever. As we entered our room, we noticed little handmade dolls on our pillows with tiny tags attached declaring "*Tsunamika*, a living symbol" "She has been handmade by women who live by the ocean, the women whose lives changed forever after the tsunami struck, the women who are exploring a new way of living: women who are empowering themselves."

I was reassured to know that the women were picking up the pieces of their lives. I understood that process very well.

As I lay my head on the pillow in the dark, with the air conditioner droning above, I remembered the night when I lay down on the empty floor in Pear Tree Cottage, heavily pregnant, feeling alone and afraid, forcing myself to find inner strength to face an unknown evil entity. I had dreamt of owning the beautiful cottage, yet the reality turned out to be far from idyllic.

Back in Pear Tree Cottage when I battled through an uncomfortable night fighting my terror, fearing for the future and my unborn baby, I had wanted to run away back to London and my busy life style but things seemed different in the early morning light. The fear drained away and as I spied with pride the delightful trees and enticing garden I wondered whether I had imagined the horror of the previous night. I stretched and looked at Chinda, who also had regained her confidence as she licked my face and wagged her tail and was excited to explore her new territory outside. I unlocked the door and waddled down the stairs into the bright light of the hallway, which was gleaming green and gold. The kitchen was bright and airy with the morning sun streaming in through the conservatory. I glanced out of the window and was thrilled to see my lawn bejewelled with dew. I was excited to own a garden and relieved not to be cooped up in a tiny flat in London. As I walked towards the old creaky gate overgrown with delicious, yellow climbing roses, the air was fresh with sweetness. I breathed deeply, relieved to have escaped the grime and fumes of the city. The night horror drifted away as I bent forwards to pick a stray rose trailing near the shed and was shocked when a ruddy face peered through the gap in the fence.

" Mornin,' Missus! You t' new owners then?" he inquired in his broad Yorkshire accent.

I nodded and smiled.

"I'm Sid, t' milkman. My farm's across t' way. You just nod, missus, if ya need owt!" he grinned looking at my huge stomach.

"Oh—er—that's very kind. Could I have a pint of milk please?"

"Have what ya like, missus: got all sorts!"

"I'm afraid my husband hasn't arrived yet, and I haven't got any money; can I pay later?"

He laughed saying, Folks round 'ere pay at t' end o' week like!"

I followed him out of the yard and round to the front of the house where the village green glistened in the early morning sunshine. Sid's lovely Shire horse stood patiently waiting with her cart laden with milk, bread, cheese, ham, chicken, cake and a whole variety of fruits and vegetables. As I stroked the horse's nose, her brasses glinted and her tail and mane, which were beautifully groomed, twitched. She whinnied as Sid slipped her a carrot.

"This is Daisy!" he announced proudly.

"Ya see, as I said afore, we've all sorts and what we've not got we can get. There's only three shops 'ere, ya see, so folks relies on us!" I was overwhelmed with the choice.

Sid helped me indoors with my delicious food. Back in the kitchen Sid took out a little red book from his pocket and wrote down all my purchases. "Ya best turn them off, what with the price an all of electricity being what it is!" He stepped forwards and took the liberty to switch off the kitchen lights. My stomach churned.

"The folks before ya was the same. Always had kitchen lights on, even at dead o'night!"

I smiled nervously as a twinge of uneasiness flashed across my face.

"Don't worry about nowt. There's plenty o'folk that'll elp ya any time. Bye then!"

I watched Sid stroll out the gate in the bright sunlight with his red hair and friendly, rugged face nodding and I felt a shiver of uncertainty stray into the calm of the morning.

Chinda sauntered back into the kitchen with her fur wet from the grass and as I bent down to stroke her, the baby somersaulted. I straightened my back and the morning sickness returned. I needed to eat something and tore voraciously into a bread bun as the sound of a horn hooted across the empty hallway. I rushed to open the front door and saw the disgruntled faces of Will and his friend Dan. They had obviously been arguing and were tired after their ordeal.

"We need hot tea!" shouted Will as he alighted from the driver's seat and swiftly pecked my cheek. They both followed inside, and I made them a hearty breakfast with all the food I had bought from Sid, explaining as I cracked the large, organic eggs into the pan, that the milkman was a veritable walking supermarket

I was so glad to see all my pots and pans again, littering the kitchen and it wasn't long before the house was full of chests and crates and our meagre bits of furniture. The rest of the day was spent unpacking and putting our furnishings into place making the house warm and cosy. We even lit a fire in the medieval grate and cracked open a bottle of Champagne as the day dimmed and the night closed in. The previous night's horror faded and I decided not to talk about it, especially as the atmosphere was different as we laughed and joked away the evening. It was fantastic to have a bed again. I drifted off to sleep almost immediately but was disturbed by nightmare images flashing in and out of my dreams and the sound of clashing steel breaking through the calm. In the morning my head ached with the intrusion and strangely Dan awoke with the same headache complaining that he had had a bad night, disturbed by crashing and banging. He thought it was the central heating pipes rattling and clattering.

"Have to get the system seen to!" he stated firmly as he took an aspirin with his coffee. The fear crept back into my head of the unknown presence, still watching and waiting. I knew it was there.

Back in India, on waking after our first night in Dune, the sea lashed out in an angry frenzy, booming and crashing into the dry earth as an electric storm crackled over the eco village. I lay in bed with the whir of the air conditioning buzzing in the heat of the early morning. I remembered the little Tsunamika doll placed on my pillow the previous night and wondered how the sound of the great wall of water rising up over the land must have made a terrifying explosive blast, greater than I could ever imagine and how the people must have fled with abject horror as the ocean monster chased them, slaughtering everything in its path. When there is no place to hide from the thunder and there is no time for fear, elongated moments of time are sealed in a lost zone and everything turns into slow motion before oblivion steals time. The tremor of the storm gradually weakened to a distant lashing as the sea calmed before breakfast. I was not very hungry because my stomach was upset and I couldn't watch my son tuck into his spicy meal, so I returned to the apartment. The heat in the bathroom was overpowering, like the jungle in the monsoon. I remembered during my first visit to India that we were invited on safari in the jungle, by a maharaja friend who had a special bungalow deep in the forest in the South. It was the most exciting and frightening experience I had ever imagined after living a sheltered life in a farming community in rural England, where the only knowledge I had of a jungle was from films.

My mind meandered back to that time and I remembered the Land Rover easing into the narrow tracks, hewn under great bamboo cathedral arches, while exotic birds, species I had only seen in books, cawed and cried. I shuddered with delight at the intimacy of being so close to the wildlife and was overwhelmed by the sights and sounds of the animals but the shifty rustle of the trees unnerved me as eyes peered through unfamiliar bushes. After bounding in and down and up and around dirt tracks, we finally came to a small, squat building with a thatched banana and rush-mat roof. The *chokidar* (watchman) met us on the veranda and we followed him to a tiny black shed. When he opened the door, two round faces appeared from the dark. His wife held her small son on her lap as they waited in the black hole. It shocked me to see their bleak faces staring, even more so as they cowered away in fear when I spoke to them. Mahindra, the maharaja's daughter, explained they had never seen a white, blonde haired woman before and that they were veering away in respect. As we walked back to the bungalow, the *chokidar* told us that a tiger a few days previous had stolen his dog and had run off with it for a light snack. He had shot but only wounded it, so he warned us that the angry, injured tiger could attack at any time. The idea of the tiger, lying in wait to pounce, scared me, even though I love tigers and every snapping of a twig or rustling of a leaf made me jump.

We were served a concoction of rice and *dahl* as we sat on the wooden floorboards in the bungalow that was little more than a wooden and concrete hut with a small sitting room and a bedroom with three camping beds laid out in a row. I only picked at the food and watched as the little woman who had cowered away from me earlier cleared away my dish averting her eyes. When the others had finished, we walked out into the clearing. I was surprised to see the servant woman with her small child cleaning our dishes with dry sand. They didn't use water and rubbed each tin plate with the grainy earth until it was shiny. The chokidar lead us through the brush, and we followed in single file. I was in the middle, with Mahindra in front and Will bringing up the rear; and I mused that if the tiger was going to spring, I hoped I was not going to be its first meal.

Just as we neared a stream, we came upon the fires and the small huts of an encampment where elephants were chained to trees and some were busy moving logs from piles to be transported to towns by lorries. The chokidar said he wanted to show us something special. I held my breath when I spied two baby elephants side by side bathing their feet in the river. He said that they were twins and that it was rare for an elephant to give birth to twins. They were so cute. I love elephants and it was a dream-come-true to stroke them. The hair on the back of their necks was sharp like black plastic strands jutting out of their crumpled skin. They flapped their ears, playfully treading the water and their deep eyes, set in a flutter of fawn lashes, smiled as I stroked their backs. I wanted to linger longer by the stream to play with them but since the camp was settling down and the afternoon light fading, our *chokidar* was keen to return in case the tiger was on the prowl.

As we passed the smoking fires, some of the women were preparing vegetables, boiling them in large pots over bare flames, which licked the sides of the blackened pots, bubbling like witches' brew. Others chopped bits of meat on rough stones as they sat on the bare ground amidst the gentle chink and clink of the rattling chains of the adult elephants swaying and shifting their weight from foot to foot in a twilight dance. In the grey failing light, trekking back through the jungle was frightening. The night cacophony struck up like a symphony orchestra tuning up before a grand performance. Creatures called one to another warning of our presence in their midst and monkeys swished through branches overhead as they leapt across gaps in the trees.

Back at the bungalow the oil lamps were lit. Food was brought to us by the *chokidar*'s wife with her little boy daring to sneak glances at me from behind her sari. Again, I wasn't hungry and began to feel nervous about snakes coiled in the rafters, as well as insects, giant spiders and mosquitoes. I couldn't sleep in the heat and the noise of the night, as I wrestled with my silly fears and phobias of snakes and creepy crawly creatures. I pulled up the heavy, scratchy woollen blanket over my head but it was too hot sleeping in my clothes. All night I drifted in and out of dreams of wild eyes glaring and staring from rustling bushes.

In the early hours of the morning, we were woken by the chokidar, who had set out our breakfast on the veranda. I ate some *chapattis* with jam and drank raw coffee, which stung the back of my throat. Then we were lead to the compound where we were to mount our elephants, which were ready to ride through the jungle on a special safari arranged just for the three of us. Our elephants were waiting patiently swinging their trunks, doing a little side–step dance. The twin babies were in a bamboo enclosure and were munching on piles of leaves with their busy heads nodding in the early morning sunshine.

Each of us had his and her own *mahout* (driver) at the head of each elephant and they quickly climbed up behind the flapping ears with great ease, but when the rest of us tried to climb to a flat board tied in with rope on the elephants' backs, it was quite a different matter. It was extremely awkward scaling up, and I had to be pulled and pushed into place by one of the attendants. Eventually after nearly falling off, I perched precariously on top of a wooden board and was tied in by rope. I wanted to get off. It reminded me of the fair when the coveted ride stops and you clamber in excitedly, then realizing you're a long way off the ground, you feel extremely unsafe and panic, screaming "Let me off"; but it's too late as the ride swings into action.

Your heart jumps into your mouth with fright as the ride lurches forward and there's nothing for it but to hang on for dear life.

The motion of an elephant's gait is very unusual and it takes a while to find the right position in which to sit comfortably. Once you fall into the rhythm of forwards, sideways, backwards you can anticipate the incline and go with it, like leaning into a bend on the back of a motorbike, rather than straining against it. The wooden board was difficult to sit on and holding onto the thick rough rope was hard as it dug into my hands. Mahindra, in front, dared to turn and wave, but I was too scared to let go and nodded a greeting, smiling insincerely. Will was behind, but I couldn't see how he was faring, as I had to concentrate on keeping my balance. After a while the thrill of riding an elephant through the jungle took over from the sickly fear that had engulfed me, and I began to enjoy a privileged experience. If someone had shown me a photo of myself riding an elephant through thick jungle like Mogli from the *Jungle Book*, I never would have believed it, but being high near the branches of sweeping trees and close to exotic birds and staring monkeys scratching each other, I was lost in a wonderland of the magical forest.

Elephants are very careful creatures. Whenever we came to a steep river bank where we had to edge our way down, my elephant, Dutaanka, placed one foot forwards holding it there for a long time, while I hung suspended, angled over one side, before she deemed it safe to place her other foot down, taking as much time and care as the first foot. Meanwhile, I hung precariously over the edge of the other side until she thought it was safe to move. Once we had cleared the embankment, crossing the quick-flowing, brown, muddy river was thrilling but equally unnerving. It was amazing feeling her anchor each foot safely in the mud. Through her skin I was part of her body like a dependent appendage totally reliant on her skill to get us through the flowing water. My *mahout* turned to smile at me wryly as my elephant dared to dip her trunk in the water and fling it backwards to spray a little my way. I was too scared to move and didn't flinch forcing a cheerful response, as though that kind of thing happened to me every day!

Back on dry land we headed towards an opening in the scrub but the head *mahout* made a signal and we all stopped in a hushed pause. To our left was a herd of wild elephants. My *mahout* whispered: "Missy Sahib, those are wild herd. We must turn away and keep smell of tame elephants down wind. If they scent us, they will charge and we will fall off elephant and die!"

I had not for one moment thought our trek through the jungle would be dangerous. I had considered it more of a fun frolic like donkey rides on the beach, not a real escapade that might be life threatening. I gulped and stiffened my position, tensing my body in a frozen panic. The head mahout steered us carefully along a different pathway far from the wild herd so that eventually we were out of danger.

The previous night, over dinner, our *chokidar* had told us of a hippy woman who was camping in the forest and who had taken to sitting in meditation along a great wild tusker's favourite path. Earlier that week, when the tusker had taken his special route, he merely whisked her up in his trunk and threw her into the brush, when he could have pounded straight through her. I imagined her shock when she was rudely awoken from her deep trance to be hurled in the air by an indignant male elephant. I thought of the incident and felt relieved to be in the safe hands of the skilled *mahouts,* who gave us a wonderful, unforgettable experience on safari through the jungle. As my mind drifted to the present, I knew that I would be eternally grateful to the maharaja who had organised a once in a lifetime event.

When Branden returned from breakfast, my jungle memory dissolved and we decided to take a swim in the pool, which was built on a raised platform overlooking the sea, high above the level of the trees, so that it appeared we were swimming in the air alongside the birds. There was a wall built around the village and a guard stood on duty by the gate day and night. The entrance to the private beach was through a brightly painted gate designed by a modern artist. After swimming we strolled down to the beach where the evidence of the tsunami's destruction was brutally obvious. Dead wood and trees lay dry and sterile in a brown parched mass along the seashore. Just as I was sucked into a depressing picture of the annihilation, a parade of butterflies flitted past, all different colours, scattering my line of vision through the sun, in a haphazard wave of beauty. I imagined the never ending flow of fluttering wings to be like the souls lost to the tsunami, with each spirit bearing a lantern of hope and every beacon of light shining its eternal fire to light their way beyond. Along the shoreline hovering above the playful sea, the butterflies flew on and on until the black silhouette of the procession dimmed to a fine pencil line before disappearing into nothing.

Branden had arranged a visit to a nearby Kali temple and hired a little yellow and black motorised *phut phut*. We trundled along the bumpy cart road and I wrapped a thick scarf around my hip to cushion the bumps as we bounced in and out of the pitted dirt track. Eventually we chugged into the busy highroad, with cars and lorries whizzing past, until we turned down a leafy lane to a field leading to an ancient temple complex in a dirty, rubbish-ridden field, strewn with litter reminiscent of piles of debris left scattered after a pop concert. We parked by a clump of trees and walked to a ramshackle shanty row of broken stalls along a dirt track splattered with fresh cow dung and old dried manure etched into the scorching earth, where we had to walk barefoot. The baking grit stung my feet. I tried to walk daintily through the excrement, but the stones made it impossible to tread easily through the waste. My son and our driver had no problems walking bare foot to the temple, but I hated it.

Near the end of the line of broken stalls, two were open for business selling all kinds of *puja* gifts. Branden bought what was necessary to fulfill his *puja* rites and I followed him to the shrine hidden below the ground. It was dark in the cave, where the holy statue of Kali stood powerfully staring through her deep black eyes. Inside the bowels of the enclave, the priest and his assistant were completing a ceremony for a family. I stared at the awesome statue with her dominant, forbidding expression.

She represented an extreme form of Durga and was terrifying. A large figurine guarded the inner sanctum and had a string of skulls dangling from her neck falling over her naked bosom. I wanted to take a photo but the assistant forbade it. The priest flicked his hand and placed his head on one side, pushing the assistant away to affirm that I could take a picture of him. As my flash lit up the cave momentarily, the dirt stained walls reflected ancient paintings of gods and goddesses with sinister faces peering from a depth of hostile poses. When I inspected the photo of the priest, I could see his young face caught in wide-eyed surprise and his plump body swathed in sweat with a pink dhoti tucked in at his waist. In the dark I could not see how youthful he looked with his boyish black curls that shook playfully as I thanked him. Back in the bright sunshine my son waited for me as we made our way to the *puja* area, and together with the driver he set up a place amongst the broken bricks to light his offering and to say prayers. I was moved by his devotion and knowledge of the religion that he followed with precision and dedication.

While they were busy, I wandered to look at the large statue, which stood elevated high into the open sky supported by a structure built like a supermarket car park. The bright blue building supported the carving of Kali, so that the deity could be seen from miles across the open field. The effigy was garishly painted in gold, red, blue and black and at the top of the dome was a fan of cobras poised to protect the icon, while underneath, the cows wandered freely leaving their excrement embedded in the general flotsam and jetsam abandoned by the daily visitors. Overhead the electric pylons incongruously formed a crisscross of wires scrambling into the unblemished sky coaxing the present to blend into the past.

As we climbed back into our little *phut phut* taxi, the driver pummelled the horn, which was as effective as a child's squeaky toy amongst the horned scrimmage in the centre of Pondecherry. We decided to visit the famous ashram where the "little mother" had lived. We paid our respects to her in the lovely courtyard, but we didn't stay long as my son wanted to have a special Vedic massage by a trained doctor who pounded, pushed and pulled the body into shape. We searched through the town with many French street signs still in evidence after the occupancy in four main quarters of the city. It was interesting that the police wore red pillbox hats similar to the French *gendarmes*. Searching the whereabouts of the specialist was tedious and tiring in the heat. We eventually found it set in a row of houses opposite a cluster of huts with an open sewer running in front of the dwellings where a child was busy squatting over the open drain, watched by a couple of thin dogs. I tried not to look at the sewer as we knocked at the door and were dutifully shown in by an old woman.

The doctor smiled a greeting and took Branden upstairs while I was shown a seat in the kitchen that had a large television and a computer perched on a rickety table. The old woman limped badly and eased herself onto a small bed where she became engrossed in an Indian soap opera, which blared across the screen. I busied myself reading a few magazines, one of which had an interesting heading, "Food is sustaining—unhealthy food is draining." As I read the words, I was aware that my mouth was very dry so I took a piece of chewing gum from my bag. The old woman looked up from the television and watched carefully as I placed the small tablet into my mouth. I offered one to her and she shyly accepted. I watched her face as she chewed on it for a moment then took it from her mouth and threw it out of the window, whereupon she adeptly worked the computer and waddled to a large fridge where she examined a round green fruit and handed one to me, miming how to eat it. At first I declined, but then I decided I should try it. I took one bite and spat out the sour juice. It tasted like an unripe gooseberry. She motioned me to throw it out of the window but I was reluctant, as I was not use to discarding waste in such a carefree manner. As she pressed me to do so, however, I copied her and threw it out feeling guilty.

When Branden had completed the treatment, I was curious and wanted to experience it but I was nervous and asked him to sit outside the room. I was embarrassed to take off all my clothes except for my pants, and I lay down on the massage bed uncomfortably with my eyes closed. The doctor, who was very professional, was dressed in a small *dhoti* with his upper body bathed in sweat and his bald head gleaming from his previous exertion with my son. I was not prepared for the treatment, which was a mixture of torture and delight. The doctor smothered his hands in herbal oil and began to stroke my hair with the substance. The motion grew fierce until he was almost pulling the hair out of my head, and I lay still afraid to move. He worked through my body on my neck, back and arms, almost twisting them off at the shoulders. He sat on my back and pummelled my spine. He pushed his fingers into my ears until I cried out, whereupon he stopped. Then he kneaded my stomach pushing his fingers into my tummy button until I squirmed. My legs were in agony as he slapped, pounded and thrashed them. The massage took an hour and by the time he had finished, I was swamped in oil from head to toe like a greasy sausage. I was given paper in which to soak off the excess oil, but Branden and I needed to get back to shower. I am sure the treatment was good for me, although at the time I wasn't sure; my son said he definitely felt much better.

The next day we returned to Pondecherry to shop but had to visit a small office where Branden could access the web. Our driver stopped outside a row of spice shops clouded in a dusty pungency. A cornucopia of aromatic smells, mostly cumin seed, garlic and licorice, stung my nostrils and lingered on my lips in the dry heat. Just before midday the temperature was rising and the sun baked the street in a hot lather of bodies. Across the road I watched a woman pushing a little girl in the back, forcing her to walk faster. She was about ten years old, and the tension in her small body portrayed her reluctance to go with the woman. Uncharacteristically, the child's hair was brushed and left free to fall around her pretty face; she wore a long, flowing skirt, with a sparkly top. I feared for the child what was in store for her, but I knew there was nothing I could do to prevent her from the awaiting pain.

Sitting in my safe seat in the taxi, I wanted to hide from the truth. My mind raced back to a time when I was teaching in a

Catholic school run by Irish nuns in West Bengal and had stood in the children's dormitory, which reeked of urine and sickly sweets and where rows upon rows of small beds were crammed closely together. I stood near the window and looked out on a primitive scene of the locals working in the fields where the women carried large pots of water on their heads and the men drove the oxen along the dirt tracks with the sound of children below me singing in English, "Onward, Christian soldiers." I feared what lay in wait for many of the little ones, knowing that once they left the safe haven of the school, life would treat them harshly. As the sun shone through the shutters and shed a golden, dusty path before me, I promised myself in those moments that I would return to India. In the heat of the moment, sitting in the scooter taxi, I was glad to have fulfilled an ambition of helping to raise some money for schools, but I was not satisfied that that was enough when there were children, like the little girl across the street, enduring torment. I reasoned with myself that each of us must carve his or her own destiny and from our clouded view here on earth, we cannot see the greater picture waiting for us beyond the cosmos. The little girl disappeared out of sight around the corner and I prayed that her pain would not linger.

We enjoyed our shopping spree and returned to the compound with a few gifts to take home. Our time in Dune was ending, and we had to pack to make ready for the next part of our journey. In the morning I was woken by the sound of the booming sea, breaking angrily across the beach, thrashing the trees and battering the buildings. Grey rain, warm rain, thick rain like a breeze blocking wall, flooded the gardens and lashed the earth in a red mud bath. The rain echoed my sadness. I had loved the feeling of Dune and the warmth of the friendly people but the next part of our journey lay in wait, and we were eager to forge our way forwards towards the Blue Mountains where our quest was to find Granny's grave.

CHAPTER 5

Madurai and Memories

Surrender to the moment. Surrender to the journey. Surrender your being to the great universe when you travel beyond your knowing. When you give yourself unconditionally to the experience, the great ones in the cosmos listen and guide you, whether the journey is short or long, direct or delayed; they live in your shadow until your safe return. As we boarded the taxi through the torrential downpour in the compound, I thanked the great ones for their guidance and asked for their help to lead us safely through our seven-hour drive across Tamil Nadu to Madurai.

    Swirls of clouds like whipped cream panned the mountains in the distance as the rain swept behind us. We drove through miles of brush scrub jungle outlined with varieties of long palm trees with smallholdings and mud hut dwellings punctuating the endless flat paddy fields. After forty years I noticed that the people and their way of life had not changed much in the outlying villages, but there were not so many beggars or diseased, people or dying children, and I noted an increase in factories and hospitals built in rural areas. It was comforting to see the general, overall improvement in many peoples' lives. I had only known India on the tail end of the British Raj rule and was warned by Branden that people's attitude to the British was not always friendly. The tempo of living changed in India for the

British when Independence was declared and when the Indian people reclaimed their heritage, they tidily locked away British Raj ideals in closed closets, except for the railways, which are integral to India's new world success. Embarrassingly laid to rest is the guilt and blame game, which occasionally rises to the surface when certain words come up accidentally in conversation, such as "servants."

As we raced through uneven tracks with our young driver chatting on his mobile, my thoughts meandered back to a time at Granny's house where the servants were ubiquitous in our lives and the very idea of living without them was totally abhorrent. Granny had a good relationship with all her staff, particularly Mary who had been a lifelong loyal lady-in-waiting. Only one of her cooks, who stole regularly from her, had eventually to be dismissed. The night he was sacked he put *datura*, poisonous snake venom, in Granny's dinner. Later that night she became very ill. She knew immediately who was responsible and turned his venomous intentions back onto him, whereupon his screams were heard late into the night. He died of the effects of snake poison, although none could be traced in his body. Granny explained the "law of intention." If you wish someone harm, it will come back on you ten times worse than you originally intended. Likewise, if you spread good intentions, they will multiply and bring you more love than you ever imagined possible.

I remembered how things changed at Granny's house when her daughter, Prudence, left her home in West Bengal after the death of Jeremy, her husband, to live with Granny in the Nilgiris. Her daughter's attitude towards the servants was very different and a ripple of unease spread throughout the household as she bludgeoned her way through everything upsetting the established daily routine. She was a socialite, always preferring to gad from party to party and was hardly ever at home, leaving the servants strict instructions to attend to everything while she concentrated on all her commitments, such as tennis, visiting army wives and the officers' mess, riding and bird watching. She did from time to time organise her own soirées, although she didn't always host them, leaving Will and me to fill in and apologise for her absence. She did, however, offer alcohol on these occasions, which Granny deplored, making her retreat to her room. Every Friday morning was Prudence's Bridge set and while we were living there, Will and I were roped in to play.

The Bridge set was a group of interesting women from different countries who were accompanying their husbands stationed at the army cantonment. They often had conflicting ideas about many things; but they wholeheartedly agreed on one thing, that they had all found their houses absolutely filthy when they first arrived. Margarite, a friendly American woman, who was an adept Bridge player said: "The stench was diabolical! Everywhere was infested with rats. Well, Dan was incensed and stripped down to his waist and took a baseball bat and worked his way through each room swiping and blasting the damn things until the whole place was a bloody battlefield; but believe me, he got rid of those goddamned creatures real quick!"

Aunt Clarisse, who was an elderly eccentric English lady, who preferred to dress in Edwardian style clothes and was totally locked in a past time zone, visited the Bridge set. She had a deep, booming voice and spoke above anyone who tried to steal her limelight. Gin and tonic was always served throughout the game, and Aunt Clarisse apparently never imbibed more than two. Her manners were impeccable, and she expected the same high standard of behaviour from everyone. Her only public sin was smoking. She smoked what she called, "camel dungs" as the brand was Camels and unfortunately there were two types—one that was for visitors and one made for the locals. That particular morning prior to her visit she had sent her bearer to buy her "camel dungs," but unfortunately he had bought the local brand, which had large amounts of marijuana rolled into the tobacco.

Aunt Clarisse duly began our Bridge game huffing and puffing on her cigarette, stuffed in a long black holder, which she wafted around the room as though she were conducting a large orchestra. The smell was unusual, but we were busy concentrating on our hands. We noticed that Clarisse's voice grew louder and her concentration diminished as she downed two large gins in one go and puffed harder on her Camels, until she was in a solo fog. Her uncharacteristic behaviour grew worse as she demanded more gin, laughing and swearing and blaspheming in an alarming manner when she fell off her chair and rolled around the floor kicking her legs in a much undignified pose. Prudence looked at Will and together they attempted to gather Clarisse up off the floor, but she was very strong. Margarite helped to push her while Will pulled, and they tumbled her into her waiting car with the help of her loyal driver. The next time I saw Clarisse was when she invited Will and me for coffee, but the Camels remained on the mantle piece. She didn't mention that unfortunate occasion and served us hot water in tiny teacups as she had forgotten to add any coffee!

The Bridge mornings were always a source of entertainment as there was little to do in the hill station. Margarite, who was a newcomer to the circle, having had her house sanitised and repainted after the rat incident, regaled us with the next installment of life in their army house saying: "And ya know, they gave us a house boy, Radhi- he was only fifteen and had no experience of working with a family or cooking. Well, I had to spend time with him and show him what to do. He was okay with the basics if I watched over him, but Dan pressured me to invite the Colonel and his wife for dinner, so I had to trust him. I asked him to cook prawns for the starter and chicken for the main, explaining that I would rustle up something for the desert. I sent him to the bazaar to buy everything but I didn't check the shopping, which was stupid of me, but I was busy with all the other stuff."

While organising the cards in our hands, we all listened intently as she continued, "When he brought the first course, I was mad, real mad, but kept quiet as everyone tucked into a plate of curried vegetables minus the prawns. You see you just have to watch them. They learn how to economise with the money, if you get my drift. The main course was passable and tasted okay. When I went into the kitchen to supervise the desert, however, I noticed in the trash can some furry carcasses with long tails." We all paused to look up from our hands as she shuffled hers and went on:

"Rats! Damned rats with their eyes looking up and their insides cut out in my trash can staring up at me! I could have strangled that wretched boy and all he could say was:

"Mem Sahib, chickens? No chickens, but rats plenty. I cook them—very tasty!"

Well, I nearly killed him and sent him packing there and then!"

We all commiserated but continued to eye up our hands. I broke the silence with an equally shocking tale of when Granny's sister, Grace, who had been a foreign correspondent for the *Times* newspaper, had wanted to give a bonfire party for her British friends in Madras and had asked the cook to come into the sitting room to discuss the party. He looked very shy and held his cap in his hands respectfully looking down at the floor as Grace said: "Now cook, I'm giving a bonfire party for all my friends; what would you like to make?"

"Mem Sahib, I do not know; what you like best?"

"Well, I thought we might give our guests shepherd's pie, since you cook that very nicely."

"That is good, Madam; for how many people?"

"About fifty!"

I watched his jaw drop in disbelief until he plucked up the courage to reply: "Mem Sahib, I can cook shepherd's pie for five people or for fifteen people sometime, but I cannot chew up all that meat for fifty people!"

Just at that moment our bearer came in bringing in a tray of hot potato cakes and we all exchanged glances. "Don't worry," Prudence reassured everyone, "he is a very reliable cook."

"I wish mine was reliable," Audrey, another army guest, piped up from the second table.

"I just can't get the damned cook to serve up hot buttered toast with my hot boiled egg at breakfast. He either gets the egg hot and the toast cold or vice versa. How does one teach him to do it?"

"Well, my dear, I never venture into the kitchen," said Lucy, a middle-aged colonel's wife (no one ever dared to step into the kitchen for fear of what they would find), "but I tell you, my man always gets it right!"

"Just find out how he does it; then I can pass it onto my man," Audrey responded purposefully.

A week passed by and the Bridge party sat down as usual to our little gathering. Audrey arrived late and when she settled herself, she thought to enquire if Lucy had ventured into the kitchen to find the secret of producing hot buttered toast with a hot egg.

"I wish you hadn't asked that question, dear. You see I did go down to the kitchen the very next morning and well, cook stood over the egg boiling in the pan while he held two pieces of hot buttered toast under his armpits!"

"Must have been salty!" laughed Will.

Since those early days in India, I have never played Bridge again.

A few hours into the journey to Madurai we decided to stop by the wayside for a cup of coffee. We found a suitable café and invited our driver to sit with us, which would never have happened in Granny's day as our driver would never have been allowed to be in close social proximity with the family or take any food or drink in our company. Such was the rule of the ruling class at the time, and I am glad that things have changed for the better. Will and I had been friendly with all our drivers and servants, much to his mother's chagrin as she continually lost patience with them. I found it hard to live that way, and one time I even resorted to stealing medicine and aspirin from the house to give to the servants for their sick children, as they could not afford a visit from the doctor. Sometimes I had secret fun with my sweeper servant girl as she used to dress me up as a sweeper woman and I used to regale her in my fine clothes. We were both very young and played games like sisters. We never thought it was wrong but if we had been caught, she would have lost her job!

The stop was fruitless as the coffee was not good, although the driver and Branden drank it. Back in the car we moved swiftly, ploughing our way through post-monsoon muddy roads and on for another three hours before we decided to stop for lunch. The grey day loomed over the tightly compact buildings as we squeezed our way into a tiny parking spot. I thought we were going to eat at a restaurant and was shocked when we disappeared inside a small, dark and dingy diner where the food was cheap and plentiful. I felt uncomfortable being the only white woman. The locals stared. Branden made himself at home immediately in the café and spoke to the server in Hindi. A large banana leaf was set before him and substantial dollops of different kinds of rice, dahl and vegetables were slopped onto the leaf. I couldn't force myself to touch any of it even though I was very hungry and sat watching in awe as he heartily tucked into the meal served from huge cauldrons. After he had finished, I was relieved to be on our way again in what seemed like an endless grey-lidded day.

Eventually when we reached Madurai, an ancient city with an amazing antediluvian temple complex in the centre of an antiquated thoroughfare, the streets were heaving with traffic, people, cows and long horned buffalo. Piles of rubbish were left decaying and fermenting in the heat. Monsoon drabness overshadowed the streets clouding the scene in a dreary veil, but it was Saturday and people were out on the streets enjoying a weekend in a relaxed atmosphere. Our driver lost his way several times, missing a vital turning in the dull rain. I dreaded the possibility of arriving at a squalid hotel with unclean beds and a filthy bathroom. Eventually as we left the fetid streets, we drove out onto a clear highway where the sun broke through the dingy oppression, revealing an amazing hotel, "The Heritance," which was another spark of brilliance engineered by Branden, allowing us a little luxury on our long journey.

The Inheritance was luxury personified set in beautiful grounds with pristinely tended gardens and small bungalows built in rows. We were shown to a massive apartment beautifully designed in a minimalist style with lovely wooden floors and heavy mahogany doors. The bathroom was created with an open Japanese elegance with sliding glass doors leading onto a small patio with a private outdoor pool that was just big enough to swim two strokes. I relished the thought of secret, naked swimming in the early morning. After the long seven-hour drive with incessant Bollywood music blaring, we were glad to relax in our new, sumptuous surroundings and shower.

Branden thought it would be a good idea to take a taxi into town and explore the ancient city in preparation for his planned Saturday evening devotion in the amazing temple. The darkness of the monsoon sky lifted and we walked in the oppressive heat of the afternoon sun. Branden bought a sugar cane drink from a street vendor and I had to turn away as I couldn't bear to watch the unclean procedure of making the juice with an ancient rusty mangle and worse still, to see the vendor wash a plastic cup in filthy water in which to serve the juice. I realized I had to come to terms with my Raj background and I had to learn not to be so fearful, but a few protective prayers never went astray.

As we walked in the scorching heat, street sellers hounded us and shopkeepers trailed after us to buy various articles, one even invited us to view the temples from the top of his shop roof. The Meenakshi Temple complex across the city was a stunning vision where history mingled cohesively with the technological, modern present. The settlers in the sixteenth century began the colossal building project and it was continued through the eighteenth century by the Nayaks. From the fantastic vantage point you could see the twelve towers majestically soaring into the sky; each tower (*Gopura*) was layered from top to bottom with statues of deities, mythical beasts, monsters and naked goddesses. Mini-pyramid outer temples painted the skyline around a square central temple, and each minor temple was built layer upon layer upon layer with identical tiny statues like a tiered wedding cake. Amazingly each level was exactly the same as the first, designed in a repetitive pattern of pink, orange, blue and green all the way to the top where a forbidding dragon looked down on the people with white–fanged teeth. The dragon's tail fanned out on a Chinese style, tiled roof painted in red and green, with half-naked goddesses peering through the fantail. It was a truly awesome spectacle.

As we were ambling down the main street, a man approached Branden to take us in a bicycle taxi around the town. He had an earnest face and although his bicycle was worn, it worked and he offered us a cheap rate. He was amazed when Branden spoke to him in Hindi and he introduced himself, "Sir, my name is Davindra and I have wife and five children." It was difficult climbing on the rickety framework, as I could not bear very much weight on my hip, but Davindra kindly assisted me. We set off on our precarious trip around the city where his acquaintance with everyone afforded us privacy from pushy beggars. His thin body laboured against our weight, but his muscled legs fought the strain.

Flower market, fish market and spice market: each quarter announced its presence long before we reached the vicinity as the smell from each was distinctive. The banana market was really interesting and Davindra helped me down from the bike to follow him down a shadowy, dingy alley where bananas clustered in clumps, thickly bunched unripe on the branches. All the way through the passage were little black holes like prisons, where the unripe fruit was kept and heated with cow dung to quickly ripen the fruit. I shuddered at the thought of huge spiders lurking in the thick clusters and felt a claustrophobic urge to get out. I spied red bananas on a branch and hurriedly took a photo of them before I scurried back into the main street.

Since we showed great interest in the city, Davindra decided to extend the tour and took us on a detour near to where he lived. It was bearable weaving in and out of the small market streets, but when we hit the main roads our little bicycle was like a tiny, vulnerable fishing boat, tossed about on turbulent waves struggling to remain afloat alongside vast ocean liners. We were defenceless against the bustling traffic, modern cars, smoke fumes, dust, petrol and the screaming and screeching of fast motorbikes scraping next to our wheels. Up the steep inclines Branden hopped off and helped Davindra to push the cycle and afterwards, would scoot back when the road evened out. My hip jarred and jostled in the foray. Each time we squeezed into the traffic lanes with cars drumming and revving out fumes on either side of us, I closed my eyes and covered my mouth. I was terrified of being squashed as we raced across the massive junctions where all the traffic met in blaring confusion and poor Davindra had to peddle hard and furious to reach the other side before the traffic lights changed. Through the rough bumps and potholes the cars sped as we struggled to retain our balance and throughout, I was afraid of being trapped in the middle of a tangled mass of vehicles.

As we wound our way to a vast wasteland scattered with litter, debris, goats and cows, I was shocked to see a large pool of dank water used as a launderette. It was filthy, muddy and shallow, but the women produced streams of clean washing from the grimy pool, which they hung in rows near the cesspool. A sacred elephant swung its trunk from side to side under the bridge, where its owner tended to its needs while men slept on piles of rags unaware of the elephant's daily ablutions. Children came out of nowhere to wave and greet us as we juddered down the dusty streets. Branden decided it would be a good idea to visit the Ghandi museum, so Davindra nodded and pedalled on through the searing heat. Just as we were turning towards the museum, the sacred elephant sauntered towards us with its gaily painted trunk and decorated regalia. I was thrilled when we stopped for it to thrust its trunk in my face to blow air into my nostrils. I pushed some notes into the holes in its trunk and it tossed them back toward the mahout. I tingled with joy still feeling the warm air from its trunk in my face. As we turned into the car park, there was a hushed reverence severing the noise and bustle from the busy city into the quiet dignity of the grounds. I had read the life of Ghandi and seen the major film several times, marveling at the man's humble ability to gain the love and respect of the whole world.

Inside the dark building school children and college students were quietly inspecting the photos and articles of clothing together with pieces of cloth on display woven by Ghandi. In one glass case set out on a black, velvet shelf was a pair of his old sandals. I shuddered at the singularly forlorn objects laid in the coffin-like encasement. Old shoes often gave me unwarranted visions of the wearer and his emotions, together with articles of clothing close to the owner. As a teen-ager I was taken on a tour aboard Admiral Nelson's ship. When we came to the spot, painted bright red, where the surgeon performed operations at sea with primitive tools and no anesthetic, I had a flash of pain and horrific visions of amputations. When I saw Nelson's blood-stained vest, I fainted and had to be taken out. I can still recall the vision that the bloody shirt incited. So it was with Ghandi's shoes. They filled me with a deep sadness and strange flashes of his life flickered in my mind, including the heated confusion before his last moments when he was shot.

We didn't linger very long in the museum and were soon out into the bright sunshine where Davindra waited patiently. The ride back was tiring, tedious and laborious, taking over an hour to get back along the main roads. It was a slow, arduous ride as poor Davindra's legs bore our weight in the draining heat. Branden had booked him for the evening. I wasn't sure whether I could take any more bicycle transport, but it was impossible to change the arrangements as the poor man was looking forward to a hefty tip. When he dropped us off at our lodgings, Branden gave Davindra some money to buy himself some food and find a place to rest while he waited for the evening's toil back into town.

We ate in the hotel and prepared for our evening venture into the city. The hotel staff was bustling to and fro in a flurry, busily preparing for a prestigious wedding. Lights with little candle flames were hung on strings through the trees and along the sidewalk, where they shone haloing yellow circles on the ceiling in the dark. The sight of them dangling aimlessly in the air threw my mind back to a time in Pear Tree Cottage just before my first child was born.

That summer was the hottest on record for twenty years and the heat wave continued throughout the summer and only slightly abated in September. My baby was due to be born early October, and the last remaining weeks seemed endless. Pear Tree Cottage had been my dream house, but the beautiful dream had turned sour as strange happenings began to reveal a secret macabre history. I told myself that I imagined the eyes watching and the hidden presence that was forever spying on me. I told myself that the silhouette I sometimes glimpsed out of the corner of my eye was not real and the sound of a child crying in the distance and footsteps on the stairs and echoes of whispers around corners were imagined. Lights continually switching themselves on and the nightly banging and crashing throughout the house were not reality but part of my dreams. I tried to convince myself perhaps one day I would wake from the nightmare and not live in fear. My husband, Will, noticed a change in me and no matter how hard I tried to suppress my depression, I couldn't help feeling I was battling everything alone. I tried to discuss my anxieties with him, but he only smiled, not believing for one moment that the house had a sinister secret. He spent most of his days at the university and didn't understand the cottage the way I did. I didn't know anyone in the village and so my days were lonely, so different from my professional life in the theatre, which had been all consuming, exciting and exacting. I suppose Will thought he was doing the right thing when he invited his Aunt to stay for two weeks before the baby's birth, to make sure I had company and plenty of rest, but her presence was the last thing I wanted.

Aunt Berry was a robust, middle-aged woman, the head matron of a Christian Science Nursing Home in Hampstead, and was used to getting her own way in all matters, bludgeoning her way through anything and everything. At an early stage in her life she had taken charge of the family fortune and doled it out when and where she thought best, staying at relatives' houses where she spent a small fortune on food and goodies for the family. To this end, most of the relatives looked forward to her visit but wherever she stayed, she took over the running of the house. I did not relish the thought of her visit and tried to plead with Will to dissuade her, but he had spent money on two new sports cars, which he didn't want her to know about, and angled to butter her up to get further financial help. I didn't get on very well with her and found her blatant intrusion into my business rude and unacceptable. On my first visit to India, I left my clothes and belongings with her, only to find on my return, that she had opened all my cases, rifled through my clothes and even given some away to charity saying, "I thought you wouldn't mind dear, giving a few things away; after all, they were not your style!"

Will told me not to ruffle her feathers or make a fuss as it might upset our chance to gain more financial help. She also infuriated me when we visited her Hampstead flat above the nursing home. She cooked us a lovely meal but when we sat down afterwards to watch some television, she insisted on holding my little dog on her lap - little did I know that she was clipping away sporadically at Cheeni's fur. When the programme finished, Cheeni shot off her knee shaking loose clippings onto the carpet and stood half bald. I was horrified to see the state of my pet.

"I thought she needed clipping, dear; she had so many knots in her fur, I thought it best to chop it all away!" I was speechless, and Will ushered me home quickly before I could vent my anger on her.

Whenever she invaded a household, the occupants, for the sake of peace and a financial reward, always turned the other cheek, but I wasn't sure I was capable of doing that. She wasn't my aunt and I didn't care about the money. Somehow I had entered a lonely wilderness where it was just me and my little dog and my unborn baby struggling against the rest of the world. I was sure Will felt I was going insane and our relationship suffered, dwindling into little more than companionship. I had no money of my own and he controlled everything, even the small amount he gave me to waddle to the shops, which consisted of a post office, a grocers and a small supermarket. My pregnancy craving was for avocado pears, and I missed the multicultural choices available in most grocers in London. My initial visit to the village grocers was not very productive. The young man behind the counter eyed me suspiciously as I was dressed in my Indian caftan and dripping with Indian jewelry. I brushed dangerously past his fine display of King Edward potatoes.

"Do you have avocado pears?" I enquired.

He was silent, thought for a moment and then replied, "Naw, we only 'av cape!"

I managed to stifle my laughter and then asked: "Have you got any garlic?"

"Naw, we don't 'av that stuff round 'ere!"

"Well, do you have peppers?"

"Naw we don't 'av them!"

Needless to say, I left disappointed purchasing only six onions and a pound of apples.

One bright afternoon, Aunt Berry whirled into the house like a buzzard and altered the furniture, changing it to suit her needs, while Will stood motionless, blindly allowing her interference throughout the house. She piled the kitchen surfaces with boxes, baskets and tins of goodies more sumptuous than a Harrods's Christmas hamper, before throwing a bloody joint of beef into the cooker. Then she marched Will into the garden, where she took control of all the vegetable planting. I bit my lip and choked back the rising anger. Two weeks would soon pass, and I mustn't let her upset me. Eyes watched, something twitched sideways but was gone immediately. Sweat dripped down my back in a swift panic as I fought to breathe. I was slowly suffocating amidst boxes of dark chocolates, Turkish delight and nut clusters. "Anyone else would have been grateful," I thought I heard her say as I stood limply by the vegetable patch, where she was heftily digging up lettuces.

Admittedly the roast beef was delicious and the chocolates delightful, but when she ushered me out of my own kitchen saying, "You look dreadfully tired dear; why don't you have an early night? Will and I can watch that detective programme we like! That would be good, wouldn't it, Will?" He smiled and nodded choosing to ignore my glare. He knew I hated the detective series and that I was furious to be dismissed to bed. However, I went quietly, much to Will's relief and stood looking out of the small bedroom window. The air was cooling and the shadows were lengthening across the lawn. The day was dying with a gentle sigh as the scent of sweet, old-fashioned roses lingered. I lay down on the bed. Perhaps Berry was right, I should be grateful and appreciate her efforts. I resolved to try harder.

Just as I was about to close my eyes, I noticed a tinge of light in the far corner of the room. It stole my focus for a few moments as I struggled to make out what it was and where it was coming from. The golden iridescent light grew to about the size of a penny and glided gently across the ceiling. I was entranced by the halo of light flickering like a candle in the wind. As I gazed downwards, I was horrified. The light was emanating from a candle that was held by a woman dressed in a long, white nightdress with shoulder length, dark, curly hair. She walked as if in a trance, keeping her gaze directly ahead. Her pallor was ghostly. I stopped breathing as she sailed by the end of my bed holding the candle at arm's length in a white ceramic holder. Her body sucked up the light as she moved in the brightness leaving dark shadows behind. I witnessed the spectre hover momentarily near my cupboard before passing straight through it. There was something about her that terrified me, and yet her frightened eyes were pitiful. I sat bolt upright. I struggled to breathe and fought my way down the stairs barging through the door, interrupting their cosy scene. I screamed and breathlessly blurted out the horror of what I had witnessed. The two of them exchanged glances as though things were worse than they thought. They sat me down and patted my back as if I were a child recovering from a bad dream. They listened to my story with mock sympathy then whispered behind my back before Will dared to surprise me with, "Oh by the way, Aunt Berry has decided to stay until the baby's born to help us- isn't that wonderful?"

I stared in horror at them both. They had secretly colluded behind my back. I turned away in disgust resolving not to share any of my visions again. I knew I had seen the woman and that she must have appeared for a reason. As I trudged ponderously back up the stairs with the faint voices of Will and Berry plotting downstairs, the ghostly frightened face of the young woman stuck in my mind. I retraced the scene in my head. I went back over the sight of her drifting past my bed and realized with horror that, just like me, she was heavily pregnant!

CHAPTER 6

Cinderella Chiffon

When a question lingers, it is better left unexplained, even when you ache to know the truth. Sometimes it is best to turn sideways to ponder the problem and view it from a different angle, as I forced myself to do after the terrifying apparition of the frightened, pregnant woman who floated across my bedroom. I knew Will and Aunt Berry didn't believe me and thought my mad hallucinations were attention seeking devices, so I kept aloof from them, keeping all I saw and heard a secret, taking myself farther inside solitude.

The enchanting, flickering lights, in the heat of the Indian evening, brought me back to the present as Branden lead the way towards the main gate where Davindra, true to his word, stood waiting by his rickety cycle. I wondered whether we should have taken a taxi because the journey was uncomfortable and trekking through the night traffic shrouded in a low-lying smog of petrol fumes made me nauseous. I tied a scarf around my face and cushioned my hip with a shawl, closing my eyes as we wobbled through the centre of a long line of buses, trucks, motorbikes and cars revving their engines at the traffic lights. It would only take one nudge and we'd be crushed. Eventually, when we arrived at the Meenakshi Temple, the dominant feature of the city of Madurai, I was more than relieved.

Davindra helped me down onto the dusty, dirty road. My hip throbbed and I dreaded walking through the filthy street in my bare feet. Saturday night buzzed with crowds devoted to the Temple rituals, and I couldn't imagine the same level of commitment on a Saturday night to Churchgoing in the Christian community back home. The air was smoky and hurt my lungs as I scurried after Branden, trying to keep pace with him as he confidently strode barefoot, while I tiptoed, afraid to place my feet into something nasty. Busily we mingled with the masses heading to the ancient monument. All the devotees were attired in their finest clothes, especially the children. Even poor families decked their little ones in glittering garments as though placing all their hopes and dreams on their sequinned clothes. I noted many of the children had shaved heads and was told that it was a sign that the parents had offered them to the temple.

As we passed through the main entrance down an alleyway brightly lit with glaring electric lights, a line of street vendors sat comfortably behind their stalls selling all kinds of *puja* gifts. The large, brown stones vibrated from myriads of feet pounding down the centuries and I was astonished at the slabs' texture worn so smooth. Our fair faces stuck out amidst the deluge of locals as Branden led me towards an amazing figure of Durga, erected almost to the ceiling with her large, black eyes powerfully dominating the scene in a sea of golden, gleaming candles. Branden purposefully handed me a primitive candle to light our prayers. I watched him in his moment of religious observance and admired his zeal. I followed suit and felt a little awkward trying to emulate his piety as I quietly made my own sincere prayers and hoped they would suffice.

As I stood under the awesome gaze of the goddess, time rolled back, peeling layers of prayer-soaked emotion down to the core. I was just another human being standing before the goddess as countless had stood previously down the centuries. My prayers fused with those gone and those to come. In the frank moments of my self-conscious entreaty, I merged with a multitude of supplications accompanied by a tirade of chanting, bell ringing and the general chunter of the masses as they mumbled mantras into the wax-filled atmosphere. I imagined the scene was the same as it had always been since the very first prayers were offered on that spot.

The floor was untouched in parts since the eighteenth century and in others not since the sixteenth. It was a thrill to tread the ancient tiles where countless parades of people had promenaded. It was living history, breathing, surging on and protected by an invisible raiment of seamless hope. After we had paid our respects to Durga, Branden wanted to complete his *puja* in the main temple, where apparently a lamp holder blazed with one thousand and eight torches mystically heralding Shiva's presence. As we sped past smaller side shrines, I noticed the elephant that had blown air into my face earlier that day was swinging his trunk, triumphantly encouraging more devotees to slip money up his trunk. I wanted to stop and admire him, but Branden was in a hurry.

When we reached the inner sanctum, we were disappointed to see a sign preventing foreign visitors entering into the sacred area. Branden went in search of a priest to see what could be done, while I was left people watching. I spied three other white faces in the crowd, but they were quickly sucked into the multitude. Branden returned with a priest dressed in the familiar orange *dhoti* tied at his waist with his naked, oiled upper body rippling with holy signs and symbols. He took our offering and our money and went inside to complete the *puja* for us. About twenty minutes later he emerged asking for more money, but Branden was wise and spoke in Hindi, stating that we had already paid enough. The priest shrugged and returned to his chores in the inner sanctum.

We then strolled out to the Golden Lotus tank, where people sat on high, tiered steps talking quietly. During part of the year the tank was filled with water and ceremonies were conducted in small boats glimmering with candles. It was odd standing amidst the masses, merging quietly into their special time. Was it yesterday that mocked the senses and spoke of never ending glory? I was once a tiny ligament joined to the main arteries of the British Raj many years ago, but in that moment with

Branden, I was happy to be a particle of dust merging into the ancient ashes of the past. The peoples' religion and faith were the past, the present and the future. Granny, as part of the British Raj, would never have ventured into such a place, although she confessed to me that once she and her sister had crept out in secret, dressed as servants and stole into the bazaar, where her sister had been put under a spell by a magic man and had to have special healing by a local Satu magic woman to break the spell. The two teen-age sisters had learnt their lesson and never ventured into dangerous places again.

I was proud to stand in that time-honoured place by my son's side witnessing the flow of devotion curling heavenwards. It was humbling. I felt disembodied yet raised to a state of awareness where words were colours; where thought was feeling; where feeling screamed: "I bleed where I have no wound; I ache where there is no muscle; I yearn where I had a heart; my eyes cry but I have no tears." The prayers rose and fell over our bodies and through our heads in a wave of constancy, binding the flock to the shepherd.

The night accelerated its pace and we were carried along in the underlying current of incense and rising voices. Not wishing to get caught up in the milieu, we hastened towards the myriad of corridors to explore different pockets and alcoves shrouding mini shrines. As we meandered through a long, pillared walkway, we came upon a ceremony with crowds of devotees chanting responses to the priest's prayers. We stood behind a family, and I was distracted by the antics of a small boy who was playing his own little game while his family was preoccupied with their prayers. I couldn't help teasing him and patted his head when he wasn't looking. When he turned around, his eyes stared in horror at the white woman smiling down at him. His mother cuddled him and smiled shyly back at me, but the little boy was shocked and curtailed his unholy disturbance preferring to stay locked in his mother's embrace. I had momentarily forgotten I was a foreigner!

Branden lead the way making a move before the crowds dispersed and we found ourselves outside the main building walking on the rough brickwork where puddles had formed, which I took great care to avoid. We passed smaller, inner chambers where priests were teaching the crowds, handing down the ancient knowledge to the masses. We decided not to venture further and after a few wrong turns in our attempt to find the entrance, we eventually stepped into the evening of bright fairground mirrors reflected in the small stall holders gathered around their night fires. Shades of brazen gold glared back at distorted figures swaying in the shadows down alleyways, and I was grateful that Davindra waited for us. Once we collected our shoes, I was happier to walk in the dusty street, even though the atmosphere was clogged and polluted with specks of grime, dust and fumes. The night air was visibly hazed in a poisonous veil and I covered my mouth and nose with a scarf so as not to inhale the contaminated air. I took photographs of the low-lying pollution and did not relish the long, tedious haul back through the night traffic.

Poor Davindra had pedalled hard all day and been a wonderful guide, so I gave him all my spare *puja* gifts, which he gratefully accepted. He was extremely respectful of our mother/son relationship and spoke of his own family with love and pride. He stopped by the wayside and bought me a small garland of jasmine flowers and asked the woman to weave it into my hair. Inside my head alarm bells rang as the voice of Prudence, Will's mother, rang: "Don't let them touch you; you never know where their hands have been, and they will contaminate you with their diseases!" I smiled at the memory, inwardly rebelling and allowed the woman to fix the flowers in my hair. Just across the road a troop of male dancers were shaking their shoulders and hips in unison, pounding their feet on a raised dais on a makeshift stage where disco lights beat to the rhythm and strobe lights cut through the polluted air like sharp razors hacking a pathway of light through the night.

On and on we ploughed with Davindra sweating in the heat of the night under the strain. Branden as usual climbed down when the going got too tough up steep inclines until we eventually reached the heavily guarded gates of our hotel. Davindra had his photograph taken with both of us, and Branden paid him a fair sum. He pressed for a hundred pounds, but Branden, in his kind but immovable manner, told him that we were not millionaires. So courteously he backed away into the night as we walked into the reassuring grounds of the luxurious hotel and into our stylish apartment where we ordered a bottle of wine to drink sitting around our tiny swimming pool in our private courtyard.

Wary of night insects and unwanted creatures straying into our living quarters, I inspected the pool and was happy that we were safe. The wine was palatable and we drifted into easy conversation, tired after our long day's exertion. My mind drifted towards a time when Will and I were visiting friends in Bombay and were invited to a special luncheon hosted by a flotsam of well-known film stars. A Parsee friend had bought me a beautiful sari to wear for the occasion, and I felt like royalty as we sauntered up the red carpet into the lobby, cheered on by the people who had come to gaze at their film star idols. The tables were set out on a beautiful veranda overlooking tall trees and well-sculpted parkland and were interspersed with floral bushes and basket displays. We were privileged to be sitting with two of the main male film stars and their wives and a couple of prominent politicians. I sat next to one of the spectacular bushes ablaze with striking red and yellow sweet-scented blooms. Just as we began the entrée, I noticed something twitch in the bush and turned my head to the left to investigate. I saw the creature and glanced back to the table to eat, but the vision was so shocking that momentarily I froze half way to placing my fork to my mouth. Reason overtook the flash, and I pushed away the image, managing to eat the mouthful perched in midair, but the idea of the creature sitting next to me, almost crouching on my left elbow, tormented me, and I dared to look again to make sure I had really seen what I thought I saw.

Next to my left elbow, perched on a massive stalk was a creature the size of a cat. Its stick, stalk-like legs were folded underneath its green body. Its poky antennae tipped forwards above its massive bulbous eyes. Its opaque glaring orbs dared to stare straight back at me. The Praying Mantis blinked and my body involuntarily went rigid. I had never seen a real Praying Mantis, never one that big and never so close that its wings brushed my arm. I couldn't speak. I was completely traumatised and frozen in a freeze-frame pose. No one really noticed for a few seconds as the conversation flowed, but when attention turned to me, I was unable to move. The table went silent and Will suddenly realized what had happened when he saw the creature next to my elbow. Somehow I was removed from the table in a state of shock amidst a hushed pause, which spread throughout the prestigious party. A doctor present attended me, explaining that I had experienced what he termed a "wide-awake faint." When I came to, I felt dreadfully sick, but also extremely embarrassed that my phobic fear of insects had disrupted the esteemed luncheon party.

I shivered remembering the horror of it and sipped more wine. When we had finished the bottle, we retired and I sprayed my bed with anti-mosquito solution, afraid to be bitten as the malaria epidemic was on the increase. Branden was not as vigilant as me and was not afraid of night creatures. On my side of the room I closed my eyes in the dark and was immediately overwhelmed with visions of distorted gods' faces looming in and out of focus from behind ancient, wooden doors. I opened my eyes quickly to dispel the nightmare images. The visit to the Meenakshi Temple had stirred up feelings hidden in the fabric of my brain, and I didn't want to examine the pictures. Travelling, with its tedium, and apart from the obvious highs, places you out on an unstable ledge where sometimes you have to creep forwards regardless of the outcome. I dared to close my eyes and spectres formed of unholy sacrifice with screams echoing along ancient walls. Raw travelling does not allow lies and whatever you experience is what it is. When there is nothing left, no portholes through which to escape, you have no choice but to feel the force of the power that leads to nightmare scenes and dreams of things hidden and forbidden, along paths of worn-out places where bloodcurdling faces wait to be unleashed and fed on fear. Through the night my body was attacked and ached with sharp needle pricks and I slept fitfully in the heat fighting off the evil demons that flared through black eyes painted on statues of gods.

In the morning, as I sat up, the squashed dead bodies of four mosquitoes lay underneath me. I had been bitten. I shuddered at the thought of them squirming in my bed attacking and feasting on my blood. As Branden slept, I crept out into the bright, clear morning and indulged my secret ambition to swim naked in the tiny pool. The water was cold and invigorating and I didn't dare to look closely at the crevices in case I saw something crawling in the hidden crannies. It was peaceful with only the exotic cries of the birds calling through the trees dispelling the ghoulish masks that had invaded my dreams. The cold water took the sting out my bites and I was happy to face a new day. Floating furtively in the refreshing water, England seemed far away and I indulged my whim as long as I could before hunger pangs got the better of me. I sneaked out of the apartment, leaving my son to slumber on, making my way to the outdoor restaurant for breakfast feeling clean and revitalised to face a new day.

It was lovely to watch the morning quietly unfold while I was luxuriously served breakfast on the veranda. It was fun to sip coffee while sleep rolled away the corners of other peoples' dreams. Branden was peacefully sleeping: sleep but to dream, dream but to wake, wake but to live and live to take life on to the next chapter. In the tranquil moment, my stressful times back home faded into shades of nothing, and I wondered why we have to be tethered to life's carousel- can't we just jump off when the going gets tough and sprint back when the time is right? Sipping my freshly squeezed grape juice, I pondered the question and smiled to myself remembering my little granddaughter's question: "Who puts the rainbow in the sky, Nanny, and who lights the way to the stars?" Children's questions can be innocently profound and as adults we turn their minds from true magic by giving them scientific answers. Alas I am not scientific and merely replied: "Many miracles are performed with fairy dust, which paints rainbow magic in the sky and lights silver shreds of moonbeams!" She gave me a sideways glance at my whimsical response and picked up the cat whispering, "Poor Nanny!"

The bearer interrupted my thoughts as he placed a full English breakfast in front of me. It seemed incongruous with the unfolding exotic morning, watching chipmunks scamper up the trees and hearing colourful plumed birds calling through the branches. But, I thought, returning to my granddaughter's question, miracles do happen all the time and we choose not to register them. I thought of Einstein's quotation: "There are two ways to live—you can live as if nothing is a miracle; you can live as if everything is a miracle."

I smiled remembering a time when I had just married Will and we visited his family's friends on the Isle of Skye. Gilly had retired from keeping Will's family's accounts and looking after their financial interests, escaping to the Isle of Skye, where he and his wife, Emily, who was a potter, owned a small cottage. They had turned the barn into a pottery shop where visitors could buy Emily's pots.

Their cottage was in the middle of nowhere surrounded by acres of farmland. When they first bought the ramshackle pile of rubble intending to renovate, people thought they were crazy, but they loved the plot so much that they were patient, waiting months for the cottage to be restored into a quaint dwelling. An old woman called Bella Marie was the previous owner. She had lived there all her life and had never set foot farther than her local post office. Local artisans and builders who undertook the work on the house noticed a large stone outside the kitchen door, which seemed to be changing shape. At first no one said anything, but as time went by, the men began to talk about the stone, which was moulding itself into the shape of a face. When Emily went to inspect the building, the foreman told her how everyone had noticed a face appearing on the once flat surface of the stone. She acknowledged the information and kept a close watch on it. During her visits to the cottage, she noted further changes week by week. By the time the house was ready, a fully sculpted face had hewn itself into the rock. On the day when she and Gilly moved into the house, a local man who was moving their furniture into the cottage, noted the stone and said, "Well, will ya look at that—Bella Marie has returned?"

The stone had moulded itself into the likeness of its previous owner, Bella Marie and so Emily placed her inside the house on the hearth where she belonged and where she has stayed ever since.

On my first visit to their cottage, I marvelled at the sculpture of Bella Marie and smiled as I wandered into the kitchen to find Emily making marmalade for breakfast. She was a wonderful old lady with a warm, kind heart. As we stood by the kitchen window, a mist slipped over the fields encasing us in a thick, white shroud. Will and Gilly came into the kitchen and as we began breakfast, the fog wove a thick blanket around the house, curling and pushing at the windows as though to force an entrance. An eerie silence seeped through the bricks. We hardly spoke, but when we did, our voices reverberated through an empty shell as we floated mysteriously in a sea of white vapour. I got up to get a cup from the sink and was relieved to see the mist clearing as a huge mountain poked through the low cloud. "Oh, I didn't know there was a mountain there?" I questioned.

"There isn't!" said Emily. We all rushed to the window. A mountain loomed ominously through the misty veil, dark, brooding, almost menacing. We were silent as the same questions thrummed through our minds. Where were we? Had we been miraculously teleported somewhere? Were we the victims of mass hallucination?

"Let's go outside," said Gilly breaking the silence. We followed. The garden, what we could see of it, was the same but the mountain remained. Will thought we should take a walk through the mist, but Gilly decided we should have a cup of tea and wait until the mist cleared. Emily agreed and we followed them back inside. Gilly and Emily put up a good show of being unaffected by the presence of the mountain at the bottom of their garden, but behind their eyes fear hovered. To make light of the situation Gilly brought out some contraband whiskey from the hidden cupboard behind Bella Marie's stone, and we were glad to take comfort in the warm, fiery liquid. As the morning wore away, so did the cloudy mist and the mountain retreated back somewhere over the rainbow, until the garden and landscape regained normality and the sun shone gloriously, mocking our experience. No one spoke about the phantom mountain again as we settled back into our daily routine, but none of us have ever forgotten it.

Months later, back in London and during a heavy winter, I had a dream about Emily and Gilly on the Isle of Skye, trapped in their little cottage. They were both ill in bed with the flu and couldn't move out of their beds. The dream had a real urgency where I saw Gilly struggle out of bed to show me important documents pertaining to the family's estate. I gave Will the instructions that Gilly made me memorise. I was so worried about them that I phoned the Isle of Skye Post Office, and the manager said that the snow drifts had been so bad that they couldn't get through to the elderly couple, but as I was concerned, they would try a snow plough. When the postman reached them, they were critically ill and had to be taken on stretchers to the mainland hospital. I am glad I acted upon the dream; eventually when they regained their health, they thanked me profusely, for if they had been left a few more days, they both would have died.

Branden appeared through my hazy thoughts and brought me back to the moment. He had slept well and was looking forward to the next stage of our journey. He ordered his usual *masala dosa* and voraciously tucked into the pungent, spicy dish. He had organised a taxi for the long trip to Coimbatore and after haggling, procured a good price. It was sad to leave the magnificent hotel, but we were keen to begin the next stage of our journey. I was excited to think that soon I would glimpse the beautiful Blue Mountains that held so many memories. It was hard to believe that I was returning without Granny being there to greet me.

After my marriage to Will, Granny accepted me into the family and we grew quite close. She taught me many things about healing energy and how to tackle problems using a spiritual focus. She taught me how to deny evil, explaining, "When you reject the existence of the 'devil,' you take away the power and strength of anything that is remotely connected to the evil force. Remember, *there is no devil.*" I found it perplexing at the time but have grown to understand her teaching. Living next door, just down the drive from Granny had been two famous sisters who were both authors. The sole remaining sister died quite tragically while I was staying with Granny. There was hushed gossip of her being attacked by a thief in the night. One afternoon, a few days later, I found Granny on the veranda deep in meditation. I didn't mean to disturb her; but when she opened her eyes, she explained she was helping the lady to pass over to her spiritual home, as her death had been a shock and she was still hovering in the realm of the living. I was intrigued to learn more about this, not knowing that years later I would help many souls to pass over.

Some of Granny's old-fashioned ideas were hard to take seriously, like the time Will and I were invited to go trout fishing with the Colonel of the regiment in Coonoor and some of his officers. I was treated like a Princess travelling in the Colonel's Land Rover, which lead the small convoy out to the forest lakes. I was the only woman and was dressed in army gear like the men except that my fashion boots were pink. The mountain air was fresh and the sun was hidden behind a grey thick lid, so I didn't bother with any sun protection.

We parked by a clump of trees and traipsed down to the lake. The men spread out along the edge and began to prepare the rods. The Colonel, a very large, powerful man with a bushy beard and prickly upturned moustache was a keen fisherman and displayed his skill by flicking his line far out into the middle of the lake. He nodded for me to do the same. One of the soldiers, quick to obey orders, jumped to attention and handed me a rod fully prepared with bait. I gestured to flick the line, but as I did so, it flew behind me and caught in a tree where it swung comically. One of the men at the Colonel's command quickly climbed the branches to retrieve the swinging line, while a soldier handed me another rod. Not wanting to make a fool of myself again, I stretched my arm far behind me to get the best possible aim, but as I flicked my wrist into action, there was no response. I pulled harder and realised the hook had jammed into my bottom. The men stifled their laughter and their embarrassment as Will came to my aid to dig and pull the hook from my backside while everyone politely turned away.

Eventually I was free, and the Colonel decided to help me and he took my arm and flicked the line far into the water. The men clapped politely as I stood awkwardly waiting for the line to respond. The Colonel called his men over to stand in our places holding our rods, while we retired to a picnic lunch, which was served by a bearer and two other servants. They carefully unfolded beautiful treats from snow-white linen. Wine was served in cut crystal glasses as we perched on foldaway chairs. It was a royal feast. Not long after we had finished, one of the soldiers called and I ran down to the lake's edge to witness something wriggling and swishing on the end of my line. I wasn't sure what to do, so the soldier helped me to land the tiny fish. When it flounced on the wet stones beside me, I panicked. I looked to Will for help; he had also caught a small trout and was manoeuvring it off the hook. In haste and confusion, I jumped on the fish with both feet to hold it still. The soldier helping me blunted his laughter, got the hook out of the fish's mouth and swiftly knocked its head on a stone to end its misery. He handed it to me ceremoniously and the soldiers clapped. The Colonel caught several large fish, and our two tiny specimens were placed in a basket to take home.

Back at the house we handed Granny our prize catches. She smiled wryly at our two meagre offerings and took them to the cook to bake for supper. It was a rule in her house when Will was a small boy, that whatever he shot in the garden he had to eat, so for a time his diet consisted of small birds. I think Granny viewed our baby trout in a similar way. I suddenly felt flushed and caught a glimpse of my face in the mirror; it was bright red.

When Granny turned to me she was horrified. Quite suddenly my face was a glowing beacon, beaming in the dim twilight. Granny scolded me, saying that when the sun was not apparent, it was the worst time to get sunburnt. She hated the thought of me turning brown. She said she would pray for me and that I was never to do that again and went away to her room to meditate. Needless to say, I did not suffer with sunburn but turned a mild caramel, which Granny had me rectify with plenty of face powder.

Another occasion on which I found Granny's ideas a little harsh was when Will and I were invited to a prestigious wedding, which was a three-day affair, and I had to have stunning outfits for each day. I had nothing vaguely suitable, especially by Granny's standards. So she arranged for her dressmaker, Timonis, to undertake the task. He was a Hungarian dress designer, who had won world acclaim for his creations when he was a young man before he settled down with his Indian wife in the Nilgiris to open a chicken farm. Rich ladies came from far and wide to have their clothes fashioned by him. Three reams of material were chosen for me and were sent to Timonis to interpret. I had no idea what to expect and just accepted that Granny knew best. Granny's driver, Dickie, drove me to the chicken farm and before we rounded the corner, the smell of chicken excrement was overwhelming, affecting my preconceived image of designer, *haute couture* creations. Amidst the clucking and cawing of the penned chickens, I tentatively entered the master's studio, which also stank of chicken manure.

In a flurry of artistic gestures, Timonis appeared from nowhere like a magician in his silk pyjamas with his white hair sticking out at odd angles from beneath an embroidered pill box hat. His white moustache was meticulously groomed and twitched from side to side as he peered at me from the top of his glasses clapping his hands with glee, like a child with a new toy. A small girl ran out from a recess with a tape measure and began jotting down copious notes in her book as Timonis zapped the tape around my body, whipping it sideways like a cowboy lashing cattle. The session didn't take long and as he worked swiftly, he said, "Leave zis all to me! I vill conjure somzing beautiful. Come back in a veek!" I thanked him but was puzzled. I hadn't even seen the material and had no idea what to expect.

A week later I was excited to go for my first fitting. I gasped with delight when Timonis produced the most exotic and fantastic costume I had ever seen. It was a mogul outfit in bright orange with real gold thread woven into the fabric. The trousers fit beautifully and had a matching blouse. The overcoat flowed out delicately and had a high neck, mogul style, with tiny gold buttons hand stitched all the way down the front. I felt like a princess as I paraded up and down. "I absolutely love it!" I gasped; "but I wish I had longer legs!"

"My dear, you 'av no idea about zis. Take eet from me when I say, zee smallest chillies are ze 'ottest!"

The second outfit was a dark green and gold, gypsy-style, long, tiered skirt with a fringed waistcoat and a small white blouse. The gold pattern was real gold thread, and the skirt made me want to dance flamenco style, whipping the skirt around me, whirling like a small child dressing up in her mother's best dress. Timonis laughed at my antics and applauded my dancing:" And now for ze third creation, my dear. Come along, come along, Marta, and clear this mess away. Bring me ze garment. Don't dilly dally, girl!" I waited with bated breath as the curtain opened revealing a sea nymph ball gown. The gossamer film of pale blue, green and turquoise swirls in a blue sea of silk, with fine wisps of pale blue silk, was spun into a Cinderella cloud of chiffon.

I was shocked when I saw the plunging neckline. The front of the dress was cut under the bust in tight pleats, but the décolletage was open almost to my waist revealing the outline of my breasts. I was embarrassed and tried to pull the material together. "Look, my dear, eet is no use doing zis. I av designed zis for you; you know if you av eet, you must flaunt eet; I am not changing zis. You will see you will be the belle of ze ball." I was barely twenty and had never worn anything so beautiful or revealing but to protect my modesty I secretly decided that I would wear a shawl.

The day arrived for the first part of the wedding and I wore my orange and gold mogul outfit. The moment I felt the soft silk next to my skin I was transported into a fairy-tale world. I glided into the milieu of stunning guests wearing more golden jewellery than I had ever imagined. Nose jewellery glittered brightly on women decked from head to toe in diamonds. Red and gold saris wove paisley patterns of colour through silken clad men wearing traditional mogul style trousers and tops. I understood why my gold and orange outfit was chosen as it was ostentatious and flamboyant, which the event demanded, without giving offence to the relatives of the bride, who all wore magnificent red and gold.

I had never attended an Indian wedding before and had no idea what to expect. The bride was hidden in a tent from the general gathering; only the women were allowed to see her. When the bridegroom appeared riding an elephant, a fanfare of horns blazed his auspicious arrival. He paraded amongst the men and then was escorted to a raised platform where he waited for his bride, who was lead into the arena by her mother. The young girl bent her head low as she was ushered alongside the groom. Will disappeared in the crowd to take photographs and I was left alone, mesmerised by the drama of the ceremony, witnessing the bride being tied to the groom with a silk scarf, while the mother lead them in a parade around the platform amidst chanting and singing.

I did not see the eyes staring opposite me. I did not see the man's face. I was not conscious of his intense gaze. I was not aware that he followed my every move, until I looked up and met his eyes. Through the heat of the candles, the crashing of cymbals, and a haze of red and gold the moment froze. He stood with his hands together as if in prayer and raised his royal hands to his forehead in a gesture of greeting and devotion. His simple signal was intimate, shocking and thrilling.

I looked down as the blood rushed into my cheeks. I attempted to lose myself in the dignity of the occasion, but his body called to mine while his eyes held me captive. What was I doing? My newly wedded husband was in the crowd and I was secretly flirting with a stranger. But it was not flirting; it was frighteningly much more. It was a rare moment in life when a pearl of energy between two people materializes spontaneously and spins dizzily before falling into the sea, sinking without trace, while hungry seagulls screech and claw the air in disgust at their loss of a possible morsel.

I did not see that he followed when Will appeared and stayed close behind me when we were escorted to the banquet. I only know that he was there while I perused the feast. I had never seen food like it before. Many dishes were laced with real gold. I had never tasted real gold before and daintily picked at the food. Invisible eyes bore into my soul, stealing my thoughts, stunting my actions with guarded intention. Will managed to eat plenty and when he was spooning his last mouthfuls of Indian sweets wrapped in a thin, gold coating, he was approached by a man who wanted to take us to meet people at the bar. I did not see the prince arrange our meeting, I only saw Will being taken to greet a group of men from the army, while I was left in a quiet space near the entrance to the bar. From out of the noisy throng, eyes moved towards me, hypnotically rooting me to the spot. His regal body stepped with grace and ease to stand close by my side. Locked in each other's gaze, we talked. He bought me a gin and tonic and we chatted about everything and anything. I don't remember the details except that he was from the north of India and had six brothers. He was a prince and was soon to marry a girl of his parents' choice. Two gin and tonics later we were still talking. The room faded. Just the two of us sailed through a cosmos of eternity riding on orange mists of golden opportunity. Our laughter was heard from afar, polite and controlled. Our voices were genteel and respectful, but our eyes ravaged each other in a multidimensional fantasy. Our controlled conversation fooled no one. We were watched. With my head in a whirl of lavish beauty and fairy-tale fantasy, I was hauled back to reality when Will returned. The prince pressed us to stay, but Will insisted that we had a supper engagement.

On returning to Granny's house, I was floating in a shimmering haze. She asked me if I had a lovely time and I told her, "Oh yes, and I had three gin and tonics!"

The world exploded. Granny was furious. I had committed a huge crime. To drink anything at all was an offence, but to have imbibed three glasses of alcohol was a mortal sin. Will looked uneasy, whispering that I should never have told her, but I reminded him that back in London we were used to drinking at parties. Granny's panacea to everything was to go away and pray. "I will pray for you!" she stated with stern determination and disappeared into her room.

Back in the taxi in the present of forty years on, we sped across the city, past the Meenakshi temple on our way to Coimbatore. I recalled the prince's face with a melancholy ache as through all the years I had never forgotten him. Watching the ancient city fade behind us, I allowed a stray thought to tease my imagination—could we ever meet again? Would it be possible that he might stray back to Coonoor to visit the army encampment? The heat of the day already beat through the windows and the cracks in the road jarred my hip. It was a foolish thought. We had grown old and we wouldn't even recognise each other. But "what if's" taunted me and reminded me of the yearning and longing to see him again that had never quite died. As the landscape drew me closer to the mountains, my mind meandered back to the second day after our first meeting at the wedding. I was dressed in my green and gold gypsy outfit and although eyes watched from afar, the prince and I were never given the opportunity to spend time together. I knew somehow things had been engineered to boycott any further liaison. The whole day passed in a processed cyclone of rituals, but I was not part of it. I was encased in rising expectation that gradually slipped through my fingers like grains of sand on a beach scattered by the wind to the far ends of the earth.

The third part of the wedding was to occur at the weekend with a large ball at the grand club. My sea swirl gown was hanging ready for the event where I hoped to meet the prince and perhaps steal a dance with him, but a surprise visit to the military cinema hijacked fate. One moment, one glance, one word, one slip of the hand changed everything. My mother-in law took Will and me to the military cinema for officers only and as we were honoured guests, we were privileged to have special reserved seats. When we walked in to the packed house the audience was buzzing with anticipation to see the long awaited James Bond film and as we sauntered along the main centre aisle, the prince appeared directly in front of me. I stopped to speak to him briefly while Will and his mother brushed passed us disapprovingly. I wasn't aware that suddenly all eyes were on us and that the noise fell to a shocked silence. In the middle of the arena we were sacrificial lambs to gossip's sharp knife. We only spoke for a couple of minutes, but it was enough for everyone to witness our feelings. We planned to meet each other at the ball.

That evening back home Will's mother taunted me with "Your boyfriend this and your boyfriend that and your boyfriend . . . !" She shamed me into feeling that I had made a public fool of myself, but I clung helplessly to the hope of seeing the prince just once more. During the next couple of days, I was unable to concentrate on anything and was glad to spend an evening for dinner at a famous classical dancer's house. She and her husband had invited many other guests, and the atmosphere was jolly. Rani was beautiful and had held film star status when she was younger. She eyed me cautiously because I was also a dancer and she kept a close watch on her husband. Nasty gossip from malicious tongues had spread the news of my meeting with the prince and although we had only met in public, we had already crossed boundaries. I was British, and he was an Indian Prince. He was betrothed to be married, and I was a married woman. We had, in the community's eyes, dared to cross the line by our show of familiarity towards each other.

On the evening of the ball I was a tangled mess of nerves. I was embarrassed about the neckline of my ball gown and covered myself up with a delicate white shawl. When we arrived at the club, the band was playing and the hall throbbed with guests. Rani and her husband stood in the middle of the dance floor talking to a small group and when they spied us, the people parted making a pathway for us to enter into their circle. The band stopped playing pausing for breath, and Rani's affected voice screeched through the hubbub. She took one look at me and moved forwards like a cobra ready to attack with her head and chin poised toward me. Deliberately she looked me up and down and then snatched the shawl off my shoulders. I felt she had ripped off all my clothes and that I was standing naked before the whole world. No one spoke. Everyone was shocked. Publicly I was shamed. She was triumphant. Rani's husband was angry and gently walked me to the back of the hall. I didn't cover myself up but let the shawl dangle by my side and walked proudly through the crowd with my head held high. I was not going to let her win. Someone placed a drink in my hand. Outwardly I was composed, while inwardly quaking. I gently walked towards the open veranda and stood alone watching the night. Someone stood beside me.

"He sent me to tell you that he can't come. They have placed him on duty. He is so sorry!" His friend had kind eyes and knew our situation. I understood only too well.

"Tell him—er, tell him—er—it doesn't matter, thank you," I whispered.

We both had to bow to the establishment, but I put up a fight. I danced almost every dance in my beautiful ball gown despite my initial shyness and became, as Timonis had predicted, the belle of the ball.

The countryside sped past in a whirl of memories as we raced closer to the Blue Mountains. I never saw the prince again; but the following summer when I was in living in London with Will's aunt and uncle, he brought his new wife to the flat in the hope of finding me. I was out. My aunt entertained the visitors with tea, but I never knew that they were looking for me. I was shocked and upset to know that he had tried to find me, but perhaps it was for the best. He left a tiny hole in my spirit, like a cigarette burn on gossamer: pale blue gossamer with seascape swirls and Cinderella chiffon from en era long gone.

CHAPTER 7

Return to the Blue Mountains

It was Monday morning, and the early city traffic throbbed through the highway as we made our way out of the suburbs, escaping the city's congestion where miles and miles of palm trees and banana plantations were our only vista. Frills of white energy flashed like silver swords lashing across the sky, striking the earth where cloud and horizon mingled into the blood red soil like sacrificial lava. Beyond the mountains blackening clouds gathered threatening the last of the monsoon rain. The driver, young and keen to complete the journey quickly, sped through the empty roads. Words sifted through my mind, and I caught the message planted in my brain from another dimension: "In and out of the rhyme of time your song will thread through a harmonious galaxy where your melody twinkles like a Christmas bell leaving a silver trail like a snail, on its early morning journey."

I pondered the meaning; none came, but I understood that all our energy is stored in a universal grid of knowledge. The voice persisted: "Do not be afraid of ridicule, for you have to speak the truth even when many do not understand or believe; but remember, no one can damage your song—it is too strong! Everyone's rhymes are unique; yours are created for a purpose, for you are a star-child from a distant planet. One day your world will not be as you know it; everything will change, and you will understand that your vibration, when it is pulled taut like a violin string, will catapult you in and out of time, across the universe and out beyond your planet; there you will find understanding and be embraced by your true family. Be prepared. Your earth will not be the same for very much longer as it is about to enter a time of destruction. Humans must learn to latch onto a higher consciousness; otherwise, they will drown in the mire of their own destruction. Water cleanses and your planet must pay. This time is coming. Nature seeks revenge and your planet will suffer. Heed my warning!" The words faded and I shivered in the heat.

My dreams had for some time showed me tsunami destruction in major cities of the world. Moreover, burning fires lingered across devastated wasteland, where once thriving towns had flourished before radiation seepage from nuclear plants polluted the atmosphere and many people died. I dreamt I woke one morning to a dark world with no electricity or power of any kind. The streets were silent and the houses abandoned. This dream persists and I am anxious, but the now is all embracing and the now leads me on. Farther forwards, on and on we drove and my mind raced with memories from the past. The prince was probably bald and fat by now, and he would find me changed from my sylphlike self of those days. What would I find nestling in the Nilgiris? Who would I meet? I didn't want to shape my new experiences with past preconceptions.

When we arrived at Coimbatore, the sandy streets had metamorphosed into tarmac rubble with rows upon rows of westernised stores and shopping malls. The hotel was a one night stop, cheap and convenient. The driver sped off before I could claim my suitcase in the boot, and the manager of the hotel acted quickly to contact the driver before he had sped out of town.

Anxiously I waited in the reception while the driver made his way back to the dingy hotel with my suitcase. My stomach was upset and although I was hungry, I daren't eat. Besides our allowance was running low and we didn't want to spend too much at that stage of the journey. We had arrived much earlier in Coimbatore than expected and we could have travelled up into the hills, but we had been advised not to take any risks travelling at night and couldn't change our plans at the last minute. Forty years previously it had been safe to travel with a local driver any time of day or night.

After placing our luggage in our room, which was adequate for our needs, Branden wanted to find a bank, so we walked through the rubble and building debris to the modern shopping mall. We eventually found a small bank and decided to have a cup of coffee in one of the modern stores. It was like many other stores back home with the perfume and cosmetic counters in the entrance hall set out to tantalise and suck the shoppers into the bright lights. We took the lift and walked out into the toy department, which was like many back home. The coffee counter was set back behind the cuddly toys. We ordered two coffees. Mine had been presweetened, which I couldn't drink, but the men behind the counter obliged me by making another without sugar. Time hung heavily in the dull afternoon amidst the westernised shoppers, as we were impatient to make tracks up the mountain. We were so close, yet still so far away.

As we walked back to the hotel, we passed the eye hospital and I remembered how Prudence used to travel down to Coimbatore from the mountains for regular eye examinations and would come back laden with reams of shopping. That evening Branden suggested we eat in a local café that was recommended in his guidebook and inexpensive, but when we got there, it was not up to my standards of cleanliness. I didn't feel well but appeased Branden by ordering soup while he tucked into a spicy local dish. I couldn't drink it, as it tasted greasy and looked like grey dishwater. After the meal we ambled back to the hotel in the heat of the night and decided to have a drink on the roof bar where the panoramic view of the city was pleasant at night with the bright lights washing the black sky with a neon glow. There were seven waiters standing idly in the restaurant as Branden and I took a seat out under the stars near the advertising billboards. A whiskey helped to soothe my stomach, and we sat for a while discussing our final trek to the hill station early the next morning. The restaurant began to fill up and a light drizzle of rain brought an end to our evening as we retired for the night in preparation for our early start.

The room was adequate but not up to our usual standard of cleanliness and when we turned off the light, the noise from the corridors and surrounding rooms echoed through the walls. I tried to block out the commotion, but the sound of a girl crying in the next room disturbed me. Sometimes it's difficult to interpret crying, especially when it's resounding through bathroom walls. Was she in pain? Was she frightened? Was she in need of help? I tried to imagine all kinds of reasons and wondered if I should go and investigate, but Branden seemed to think that I ought not to interfere. Crying internally is not the same as crying externally; crying secretly is not the same as crying to alleviate frustration and crying from another dimension is like a memory played and relayed down time, locked in the bricks and mortar of the fabric of a building, like the crying of a child heard on my first Christmas Eve in Pear Tree Cottage. It was the crying of an infant long dead. Through the din of the moment, I allowed my mind to wander back to the first Christmas in my dream cottage, not aware that the dream was about to become a nightmare.

It was Christmas Eve and the snow was falling in a lacy haze through the dense blackness weaving an unblemished white mantle over the hushed village. I gazed out of the window holding my sleeping baby snugly in my arms. It was her first Christmas. She was just two months old, and a winter wonderland of magic was being spun just for her. I was glad to be inside with our crackling log fire blazing in the ancient grate, glinting brightly on the polished horse brasses. I wanted everything to be special for my family in our lovely cottage to celebrate our first Christmas in my dream home. My parents arrived bundling into the sitting room with presents to stack by the tree, while Will played host handing out drinks. I went upstairs to put Sarena to bed. She looked so sweet and cosy in her little basket cot. I stood over her smiling, feeling wonderfully contented that after her birth everything in the house had settled down and there was no hint of anything untoward. As I crept downstairs, I heard children laughing outside the front door. The voices were loud and pierced through the silence.

"Don't say we've got carol singers at this time of night?" grunted my Father warming his hands by the fire.

"Surely children aren't out playing in this weather?" asked my mother settling down in a large armchair.

"This is Yorkshire, remember?" teased Will.

I peered through the curtains expecting to see a group of children outside, but I could only make out the bright golden halo of the street lamp highlighting the downy white flecks falling fast through a carpet of speckled down.

"There's no one there!" I added nervously.

"They're playing games!" said my father, who didn't trust teen-agers, suspecting it might be a gang of boys out to cause some Christmas mischief.

The laughter echoed round the room and we all looked puzzled. "I'll just go and have a look."

As I opened the front door, a flurry of snow gushed into the hall and the cold stole my breath. The eerie silence was strangely beautiful. As I looked up into the white, swirling mass, my hair and face became embossed in a lacy veil. I wanted to stay outside alone, away from everyone and blend into the dense whiteness. The cold seeped through my jumper and I shivered. Looking for footprints or evidence of the noisy children, I padded through the soft snow near the window; but there were no footprints, no children and no evidence of anyone having been near the window or the door; yet, we had all heard voices. Back inside, the warm glow of the fire was welcoming, but I was puzzled. "There was no one there, not even footprints!" I said.

My father looked uneasy and shuffled his feet. He was a war hero and was used to dealing with all kinds of situations and was not afraid of anything. We all shrugged. It was nothing. We had been mistaken, but secretly we all knew what we had heard. We sat down and toasted the new house. Suddenly the sitting room door flew open banging against the wall. A gust of cold air breezed in and dampened the cosy scene. My father shot up out of his chair and went to investigate saying, "Someone must have come in through the back door!"

"I've locked it!" stated Will confidently.

We all paused in the silence as we heard my father checking doors and twisting keys in locks. When he returned, he looked puzzled, "Well there's no one there and all the doors are locked!"

A baffled silence ensued which was suddenly broken by a baby wailing. "Oh dear, the banging must have woken her up, sighed my mother, I'll just go up and check her."

I knew in my heart it wasn't Sarena crying. I knew it was all starting again, the haunting and taunting from the terrifying presence. Everyone in the room felt the macabre spirit hovering, waiting in the wings to dampen our celebration. My mother came down the stairs quietly, also baffled, "She's fast asleep!"

We were silent inside our thoughts. Will offered to refresh everyone's drinks, but somehow the festive atmosphere eluded us, smothered by a dark secret. We all experienced the change in the air. My little dog felt it as she sat with her tail between her legs and my father's dog, curled up by his feet, also knew it; but none of us acknowledged it, preferring the safety of our own denials.

"I think it's time for bed. It's been a tiring journey," said my mother. I nodded, disappointed that our evening was not the jovial family gathering I had intended. We all retired. I closed my eyes. I was afraid. Will went to sleep, but I was perturbed remembering the ghostly apparition that had sailed past the bed before my baby was born and the strange sounds with the watching presence that waited furtively in the shadows. Eventually I drifted off to sleep with alarm bells ringing on the edge of seasonal goodwill.

Morning white light sifted through the curtains with glaring intensity. I parted the curtains on a snow-white landscape, a Christmas morning landscape. I hurried to Sarena's room just as she was beginning to make her puppy snuffling noises and picked her up to kiss her soft warm cheeks. Her eyes smiled. In the quiet of her little nursery, I fed and changed her before walking downstairs to the kitchen, where I found my father alone sitting at the table and sipping tea. He looked worried. "You can't stay here!" he whispered. My words dried. "There's something here that's—Look in there."

I followed him into the dining room where I had carefully arranged three large vases of fresh flowers on my lovely baby grand piano. The flowers were strewn and mashed over the floor with the vases left upturned, dripping water onto the highly polished piano lid and draining into the carpet in puddles. Both dogs cowered in a corner. Piles of yellow bile and sick had dried on the green carpet. "The dogs are terrified; look at them!" scowled my father. I held baby Sarena tightly and turned away from the shocking scene.

"What happened?" I gasped.

"I'll tell you what happened all right!" His voice rose, but he curbed his tone. "Last night when you all went to bed I thought I'd make one last check to make sure everything was all right. You see I thought I heard someone switch on the kitchen light so I came down to investigate. You had obviously left it on, so I thought I'd leave it as it might scare away intruders; you never know on Christmas Eve. So I came back upstairs and was about to climb into bed when I heard someone playing the piano. It was one-handed playing like a child's playing a single melody tapping on the keys. Well, you know me, soldier, war hero the lot, but I tell you it scared me stiff; in fact, I couldn't move; I was rooted to the spot. Your mum was fast asleep and didn't hear a thing. But I know what I heard, and it was right below me in the dining room. When I managed to get back into bed, I lay awake most of the night listening. I tell you, there's something here that's—well, that's not right; I can't let you stay here!"

Baby Sarena gurgled and pulled at my long hair. I was silent. I suppose I had known all along that it, whatever it was, had not gone and I had kidded myself it had disappeared. I was not going to leave my house. I was determined to stay and fight it. "We're not stopping! We're leaving right away, and I want you and the baby to come with us!" growled my father.

"But you have to stay; it's our first Christmas here; you can't go; I've prepared all the food!"

"No, no!" he said quietly touching my arm. In the quiet of the kitchen, I cried silently—secret tears, which flowed onto my baby's head. I smiled at her lovely, innocent face. She made everything worthwhile. I would conquer the world for her and was not prepared to let anything push me out of my new home, but knowing that the "thing" was real and not a figment of my imagination intensified my terror. It was like living on the edge of a precipice, fearful each footstep would crumble, shaking the earth beneath me, and I would fall into a black abyss.

When Will came down I was cleaning up the mess. He dismissed the piano playing with mild amusement as he was sceptical about the whole thing and thought that the dogs had been sick because they had eaten too much. My father tried to tell Will that it was a serious matter, but he was too busy studying for his pending exams and had no time for what he considered fanciful reactions. He excused himself, explaining that he had work to finish at the university. I watched in disbelief as he managed to dig the car out of the drive and wave as the car skidded out of sight. It was Christmas morning and everyone was abandoning me. Fear bubbled and blistered inside my head as I said goodbye to my parents. I didn't want them to see how worried I was to walk back inside the house. My father with his dry sense of humour tried to make light of the shocking events by saying, "If that ghost appears again, you'll have to charge it for piano lessons."

I forced a smile knowing it waited inside. I held Sarena close to my chest and watched until the car coasted out of sight. It was Christmas morning in my dream cottage, but it had turned out to be a nightmare. The poltergeist had resumed its tactics; but worse, it had returned with greater strength to terrorize everyone with phantom voices, laughter and sounds of a baby crying. Everyone felt the cold chill when the door was thrown open, but everyone chose to turn away, except me. Somehow I had to find the determination and psychic power to deal with it.

Back in Coimbatore, through bouts of sporadic sleep, the morning came. As I shook off the haunting memories from the past, a flood of excitement gushed through the present.

We were due to leave that morning and head up into the hills, so we hurried breakfast and checked out to board our taxi for our final haul up into the mountains. On the edge of the city we parked to allow our driver to collect some parcels, and Branden and I explored the bustling street. Buildings were strung together in a ramshackle hotchpotch, with tiny, decrepit stalls leaning side by side next to cheap hotels and food stores, all enclosed under a spaghetti tangle of overhead electric wires and pylons. Farther down the road the mountains brooded, shrouded in a hazy cloak of meringue clouds. A sudden pang of longing to be there and a yearning to see familiar faces overwhelmed me. It was forty years since I had looked upon those magnificent, grandiose, forbidding sculptures of nature and I was awed, just like the first time.

I stumbled over piles of rubble in the street and tripped up on broken slabs left unattended. The usual mounds of decaying refuse were stacked high along the walkways. The stagnant stench of the rotting garbage wafted through the food stalls together with the smell of fried onions and spices. A banana seller set up a rickety stall next to the gutter. A flower seller arranged her meagre tray on a tree stump displaying her strands of pink jasmine laid on newspaper. A woman sauntered by carrying a little white goat and I stopped to take a photo as the kid snuggled under her chin. She explained she was carrying him to the vets as he had an injured foot. As she ambled out of sight, our driver appeared and we settled into the back of the car to enjoy our long-awaited journey up into the mountains.

After we passed the general hustle of the early morning traders, the noise gradually abated and the road shed its rush hour traffic making space for us to pick up speed. On the outskirts of the city our driver stopped near a dilapidated garage, which was no more than a derelict hut with a few spare, worn-out tyres stacked up against a tree.

"Change tyre, sir; mend tyre sir!" stated our driver.

Branden looked at me with disbelief. We had waited a long time to travel back to the Nilgiris and at the last post we were delayed by a puncture. We got out of the car and I mooched along the dusty road strewn with decaying junk and debris. A couple of men came to help change the tyre, but the replacement was just as worn out as the old one. Tantalizingly the mountains were in sight, but we were stuck unable to go anywhere. By the side of the ramshackle hut, open fields of rice grew shielded by palm trees, and a single grey buffalo grazed on a straggly patch of grass. Towering above, the Blue Mountains undulated in ridges, majestically outlining the opaque sky, and low lying clouds sailed below in small puffs like misty smoke drifting from a bonfire and I ached to be back there, except this time it would be different. This time Granny would not be there to greet me.

The repair seemed to take forever and to while away the time, I sauntered down the road. Next to the ramshackle garage was a small flat-roofed building with a corrugated iron roof and wire netting barricading the open window frames. The sign read, "Wine Shop"; but I couldn't see any bottles of wine, only plastic bottles of Cola and Sprite all tied together on a shelf with thin wire. I peeped inside and a few plastic tables and chairs were laid out on a dusty concrete floor with two men cooking spices over a greasy pan on an open fire. Eventually our tyre was replaced with an equally worn out specimen, but our driver seemed to think it was safe to continue our long haul up the mountain. Branden and I got in and were relieved to begin our ascent again.

A ball of emotion rolled in my stomach. I was excited, apprehensive and sad at the same time. It was difficult to view the present without contrasting it with the past. The forest vegetation at the base of the mountains didn't seem as lush or exotic as it had the first time I saw it. I was impatient to begin the long awaited ascent and to be encapsulated again into the unique tranquillity of the hills, which was unlike anywhere else in the world except for the temple compound at Palenque, Mexico, where the vibrations of energy are profoundly peaceful and where silence is a state of extreme nothingness, saturated in pure serenity and motionless as a frozen pond in winter. Coonoor has the same tranquillity with a similar vibration. Living in the clouds adds a mystical element to routine existence. In the early morning you wake inside a cloud, which descends below the trees before lunch, and you look down as though viewing the rest of the world from space. In the late afternoon when the mist returns, it seals the landscape in a secret, hazy vapour, shrouding the hills in a net that catches stray sounds and when the night folds in, the cloudy mystery begins again, like earth's diurnal round forever turning.

Our driver was better than many others, but even so, he took liberties, carelessly racing around blind corners. In my mind everything was bigger in my memory than the reality. The waterfall where we stopped on our first visit to Granny was much smaller than I remembered. The rocks, the gullies, the cracked and jagged outcrops were not as imposing. The monkeys still paraded in bands searching for food, sitting on the roadside waiting for visitors to feed them. The overhead canopies of lush trees were the same, but I never thought that forty years ago when they shaded Will and me, that one day I would return with my son. Spasms of reconnection to the past threw up visions of the then British Raj etiquette and of long lost sayings like, "Play fair, old boy; it's not cricket you know!" I had visions of teatime trolleys and Friday morning Bridge; of crackly wireless sets and the World Service; of Victorian households with locked cupboards storing hordes of flour and sugar; of drivers in uniforms and black shiny cars; of early afternoon military band practice and squeaky trumpets; of trout fishing with the Colonel and Batique lessons with his wife; of classical Indian dance lessons; of the smell of fresh curry at breakfast; of snooker tables at the club and gin and tonic in the evening; of dead rats served up for dinner and dinner parties; of a prince's smile; of long lost characters buried on Tiger Hill; and of custard apples and the clicking of cicadas at night—so many, many memories tumbled from the bygone years.

It was Tuesday morning and the midweek traffic was not unduly heavy, so we managed to make good time through the winding mountain roads and up steep gullies until we finally reached the main town. I gasped. A myriad of memories superimposed themselves on the moment. I could see the bus station as I remembered it, but also how it really was. So many things I recalled were slightly altered but in essence were still the same, like the bazaar, the church and the houses elegantly perched on the hill. The quiet station had become a bustling, thronging community with a different feeling of modern day technology buzzing on the high street by way of Internet cafés and Internet banks. The new world had taken over from the sleepy past. I could see why my son had warned me that things had drastically changed. Progress had forged a new path destroying the old ways.

Gone were the government propaganda billboards giving contraceptive advice and warning that "Two children are enough." That advert had been designed by the British, who had not quite understood the nuances of the language, and so instead of relaying the message that two children were enough, the locals interpreted it as a question—"Two children are enough?" The government promise of giving men a free radio in return for a vasectomy was ignored and the population grew.

Eventually, after winding up and down and around uneven roads, we came to a small bungalow next to a small community of houses on top of a hill overlooking the valley. Our hostess, Diana, came out smiling, warmly greeting us with a hug. She was a large woman with a huge heart to match. She bundled us inside and showed us to our rooms. She let me decide which room I wanted and I chose the large dark one; but there was something disturbing in the vibration of the room, and I regretted not choosing Branden's, which was light and airy with a sweet bathroom. How different it all was from my first visit to the Nilgiris where the monkeys congregated in the trees above my bathroom and stole my toothpaste. It was odd staying as a paying guest in a place I knew so well. It was strange sitting in a small garden with the sounds of the houses surrounding us in a compound of domesticity, as Granny's garden had been massive and totally private. It seemed peculiar being in a stranger's house; I felt that at any moment the driver would collect me and take me home to Granny's.

I ached to get a glimpse of Granny's house to see if it had altered, and after coffee Diana offered to drive us past it on her way to visit the army bakery. The bakery was a place I had known well and had not been inside for forty years. The last time I visited the barracks was the night of the ball, and I was nervous wondering if I might see anyone who recognised me. What was I thinking? No one would recognise me, or I them—forty years was a long time! As we bundled into Diana's little car, I was excited but also afraid to be disappointed or shocked at any major renovations made to Granny's property. As we drove past the drive, however, it was pretty much as I remembered it, except it seemed smaller and without a heart; it was just like many other driveways. I spied the army barracks parade ground where most afternoons the band practised out-of-tune renditions of British marching songs. I held my breath as we drove into the army compound and parked the car in the visitors' car park. When we walked into the unmistakable army atmosphere, a flushed recollection of the last night at the ball returned and I was walking again in the cool evening breeze towards the Officers' Mess delicately holding my seascape ball gown off the ground, with my shawl wrapped firmly around my shoulders, trying to hide my racing heart beating for a glimpse of the prince.

I furtively glanced around to see any faces I might know, but of course, there were none. The bakery had undergone renovations and the atmosphere was mechanically busy, not friendly like before. Back in the car, I swallowed my memories, embarrassed to have even dared to hope to see someone from the past. Up and down and around the winding corners we bounced along in Diana's little car hurtling through a green eucalyptus cosmos.

Army bugles blared in the distance and reminded me of a time when I was invited to give some of the officers a dance workout. They were dressed in their cream, army, long-johns, which was the nearest attire they could muster to dance tights.

The evening was fun and the men enjoyed a different kind of training—dancing to rock music. The best part of the evening was the motorcycle ride back home. One of the officers offered to take me back on his motorbike, and in true army style he saluted before I jumped on the small seat behind him, clinging to his back like a baby monkey, with my arms wrapped firmly around his waist. I was terrified of motorbikes since the time my first boyfriend, at the age of sixteen, got his wish to own one. On his birthday he proudly mounted his new, shiny, red steed and fled off into the bright morning. He was killed a few moments later by a lorry.

Riding pillion, I flew through the night feeling the road beneath the wheels dip and dive. Together, my driver and I, who were strangers, joined in magnificent union gliding through ever-changing twinkling lights sparkling in the villages below. A distant explosion of stars blazed on the horizon. Through leafy glades and stark trees, wild animals were surprised by our intrusion, babbling in confusion as our headlights caught their night antics. Wild dogs stood dazed momentarily before slinking into the dense bushes, and low whines from strange animals briefly echoed as the bike revved passed hedgerows. Like a search light our headlamp sought secrets in the dark and the warm wind breathed pine freshness into our faces. I wanted the ride to go on and on forever, but sadly it was over too soon. I realised that happiness is a gift and can arrive unexpectedly, sometimes found, then lost, like a motorbike ride in the night. I have never forgotten the joy of it, like flying out of my body, free from the earth's pull.

Diana told us she was taking us to visit a wonderful couple who had been great friends with Granny and had known her since she was a child. Auntie and Uncle embraced us like members of their family and welcomed us into their home with sincere warmth. I immediately felt comfortable and sat down and enjoyed their hospitality chatting about Granny. Auntie said that Granny had been kind to her when she first arrived in the Nilgiris and that they had forged a firm friendship, lasting throughout Granny's lifetime. She said that she found it strange that a granddaughter-in-law should be so caring about someone who was not a blood relation. I explained to her that I had grown to love Granny during our time together and that she had taught me a great deal about many things. Auntie seemed relieved that I had come of my own volition to seek Granny's grave, rather than at the behest of Prudence, her daughter. Once I realised where Auntie's loyalty lay, I confided in her that the last time I saw Granny I had been very worried about her. She was bed-ridden and tried to whisper things to me in secret. She told me: "I have given Prudence all my money, and she can't even buy me some lip salve. My lips are so dry. She never spends time with me or talks to me; I am left alone most of the time." She had tried to whisper more, but Prudence came in and our conversation dried up. It was distressing to see Granny reduced to an invalid, powerless to help herself and imprisoned in her own bedroom. I tackled Prudence about buying Granny some lip salve and she acquiesced, but I wondered whether she meant it. I also suggested that perhaps she might spend some time talking to her mum. I don't think the advice was met very kindly, and I might have made things worse. I also felt guilty feeling that I might have done more to help Granny, but I had two children to look after and one of them had almost died on the journey.

Auntie looked concerned and told me, "A few days before she died I visited, but I was not allowed to see her. Prudence was out and the servants were left in charge. They would not let me in the room, as they feared Prudence would be angry with them and they might lose their jobs. I could hear sounds coming from the bedroom. She was calling out, but they wouldn't let me through the door."

I burst into tears. I couldn't bear the thought of her dying alone in pain, crying out for help. Auntie and Diana consoled me. I was embarrassed by my outburst of emotion. I had had no idea what had happened to Granny and it was a shock to realize her ordeal. Thoughts of her loneliness and anguish beleaguered me. Visions of her last moments flew in and out of my imagination, and I fought to keep calm. I thought of her grace and love and serene beauty. All that she was and all that she strove to be are not dusty in my memory. I was angry and wanted to know answers to questions. Someone held the balance, and someone was responsible for her willful neglect.

As we drove back to Diana's house, the landscape, once so familiar, screamed a new melancholic melody. I had travelled far to find Granny's grave and rejoice in her memory, but I was incensed with anger at the unfolding picture. I tied myself in emotional knots reeling forwards and backwards trying to come to terms with the truth, but whichever way I viewed the evidence of Granny's last days, the picture of her tortured face remained in my brain. I tried to wash it away with good thoughts and followed Diana, who stopped off at the bazaar to buy fresh food for her amazing dishes. In all my time in Coonoor, I am ashamed to say, I had only visited the market three times and that was in secret with Will. Granny did not allow us to go into such public places for fear of being kidnapped, or catching diseases, or like her sister, being put under a spell by a black magic sorcerer or just being seen by neighbours or friends. Will and I had no such fears and enjoyed our secret forays into the forbidden territory. In Granny's eyes, it was the equivalent of Prince Charles and Princess Anne going to a public lavatory—it just wasn't done! The smell inside the bazaar was overwhelming, especially the fish section, which was so overpowering that I had to cover my nose and mouth and stop breathing until we passed the offensive stench. Diana knew exactly what she wanted and headed for the vegetable stalls, picking only the best and haggling with the vendors. It didn't take too long before we were piling back into the car with a cornucopia of exotic vegetables.

Back at the house, I took time to unpack. The room was dark and the heavy, mahogany bed with a thin, hard mattress blocked out light from the small windows. A high glass window in the dividing wall let in extra light, but there was something lurking in the shadows. Perhaps I was tired, or was I subconsciously remembering my very first night in Coonoor at Granny's, where I had been terrified of everything, even my own shadow? Diana told me an interesting story about the house that had belonged to her grandfather, she said that her family were devotees of Shirdi Sai Ba Ba, who was a famous Indian Saint and had lived a holy existence healing people, and related how ash used to fall from his forehead from the picture in the sitting room. She also said that Sai Baba had been seen in the house, long after his death. I was interested in the story as I knew very little about the saint and wondered if the vibrations in my room had anything to do with him?

Before dinner, Diana drove us to the Club, which I remembered well, as it had been the heart of social life in the hills. Granny's husband had once been the Club Chairman and had his name inscribed over the door, along with many other notables. The drive through the heat of the early evening was like old times when our driver, McGregor, used to take us everywhere. I remembered with affection his small, round, ebony face smiling through the mirror. I was amused that he had a Scottish name and enquired about it. He laughingly explained: "Grandfather, Little Missy Sahib, Grandfather he like name and gave it to all grandchildren!"

As we neared the club, I wondered how it had changed and how Granny would view it. The entrance was still, as it had been and Granny's husband's name was still there, brightly polished and bold. As we entered the main bar, however, I was shocked. The quiet hush of a gentleman's establishment had dissolved into the low hubbub of a middle-class social club with a television—a television! Granny would not have approved. The television blared out in the main bar, which had become mundane and ordinary. I remembered it to be a solemn, almost hallowed, place, where a woman was not allowed to buy a drink and where peace was preserved at all costs. I was shown into the main hall where the dignified grand piano was pushed into to a corner to allow members to race up and down playing badminton. Granny would not have approved! On returning to the main social area, I was amused to see clutches of people sitting around small tables playing Bridge. I smiled remembering our little social gatherings. Auntie was sitting at one of the tables and Uncle was alone reading the paper. We joined him and he graciously bought us drinks.

Uncle was an amazing man with a great depth of knowledge about almost anything and it was a joy to exchange views. We spoke of his great friend, Leonard, who was Granny's husband, and how before his death he had suffered with terrible stomach problems. After his death traces of rat poison had been found in his body. I suddenly remembered with a jolt the last time I saw Granny, she had tried to whisper things to me, but I had not understood. Disjointed phrases about her husband and rat poison remained in my brain like fragmented pieces of a jigsaw that suddenly slotted into place. My mind raced back to Granny's pale face and her sad eyes as she forced a smile when Prudence entered the bedroom and her words dried under her daughter's watchful presence. The thought of Granny's discomfort troubled me- I had not travelled half way across the world to find her in anguish. I wished only to celebrate her life joyously and place flowers on her grave.

It was ten forty-five before we sat down to eat back at Diana's house but it was worth the wait as she had cooked a lovely fresh pea soup, with prawns and rice yoghurt, together with Parsee chicken and grated fried potatoes. After supper we were so tired that we immediately headed to bed. In the dark bedroom old fears returned and the long buried memories of my first night at Granny's rose up through dormant corridors of phobias and silly insecure worries. I thought of the voices that had crept inside my head early that morning, warning of changes to come affecting the world. Questions from outside my mind rose out of nowhere like a tidal wave sweeping the land. What if night leaked into the day and what if the day exploded into oblivion; could we escape? I closed my eyes and held onto the thought of love weaving a soft lullaby through the spiky world of radiation and electromagnetic war, guiding lost souls to safety. The questions arising from my dreams of dark times bombarded and stifled my mind. I was enveloped by visions of everlasting blackness covering the earth, together with images of Granny's arms flailing in the air in a final attempt to call someone before her last gasp of breath dried. I couldn't shake off the night terrors, so I took a herbal sleeping tablet. Plink, plink—imaginary mandolins plucked a melody in my brain and with the sound of dogs barking in the distance, I began to relax drifting into a dreamless, seamless nothing, leaving the darkness behind.

CHAPTER 8

Tiger Hill

Fear can be manifold and shape-shift into many forms. It can be razor sharp; or quiet and lurking like a fox; or booming like thunder; or intelligent like a cat; or sly like a deceitful employer or a lying husband; whatever its disguise it must be destroyed, for it is a control method to keep us anchored to lower vibrations. Visions in my dreams show me dark times, when on almost every level, we will be lead to believe that everything is turning sour though it is not the truth. As a small child I was plagued by night terrors, which everyone thought were nightmares; but they were not. I used to hide, unable to breathe under the covers, as invisible entities padded the blankets and ruffled the sheets. The nightly horror was intense and unbearable but taught me to be strong in the psychic realm, however, the first night back in Coonoor I was not brave enough to fight the overriding anxieties that were striving to keep me awake. I reminded myself of the vow I made never to be afraid of anything, never to utter the words, "I am afraid"; for in admitting the destructive emotion, it empowers the perpetrator with controlling force.

The fear coiling in my gut was like that in Pear Tree Cottage the Christmas morning when I was left alone after everyone deserted me. A whole feast was ready and there was only me to enjoy it. I went back inside the cottage pretending to be fine. Lightheartedly, I laid Sarena in her pram in the kitchen where I could watch her and return to my chores with the radio blaring, bombarding the space with sound to block out my fear. At the sink, doing the washing up, I felt the "thing" boring into my being. I knew it was watching again from close behind. Inwardly I cried, but made no outer show of emotion. I was going to be strong for my baby. Highs and lows, like the sea, take us up and down and we comfort ourselves with the thought that tomorrow will be good; tomorrow will smile a new dawn; tomorrow will be calm; tomorrow will lead us into new waters. I shouted inwardly: "Let there be fun, let there be light, let there be laughter." Yet the bleak winter snow imprisoned me and I was trapped inside routine living.

In the morning in Coonoor, a dog barked and a bucket clanged outside my window as hushed voices drifted from the kitchen with light streaking through the curtains. I sat up feeling refreshed after my aided, uninterrupted sleep. I was looking forward to visiting Granny's house and as Diana drove us, I was nervous wondering what I would find. I couldn't help superimposing the past on the present and I kept seeing myself as a young, inexperienced student, naive in a strange new world and totally unprepared to share Granny's life, which was ensconced in Victorian ethics and saturated in protocol and good manners. I would never forget my embarrassment on the first Sunday as I sat next to her in Church and her eyes disdainfully looked down at my naked knees in my miniskirt. She had insisted on placing a mohair shawl over my legs in a vain attempt to shield my modesty; the mohair had itched my legs and I had longed to be back home where life was normal.

As we drove through the main gates I tried to suppress my emotions. A whole kaleidoscope of pictures encircled my brain. The gardens had a semblance of before but had been landscaped and grandly designed, with a pond and water feature flowing next to where Granny's dressing room used to be. The porch had new windows, but through my eyes, it was as it had always been, with Granny waiting, immaculately turned out in her blue blouse and grey skirt. I blinked away the vision and forced myself to adapt to the changes. I hesitated before climbing out of the car. The sun was shining, but in my heart it was raining. I could not shake off the thought of Granny's last moments, crying out in pain. I gulped and walked sedately towards the new owners. They were charming and gave us a warm welcome. Everything had changed. It was lovely, yet I could still see the old porch with its dilapidated furniture. Beautiful new windows and floors gleamed where the old, worn out tiles used to bear a grey welcome. I marvelled how the dark rooms and high ceilings were transformed into a fantastically modern living space, with a sparkling new kitchen where Leonard's dressing room used to be, with all his old tools laid out on the dresser. As we followed our host into a modern, fully equipped kitchen, I stared in disbelief out of the window at the space that used to be mine and Will's bedroom. I gaped at the fantastic gardens where the *dhobi* used to wash the clothes on an old stone and iron them with an ancient, heavy iron heated over a fire. The servants' quarters, which were raw concrete sheds, had been replaced with luscious bushes.

"That's where the servants' quarters used to be," I pointed out to Branden.

"We're not allowed to use that word anymore," stated our gracious hostess.

"Could I take a peep at the dining room please?" I enquired softly. Our hostess smiled and lead us into a room I knew so well and which had not changed at all. It was like stepping back in time. The large dining table had retained its mirror-like finish, and the silverware and candlesticks glistened from their usual stance on the sideboard. The glass cases with the delicate china, silver trays and tea service were flawlessly preserved; for a moment I was back staring at Granny across the dinner table enduring untold embarrassment on my first evening with Will.

I blinked away the memory as we were shown into the adjoining bedroom where I had seen my first firefly and although it remained in essence the same, it had been transformed with new furniture and fittings.

I was uncomfortable in the new surroundings and didn't want to linger, but I did wish to see Granny's bedroom. Our kind host showed me into what had become her bedroom and left me alone for a while. I could envision Granny propped up in bed with white linen pillows billowing behind her. A new vision claimed territory in my brain and I fought to beat it away. To describe what I saw would take away my beautiful memory of Granny, but all I can say is that the poor, thin creature left to decay was not her. Something had happened to her right arm and I dared not look. Tears welled and I struggled to regain my composure before I rejoined Branden, who was entrenched in a deep philosophical conversation with the owners. When we walked into the garden, the magnificent view was as breathtaking as the first time I saw it. The colours of the Blue Mountains and the rich flowers shaded by waving eucalyptus trees were heavenly. Tea bushes had been planted making good use of the surrounding land, and the sight of the empty army parade ground made me wistful to hear the out-of-tune and out-of-time strains of the band echoing across the valley.

Back in the car we journeyed to Ooty, short for Ootycamund, the town had recently gained a long, unpronounceable name that I rejected. I was shocked to find that Spencer's, the main store, which had once been "the" only place to shop, was closed down and left decaying. It reflected the decline of British influence in the area as Spencer's had been the hubbub and core of generations of wealthy people in the hills and to see it rotting in an undignified heap was disconcerting. Ooty had been a quiet, thriving town but it had grown into an almost unrecognisablee thronging thoroughfare blasting with noisy cars and jostling shoppers. Diana was searching for bedside tables and took us to an old warehouse brimming and bursting at the seams with antiques left over from the British Raj occupancy. Strolling down the aisles that reeked of dust and lost hopes, I could envisage the furniture in affluent settings. I imagined genteel ladies pouring tea from china cups and could hear the clink of cutlery and a smattering of muted conversation in secret corners, where army wives gossiped, watched over by Queen Victoria, who glared down from ornate, gilded picture frames, keeping a watchful eye on protocol.

It began to rain and the dingy, dark warehouse oozed a damp, dank smell; I shivered. Branden was becoming impatient as Diana stalked up and down the congeries of chairs and tables piled high like leftover scraps thrown haphazardly to a flock of hungry birds. The light was dimming, and I wished I'd brought a coat. The day's events back at Granny's house had drained me emotionally. The rain drizzled like a grizzly child, tired and hungry at the end of a long afternoon. A lonely trickle of emptiness caught me drifting back to Pear Tree Cottage, to our secondhand, antique furniture and old armchairs, which Aunt Berry managed to procure from her nursing home.

We couldn't afford any new furniture, so we mixed and matched whatever we had to make the rooms presentable. I tried really hard to settle down to domesticity and I even invented a sling with an old sheet so that I could tie Sarena to me, papoose style. I carried her everywhere, even while I was doing the hoovering. Our open fire was lovely on cold evenings but Will didn't allow us to the have the central heating on during the day, so Sarena and I spent our time in the kitchen, with the heat of the oven to keep us warm. Even when I returned home from the hospital only twenty-four hours after giving birth, there was no heating on in the house and no food; luckily a kind neighbour, Sue, had gleaned my situation and arrived on the doorstep with a little blow heater and a cooked meal. Will was always busy at the university and had very little time for house husbanding. His upbringing in India with servants and his *Iah* to replace his mother gave him very little idea of how to behave as a husband.

Return: To the Land of Durga

Standing now in the graveyard of old furniture that once embellished beautiful homes, indulgent in the pomp and ceremony of privileged ways, it saddened me to see layers of dust settling over the decaying wood. The craftsmanship and the beauty of fine things had been brought to nothing; not even one clock in the whole of the emporium ticked, and I knew the heart of the British Raj lay dead amongst mouldering antiques.

An old piano was hidden behind stacks of antique, high-backed chairs; I gingerly lifted the lid and pressed down a key, but no sound came. My mind drifted back to the eerie resonance of a simple, haunting melody played with one hand, one tiny finger, a child's finger, an invisible finger.

It was the simple melody that had driven my parents away on that fated Christmas—my baby's first Christmas. That had been a lonely time, as had Boxing Day and New Year's Day, so I was more than relieved to be invited out for coffee at a neighbour's house in the first week of January. It was Tuesday afternoon and the winter clouds scudded over the thick conifer trees threatening a storm. I looked forward to my little outing and wasn't going to allow a few rain clouds to stop me from enjoying my first social invitation. In a light mood I went upstairs to get ready. Although living in the village had dampened my love of fashion and clothes, I still dressed in an unusual way from the rest of the conservative, rural community.

I laid Sarena on the bed dressed in her bright orange baby-grow and watched as she cooed, happily kicking her legs. Chinda padded at my heels and placed her paws on the edge of the bed wagging her tail every time Sarena gurgled. I glanced out of the window as the light dimmed and black storm clouds broke, thrashing the trees in an angry fury. I was determined that the storm would not ruin my afternoon. Just as I opened my wardrobe door, a plaintive melody drifted up the stairs. It was the piano. Plink, plink—single notes vibrated through the ceiling from the dining room below. Ding, ding, dong—each note was carefully picked like a child repeating a single melody again and again. I froze. It was the moment I had dreaded ever since my father had related his experience. Common sense fought to take control arguing that it couldn't be happening as it was not possible for the piano to play by itself, but the strains lingered. Ding, ding, dong! Ding, ding dong—the single keys plucked the minimal strains. Three simple notes went plinkety-plink as a little hand hit each note, deliberately striking fear in my being.

After the initial shock I rushed to the bed and picked up Sarena holding her close to my chest. Chinda barked protectively jumping up at my legs. Anger bubbled inside, raging like a tormented tigress protecting her cub. I was not going to let anyone or anything hurt my baby. I rushed down the stairs clutching her and crashed through the dining room door, flinging it open with gritted teeth. There was no one. The playing stopped. Outside the window, the rain lashed the trees, hurling large pellets of hailstones against the window like gunshot on a firing range. I stood in front of the piano and a yellow flash of lightning streaked across the black and white keys in an electric explosion of energy whirling across the walls like a fire blast. Thunder cracked and shook the house. I clung to my baby with her head resting on my shoulder. She did not cry. My little dog at my feet whined. I stood in front of the piano and threatened the spirit. I demanded that it leave and used Granny's mantra—"We are perfect children of the universe; nothing and no one can harm us!"

Through the tempest I stood for an hour standing my ground against the invisible force, which like the storm slowly retreated. When the sun pushed through the black clouds sweeping away the storm with pale blue ribbons of bright sky, I relaxed. My baby had peacefully slept through the ordeal, and Chinda scratched at the door to explore the wet grass. Out in the sunshine the earth smelt rich, and it was hard to believe my ordeal. I phoned Kate and apologised for not attending her coffee afternoon using the terrible weather as an excuse. She understood. She had no idea how disappointed I was and how at that time any social contact was like a rope being thrown to a drowning person. I was confused and dazed by the experience as the piano playing was not like the stalking of the evil energy. Perhaps the child playing was calling to me? For what reason, however, I had no idea. One thing was for sure—I was not going to be pushed out of my house; I was going to win through, whatever the cost. The strength of my conviction brought me out of the memory and back to the present as I stood before the broken, old piano shivering in the damp. Diana at last made a move, and Branden and I were relieved to be driving back. We were looking forward to Diana's cooking, as she conjured up the best Indian meals I had tasted for a long time.

Back in the dark bedroom in Diana's house, I was still uncomfortable with an energy that seemed to hover, waiting and watching and I confess that night I resorted to taking another sleeping tablet as I could not face the invisible entity. It is hard to describe the panic that totally invades your body when you know some unknown force is lurking. Having experienced these phenomena, since I was a tiny child, as an adult I preferred to execute my right to choose a simple way out rather than face the torment. So I gave in and succumbed to the natural calming of herbal tablets keeping my mind on the next day's visit to Tiger Hill Cemetery to place flowers on Granny's grave.

The morning quietly crept into my room dispelling all bleak energy and I wondered if I had imagined the strange force hovering over my bed. I was not going to allow yesterday to journey into the day and so I got up and pushed back the curtains with resolved strength, looking forward to finding Granny's grave to place flowers on her hidden tombstone. As we left the little bungalow, the bright morning throbbed with activity as the locals set about their daily business and we chugged on with the glimmering light from the hills smiling on Diana's dinky car springing from pothole to pothole. We were in good humour after a large breakfast and as Diana had no idea how to get to Tiger Hill Cemetery, she had arranged for us to visit the people at Granny's house who knew the way. Unfortunately, as we followed their car, a lorry squeezed in front of us and drove agonisingly slowly and so we completely lost our guides.

The heat of the morning cut through the cloud and the streets were filmed in a layer of dust descending from the dry hills. We decided to carry on regardless and find our own way to the cemetery. Relentlessly we climbed through the winding roads and out towards the tea plantations where Diana thought the little church lay hidden from the beaten track. A trickle of memory dribbled back as I vaguely recognised certain houses and knew that I had been there before. As we turned another corner, I was sure I had taken tea at one of the plantations with Will and his mother.

"There used to be tigers around here, you know, once upon a time, hence the name 'Tiger Hill'!" Diana declared as she kept her eyes on the narrow path as it seemed we were driving into someone's back garden.

Of course it was all streaming back. I remembered the owner of the tea plantation taking us for a tour around the fascinating bushes, pointing out the place where a young girl had been snatched by a tiger while her mother watched horrified as it bit off the child's head, which rolled down the hill towards the house. I recoiled at the image; meanwhile, the seeming back garden, which was a side road, widened and we headed towards a lush forestation. The mist dipped around us and we didn't see a huge stone arch leading to the cemetery, instead, we ploughed on up a steep narrow track with trees and tea bushes encasing us in a leafy tunnel. The temperature cooled as the opaque cloud descended. We might have been driving through farmland in rural England on a foggy autumn morning.

Slowly the path narrowed turning into a rocky dirt track. Branden and I grew uneasy, but brave Diana soldiered on. It was alarming to see to our right, just a few muddy inches away a sheer drop. Diana was convinced she had to surge on, but Branden insisted on getting out of the car to scrutinize our position and stood back confidently in the haze holding a bright bunch of flowers. Diana was afraid that a bison would jump over the hedge and knock him flat as a man had been killed the previous week near the same spot. She warned him to get back in the car, but he teasingly smiled and said;" I have my flowers to protect me!"

"Some protection!" retorted Diana, who stopped the car abruptly as the track ended, and we certainly couldn't get through a rocky landslide.

"We'll just have to go back!" she stated calmly. Unfortunately the road was too narrow to turn so we had to reverse all the way back with the car slipping and sliding only just avoiding the precipitous drop. Branden did not get back inside the car and followed on foot. I held my breath as Diana skillfully navigated us back to a spot where she could just turn the car to allow Branden to climb back in.

"It must be around here somewhere?" Sighed Diana, as we slowly chugged back down the slippery path. The fog began to thicken as we descended through the veiled mist and we glimpsed a stone cross beckoning to us like a lighthouse on a hazy sea.

"It's there!" I beamed. Diana nodded and drove the car down a dank side road leading to an ornate archway. The cemetery resembled a little plot in rural England cushioned by a copse of tall trees, purposefully hidden from public view. The sun forced a smile through the clouds and it was as though that moment had been saved for us. As we stepped out of the car into a sacred sanctuary, a little man hopped out of the bushes and bowed a welcome. He was the guard who spent his days in quiet solitude watching the seasons disappear one into another, policing the remains of the graveyard against marauding bison and thieves, who had already robbed much of the ornate ironwork. Reverently, we told him the graves we had come to visit and he nodded immediately, knowing the exact location.

Diana quietly hung back as Branden and I followed the *chokidar* to the hallowed ground while a soft chorus of bird song filled the air with an ancient hymn and the sky met the earth in a grey shroud sheathing the morning in a white mantle. With respect and anguished expectation, we approached two large gravestones covered in moss and leaves. The *chokidar* quickly brushed away the leafy debris and wiped his hands across the green lichen, skillfully grabbing a handful of clay to scrape away at the inscription. Magically the names appeared unscathed and boldly heralded the history of two people long buried. Branden was delighted to clearly read the names and the beautiful simple message of husband and wife lying side by side. Our silent rejoicing was deafening. I knew Granny was smiling, happily sharing our victorious moment and grateful to us for our fortitude and love.

The graves lay side by side on a small incline under a tree. A thick carpet of dried brown leaves crackled and scrunched under foot. Something bit my foot. A sharp stinging pain pierced my ankle. A small trickle of blood oozed from a fresh wound. I must have disturbed a snake, but I was too engrossed in our mission to worry about it. There was nothing in the remote silence that was exotic or faraway; only the bite was a reminder that we were in India. Otherwise, it was just a little piece of England torn off from the rest of the community that was 'home' to the exiled English. Standing in front of Granny's grave, I lost time and then found it; for when faced with the shrapnel of death, like the tide and seasons, which come and go, I was reminded that so does our earthly time ebb and flow. We dance according to the reason and rhyme of lifetimes found and hidden, abandoned and sought, cherished or hated, early or belated; life is, after all, what we make of it. Standing in a place of death, it is easy to become philosophical about life while wrapped in a dying song of silky slithers of buried wishes and withered hopes, sweeping bitterness underground, concealing truth under a hard stone. Arsenic poisoning floated to the surface of my mind when I looked at Leonard's grave. It was hard to consider prolonged pain drawn out to dismember living organs, while the last embrace of breath withers on a pillow. I was sad for Granny's husband and wished I had listened to her, but regret has no place when years later there are only questions and no answers.

Branden and I carefully placed our flowers on top of the newly cleaned tombstones and stood back for a few moments to reflect. A bright yellow flower and a crimson red head filled the cemetery with a glorious blaze of colour amidst the grey low-lying mist. The vibrancy of colour splashed against the mossy marble, echoing a disturbing emptiness. My memory was not empty but bursting with thoughts of what you were, dear Granny. Red and yellow flowers adorn your resting place and our floral tribute unites you together once more with your husband in a dazzling garland radiating across the mellow moment. Sealed in a shell, your bodies crumble; but your lives live on in another dimension. I will not forget you.

I walk away as the sun streaks through a cloud highlighting a peaceful park where marble headstones rise out of the ground standing to attention like soldiers on parade. Resting on one large marble cross is the statue of an angel. She is not victorious and jubilant with outstretched wings, but sadly dejected as she rests her left elbow on the side of the cross with her hand clutching her face, her head bent low, and her wings folded inwards. She forlornly carries a garland in her right hand as though she has despondently taken it from her head after leaving a party. Her face is furrowed and her long dress hangs limply dragging across the ground. I move closer. Somehow I expect to disturb her, but she does not stir and I get the impression that the dead beloved lady lying beneath the ground has left a huge gaping hole in her husband's life and that he has created the angel to express his own dismay and loneliness that death has brought him.

An estranged voice calls through the soft rustling trees: "On and on you walk through each day taking the drudge, like a colander, your spirit drains light as it seeps through the gaping holes of lost hope. A sigh escapes into the dank forest exhaling from your bones, and you sing the farewell song of the leaves as they sink into the earth for their little sleep of death awaiting their rebirth in the spring. Thereafter a lull of forgetting the struggles and tears, the dark times, and the grey days without the sun or moon, with nothing coming or going or slipping away, the bright time of years will be all that is left. Only the "Isness" remains. Only the "Isness" will *be*. The Isness of then and the Isness of tomorrow are unreal, as all is unreal until we are led beyond the knowing."

The voice fades. I know the answer is not there in the grave and it does not lie beneath the ground. I hold a rose to the heart of your memory, Granny, for it is and will always be a part of me. A different voice faintly emerges, like a gentle breeze on a summer's day:

"Thank you for the journey; thank you for the thought; thank you for the pain and thank you for the loss; thank you for the finding. But it is not the cross that counts, for after loss there is always gain, after night there is always day and after—after what? After the snow, there is flooding. Only gaze a while and stay briefly, for only the watchman is awake. There is no welcome under dead leaves. Leave; leave for you take us with you. Gaze no more at the mossy stones, go and live and love and rejoice for what is, what has been and what will be. The end shall have no vermilion recrimination, leave it be."

The sun creeps through the dank foliage highlighting the dejected angel in a bright halo, but it will not change her outlook; for she is forever frozen in her sad repose and waits and waits until nature brings her sweet release. I creep away leaving her in peace, knowing that everyone somehow waits to be released, but in the meantime we need to conserve our strength to die. Voices warn that all too often in living we lie to ourselves and sleep through the glory of our true nature forgetting that there is a stillness in the air that makes us listen to the birdsong. Or is it the nothingness, which hangs in the trees, that makes us alert to the other side of our being? A gentle wind stirs and whines resonating above the quiet of nowhere. I do not weep but rejoice to have found Granny at last. I will never forget those treasured moments wrapped in a fairy-tale magic of lost and found, of gone and reunited. I did not cry then, only rejoiced.

CHAPTER 9

The Thread Needle Garden

After our visit to Tiger Hill, we came away feeling happy having completed our special mission and Diana had arranged for us to have lunch with an enterprising woman, Sanita, who made pickles, jams, marmalade, cheese and various other homemade produce. As we drove into her beautiful garden, she was waiting for us on the verandah and warmly welcomed us into her home. The magic and strained emotion of the morning had dissolved with the mist, and under the bright midday sun we returned to normality. My leg stung after the bite, so I asked Sanita if she had some antiseptic cream and a plaster. She led me to the bathroom through her bedroom, which was stocked with homemade produce labelled and tastefully packaged. The bite was quite deep and I was glad to hide it with a dressing. Drinks were served by our hostess's husband, who was a very astute and intelligent man and extremely knowledgeable about world issues. The lunch was, as anticipated, a cornucopia of tantalising tastes with everything fresh from the garden. Sanita's pickles were wonderfully tangy and she allowed me to try some of her marmalade, which was the best I had ever tasted.

After lunch we were shown around Sanita's colourful garden where she grew various crops, flowers and fruits for her merchandise. I loved the small outbuilding where the cheese was made and marvelled at her ingenuity at producing everything from her home. I had at one time in my life, only on a much smaller scale, the same cottage industry desire to make and create things from my garden and home. It was in Pear Tree Cottage where I made children's mobiles and fantasy artificial flowers, a variety of jams, plus home-made elderflower wine, dandelion coffee, dandelion wine and herbal remedies. I deliberately immersed myself in my cottage industry to fight off the fear of the invading malignant entity that lived and breathed inside the walls. There was no escape and it was sad to think that the highlight of my week was a Friday when my Arts and Crafts magazine was delivered. I would eagerly search for more ideas to engage my time, as the THING perched in readiness to strike, always watching and waiting for a gap in my defence. At times it jangled my nerves and frayed the edges of my sanity, especially when I was at low ebb. I suffered from post-natal depression, which was not a subject that was openly discussed or even acknowledged at that time and so I battled on in a lonely world. After hearing the piano playing that dreadful afternoon, I never stopped listening for the same plaintive melody. Although I had become accustomed to the voices, the whispers and the footsteps, I was not prepared for a different kind of attack.

It was a Friday lunch time and I was feeling happy because my special magazine had arrived and there was a recipe for apple jelly that I wanted to try, so I was busy in the kitchen peeling apples. Sarena was asleep in her pram. I heard the children from the nearby school pass by shouting and laughing. Their voices echoed through the front door and down the hall and I thought the noise would wake her, so I went to check. Just as I passed through the kitchen, a strange noise burst in the air. It was sharp, like maracas shaking angrily, striking a "shick shick shick" and pulsing around me. It ensnared me in a malicious pen of percussive rallies like a voodoo spell being cast by a primitive force. Chinda barked incessantly at the air, jumping up at the unseen enemy. I pushed my way through the resonance to the pram where the sound surrounded my baby. I picked her up while the maracas attacked. Anger boiled as I ploughed through the dining room to the kitchen where the maracas pursued me shaking above my head and alternating down to my feet and back over my head. I shouted above the racket: "I am a perfect child of the universe; nothing and no one can harm me." I firmly held my intention to conquer the THING that was shaking around me like a swarm of bees. The invasive sound intensified and I screamed above the noise repeating my mantra until it gradually dissipated, fading away to a distant zone. I held Sarena close as it passed over us and then let go of my emotions sobbing into the quiet rack of pots and pans. She was so small. She didn't understand, but her concerned eyes stopped me in my tracks. I stopped crying and laughed; she smiled and I laughed and laughed into the emptiness so that IT got my message loud and clear—I was not going to be chased out of my house. I will never forget the grotesque attack that came from nowhere leaving me quaking and terrified of the next assault.

After lunch we left our gracious hosts and Diana drove past Coonoor club where many memories flashed, including an embarrassing event. The tennis courts were still there where Prudence used to play matches and where I had lessons. One Sunday afternoon I had been persuaded to play in a tournament. The whole club turned out to watch, including Prudence who was a serious match player and too good to enter the tournament. I was doing quite well managing to hold the racket correctly, serving the ball over the net and returning it in the right direction even keeping my feet moving—well, dancing was more like it. However, the match came to a shocking halt, not through "rain stopped play" or "lost ball" or "injury"—no, the whole tournament across four courts stood still when "Missy Sahib's skirt fell down!" I jumped—well leaped actually—to strike the ball in midair and my skirt, which was held in place by a pin, fell to the floor and I stood in front of the whole crowd in my white knickers. A gasp rippled across the tarmac. It was most undignified and certainly not the kind of thing to happen at the Club. A servant rushed forward with a towel, which he held discreetly around my waist while I pulled up my skirt and adjusted the pin. Once my skirt was in place, I continued to play amidst a polite ripple of applause, but after the incident I couldn't concentrate on hitting the ball and lost the next set. Prudence was not pleased but never mentioned the unfortunate incident or losing the match.

It was odd seeing the place again, even after all that time, I still felt a twinge of embarrassment remembering the "Missy Sahib's skirt fall down" incident. We didn't have time to stop as we were hastily on our way to Ooty where Diana had more business and thought that a trip to the Thread Needle Garden would be a good idea. Neither Branden nor I had any desire to visit it, but Diana was adamant that visitors should see it. We were more inclined towards finding a liqueur shop and sitting in the bungalow garden relaxing with a glass of wine, but Diana forged ahead with her plan of action despite not having the slightest clue as to where the Thread Needle Garden was located. The drive through the leafy glades and forestation was pleasant even though the mist descended like winter fog on a bleak afternoon in North Yorkshire. It was the kind of mist that shrouded a country cottage in desolate mystery, and I found myself, inadvertently returning in my mind, to Pear Tree Cottage and the awful memories.

Not long after the "maracas" incident Will had arranged for a floor fitter, Bert, who lived in the village, to begin work on our tattered kitchen floor. It was a cold January afternoon when he arrived and he explained that in order to loosen the floor he had to soak it, and I was not to be worried when it was flooded two inches deep in a slimy solution. I decided that it would be a good idea to take Sarena for a walk around the village in her pram even though the weather was bitterly cold. Before I left, I gave Bert a cup of coffee and we sat at the kitchen table talking about York, when noises were heard upstairs. He thought someone was walking about in the bedrooms, but I nonchalantly shrugged off the sound with the notion that it was an unwanted visitor.

He told me that York was full of such unwanted visitors and ghosts and proceeded to tell me about a time when he was asked to do some electrical work in the nun's house next to the Minster. He knocked on the door early one morning and was met by an elderly nun, who asked him to wait in the hall while she fetched her superior. An old man came out of a cupboard dressed in very old-fashioned clothes like a butler and asked him if he wanted a cup of tea. Bert enthusiastically said yes and waited politely. No one came for about ten minutes and then a tall nun appeared and told him he had permission to begin the work.

"Oh, I'll have me tea first then," he laughed in good Yorkshire humour, but the nun's reaction was stern.

"I'll see that you get some!" she retorted in an off-handed manner, shocked at his impertinence.

"Oh, it's okay; the old gent said he'd make me a cuppa!"

She squinted and looked sideways enquiring, "What old man?"

"The one that came out of the cupboard and went downstairs, he said he'd get me one."

"We don't have any men here, Mr. Green- we're a community of nuns, you see!"

"Oh sorry, Sister, but I did see him all right, as clear as day!"

"I'll see you get some tea!" she stated firmly and left to work in her study. Bert said no one mentioned the old gent again and was brought a cup of tea and a biscuit by a friendly nun.

I felt safe to relate to Bert some of the extraordinary happenings in the house unburdening a heavy load of secrets locked in my mind while the THING watched from the dining room. I whispered so that it couldn't hear and Bert looked alarmed when we heard more noises upstairs. "Well I'll best get on; it's a tough job ya know!"

I left him to fill buckets of water ready for the flooding and I hurried to get my coat, aware that the THING was displeased with me for divulging its secret presence. I left Bert busy splashing the floor with the solution and walked into the swirling fog. Sarena was snugly wrapped against the damp, and she looked happy in her warm cocoon. The cold air lay heavy on my chest and I barked a deep cough in the emptiness of the hollow streets. There was no one around. My lonely footsteps echoed in the stillness. Little Chinda's paws padded softly next to the pram wheels and she looked up at me as if I was unreasonable to take her out on such a dismal afternoon. No cars shone beams of light through the dense white curtain; no one clanged a bicycle bell; no one shuffled past or muffled a stray greeting. It seemed we were walking off the edge of the world in a hazy, white cloud. I decided not to stay out too long and meandered back to the cottage noting that Bert's van had gone. Perhaps he needed some more tools? I left Sarena sleeping in her pram in the conservatory but was shocked when, on opening the kitchen door, a flood of water cascaded down the steps. The whole kitchen floor was awash in two inches of soapy solution. I looked to see if Bert had left a note, but there was nothing. I phoned his home. His wife answered, "I'm sorry, Missus, but I'm ta tell ya that he won't be coming back!"

"What?" I retorted in disbelief.

"I'm sorry he's had ta leave ya in a mess, but what he saw he can't say an he can't go back into that house!"

"But what am I to do?"

"I'm sorry, Missus, that's all I can say- he won't be coming back!" And with those final words she put down the phone.

Rage bubbled. Whatever had happened to Bert must have been quite shocking for him to have downed tools and fled. My feet sloshed about in the deluge. I had to do something to clear up the mess, so with mop and bucket I set about the arduous task of clearing the flood, knowing that at any moment Sarena would wake and that IT watched, delighting in the fact that it had won another round. It took hours to clean the mess while intermittently feeding Sarena, so that by the time Will came home there was only a wet film left on top of the slimy floor. Although Will phoned to find out what had happened, Bert would never tell and he kept his word and he never returned.

Nearing Ooty, I cleared my mind of the past as the mist through the trees vanished and the bustling town came to life thronging with people hovering in crowded doorways. Diana had no idea where she was going and kept stopping to ask the way to the Thread Needle Garden. Not interested in visiting it, Branden and I were quietly pleased when, after driving around and around and up and down alleys, we couldn't find it. Diana, however, was intent on succeeding in her mission and proceeded to retrace her tracks and furtively probe as to the whereabouts of the establishment. Many people gave us their idea where it was situated, but it always eluded us. The words "Thread Needle Garden," heard through a haze of Tamil, became a joke and thereafter each time Branden and I heard Diana utter the inimitable phrase, we were on the verge of giggling like school children. After countless attempts to track it down, we came across a policeman who directed us straight to the building. Disappointingly it was situated in an area that resembled a ramshackle fairground with various crude sideshows and dirty stalls, further augmenting our resentment at being made to visit it.

Flushed with success, Diana bundled us out of the car to reconnoitre the place. Branden by this time was furious and took a decisive stance. He paid our meagre entrance fee and marched straight through the display without a single glance at a threaded flower. I felt sorry for the poor woman who stood attentively by the door waiting to take us on a tour, but Branden shouted for me to follow, and like a little lamb I obeyed. His visit lasted approximately ten seconds, mine a little longer. He was, however, right to be rebellious as neither of us had wanted to be chauffeured there in the first place, and to see, as it turned out, a sad, tawdry tent full of dusty artificiality with rows of grimy flowers, their faces sad and layered in dirt from the filmy atmosphere only confirmed our suspicions that it would be a wasted journey. I glanced at one or two flowers that were embroidered beautifully, but the overall impression was like a mad, eccentric old lady's garden back home, where she had painted everything in acrylic white gloss, including the soil and placed artificial plastic flowers in rows like performers in a circus. Passersby usually laughed out of embarrassment or sympathy at the spectacle, and I felt a similar response to the unsophisticated Thread Needle Garden display.

Diana was surprised when we both marched back to the car within seconds of entering the display gleaning from our expressions that we were not impressed. Amongst the grimy offerings made of thread from twine, thread from nylon, thread from cotton and embroidered blossoms from almost anything that could be threaded through a needle, had been some artistically crafted handiwork, but alas, traces of plastic were spied amongst the blooms—plastic stems, plastic leaves and even, I was sure, a few plastic flowers. The idea of so many threads sewn together to make recognisable forms and creative imitations of nature, lead me to think about sinews and veins of human beings and how we are threaded together into bodies, each one following a general pattern, but every person uniquely different. I recalled my words spoken to Jeremy on our first meeting, about our lives being pulled taut like an over-stretched violin string, until we break and are catapulted into the cosmos, leaving the earth to follow our next pathway. I did not have any notion why I described the image to him or where it came from, and I was certainly not aware that he would die the next day. I had no knowledge of what scientists have discovered since then-the String Theory, which proposes that all objects in our universe are composed of vibrating threads and membranes that interact with each other. The whimsical notion of the "stringed universe" is now apparently not so fanciful, and the poetic idea of the "music of the universe," which was once considered a fanciful concept, is now an accepted hypothesis. I read that perhaps in time it might be possible to use the threads of our own being to transport ourselves out beyond the earth while anchoring our base thread to the planet, so that we can explore beyond and pull ourselves back at will.

Carlos Castaneda, in *Tales of Power*, describes his time studying sorcery with a Mexican Indian (long before the String Theory) who taught him that humans have a nest of fibres in the solar plexus. The fibres fan out and can be seen by sorcer-

Return: To the Land of Durga

ers; the nest takes the form of "an egg, like cluster of luminous fibres, which emanate from the solar plexus." He states that "One single luminous fibre can be directed at any conceivable place." Castaneda recounts how he witnessed the sorcerers jumping from high mountains using their luminous fibres to anchor their bodies to the ground, jumping and landing safely. Other mere mortals would have been dashed to smithereens on the rocks below.

The concept of being able to use these threads within our bodies fascinates me, especially since I had experienced a long silver thread twining out of my body when I was a teen-ager. I was lying in bed and felt myself rise up out of my body with a long silver chord trailing from my spirit form anchored to my body below. I realized instinctively that I could not go further than the string allowed, otherwise, contact with my body and the earth would be severed and my body would die. I have never forgotten the feeling of dangling in space, like an astronaut tied to his spaceship by a chord from his spacesuit, floating only as far as the link would allow. Also, when I was a young dancer, one inspirational teacher described invisible strands in the atmosphere that we can latch onto and stretch our arms across, using them as invisible ropes to support our weight, enabling us to keep our arms outstretched for as long as necessary, lengthening our body's natural ability to extend our limbs in space.

As the car bounced along, I allowed my thoughts to drift to a state of nowhere. Often when I clear my mind, a teaching voice enters my head and speaks softly. I have known voices in my head ever since I can remember; when I was very small, my mother took me to the doctor insisting that I was mad, as I spent hours talking to invisible people. Sometimes, especially at night, my head would be full of sounds like a radio tuning into different stations with foreign voices and snippets of music fighting for airspace in my head. My mother was frightened by the way I spoke to invisible beings stating that it wasn't imaginary as she could tell I was really speaking to someone. Since returning to India, the voices infiltrate my mind more frequently. Perhaps it is because I have more quiet time to sit and reflect. Whatever the explanation, it seems that I am being fed information at a rapid rate and being primed to receive knowledge that is important to pass on. In the quiet of the car I listened to a soft voice in my head, which offered information about the "threads of life": "Threads of your being light up your life and that of others with invisible electricity. Your thoughts are like electric pulses that can be detected subconsciously by those around you and are projected into the atmosphere. Threads of energy fall from your being, like dead skin cells flaking from your body. Good vibrations affect people with positive electrons and bad energy clogs the airwaves with a grim density that is difficult to steer through. It is important to try to fill the airwaves with positive feelings that will feed those around you and benefit your planet. Good vibrations, no matter how small or insignificant, can never die, only blossom and grow. This is what your earth needs. Soon there will come a time when humans will harness electric vibrations to damage and destroy your beautiful world. Knowledge will be used to change climate conditions with deadly technology, which will be targeted to initiate floods, cause droughts and suck the earth dry of natural resources. There are malevolent forces that will try to destroy the very fabric of life as you know it and are following a plan to take over the earth to become a place that you will not recognize, ruled by beings that are threaded from multi-sources. *Always follow your inner goodness.*"

    The words trailed into nothing and I was alarmed. The light in the sky dimmed like falling chords in an electric symphony and I struggled to comprehend the message. Night fell swiftly as we made our way back through the town and lines of shops in the main thoroughfare flared the streets with an electric glow. We wanted to find a liquor store to buy some reasonable wine, but unfortunately the store did not stock any to Branden's taste. We trundled back towards the dense forests, past the Ooty sign proclaiming, "The Queen of the Hills Welcomes You!" and out through winding roads and dimly lit potholed lanes back to Diana's little bungalow. Along the way, we passed clutches of pink-capped women in colourful saris gossiping about the day's events and gatherings of hill men, small in stature but stout of heart willing to take on tough jobs to feed their families and farther on, past the melancholy dampness of the evening air, which hauntingly smelt of pine and eucalyptus balm, until we bumpily turned into Diana's drive.

Back at the bungalow Diana's employees waited for us and opened the gates. They were a husband and wife team who looked after the house and helped with the cooking and general running of the place, especially when she wasn't there. They were a friendly pair and were always eager to assist and help with anything we needed. In the kitchen I watched Diana cooking. She was amazing at conjuring mouthwatering dishes using fresh herbs and spices, whetting our appetites with their aroma. In the bedroom, in the darkness, a lingering echo lurked and I felt guilty at having taken a light sleeping tablet every night since our arrival. I knew that I would have to make myself face the night at some point without the herbal aid, but at that moment I wasn't ready to relinquish that support.

I wandered into the kitchen where Branden was busy trying to get on line with Diana's computer. I smiled as I remembered sitting on Granny's veranda listening to the howling wolves in the distance as the world service news kept the family up to date with events. The radio had been our only contact with the outside world, but it had often fizzled out just when an important announcement was underway. I never imagined the world so changed that I would one day be back in Coonoor with my son whiling away an evening, not in front of the wireless, but sitting at a computer, which enabled immediate communication with anyone, anywhere in the world. The threads of fantasy in my youth, concerning space travel and hi-tech communication, had been woven into the fabric of today's reality, where anything is possible- after all, people once believed that the world was flat. Not so long ago in York, England, in my own city, it had been scientifically proven that glass is a liquid and I wondered what revolutionary scientific evidence would next challenge our concept of reality.

Time was slipping away and by ten thirty the meal was still not ready. Diana was insistent on cooking Chinese pancakes to add to the banquet. I went outside to feel the damp air closing in around me, clinging to my skin like a limp, clammy rag. My mind latched onto the day's events at the Thread Needle Garden and I remembered a dream I had about threads of vibrations engineered as sound killers—sound killing minds, controlling minds with microwave emissions. In the terrible dream I saw people attending a film in an ordinary cinema. The flickering lights across the screen induced a hypnotic state over the audience and people were lulled into a semi-coma. Once everyone had been sedated, a high-pitched sound wave was emitted from the film, shattering peoples' skulls, pulping their brains into a mash of gore. The cinema lights went up and men in white uniforms and masks set about cleaning up the massacre. Bloodstained faces, oozing entrails from their ears and noses lay strewn over the walls and floor. The film had been especially engineered as a weapon of mass destruction and the high-pitched sound device could be implanted into any film at any time, so that an unsuspecting audience could be annihilated at one sitting. A spirit guide once had warned: "Beware the silver screen. Beware the flickering waves bouncing through the air, for they keep the masses under control."

Recalling the nightmare, I shivered and looked up into the velvet sky as gentle chords of light strummed softly through the evening cloud. When will it happen, I wondered? Will the new dawn of that terrible world come and wreak revenge on the light of yesterday and if so, where will tomorrow live? A voice in the stillness replied: "You will rise up through the wreckage and watch the world that was float away." I sighed, wondering what it all meant.

Ten forty-five and finally the meal arrived. Inside the kitchen, the table was full of beautiful food, and I smiled, looking at Branden, and said, "I've never had Chinese pancakes at this time of night before!"

My son wryly smiled back and whispered teasingly: "Do you want to go to the Thread Needle Garden again tomorrow?"

CHAPTER 10

Screaming Walls

When I woke the next morning, the sun was streaming through tiny gaps in the curtains. A dog barked and a bicycle bell cheerily chimed as friendly voices called back and forth to each other across the road. Quiet preparations for breakfast were barely audible as muted chinks of coffee cups clinked from the kitchen. I felt rested after a good night's sleep, having taken a herbal sleeping tablet because of my dread of the night spirits. It sounds silly and infantile in recounting, but when the night terror begins, vibrations from unseen beings hover menacingly above me and put pressure on my body touching me through the bed clothes. My stomach twists into knots; my heart pounds, almost cracking through my ribcage; my breath dies as saliva dries and the terror creeps up my back.

I remember living in student accommodation when I was eighteen years old. I shared a college house with other first year girls and I was voted the housemother, meaning, in effect, snitching on my fellow students if they stayed out past the gate time. But I never did, as I was already alienated from the others having been given a room at the top of the house by myself. One morning, very early, I heard someone playing the violin. It was

Saturday and no one in our house played the violin or would play that kind of music early on the weekend. I sat up to listen. The music wove up the stairs and through the wall. It was beautiful. The plaintive melody curled over my bed and dolefully meandered up towards the ceiling, hanging in the air like a Scottish lament played on a single bagpipe. For a few minutes I was entranced by the magic as the house slept and no one stirred.

I did not know that at the same time down in the basement a fellow drama student was woken by the violin music. As she turned to listen, she saw a young girl drifting towards her with the shadow of a man chasing behind. The girl's face was white and racked with terror. Rina, my friend, was horrified as she witnessed the man striking his victim from behind, dragging her to the floor and finally strangling her. Rina, traumatised by what she witnessed, turned towards the wall to scream, but it sucked in the sound and took her voice. As the music died, a girl from the basement came to enlist my help because poor Rina was locked in shock, unable to speak. Her gaunt, ashen face had aged and her eyes were black, lifeless sockets. We dressed her and took her to the infirmary, where she was given a sedative. Later, when she recovered, she was able to tell us what she saw. Older students whispered the story, which had been passed down through the years. It seems that two musicians had lived in the house previously and were well known locally through playing at concerts and weddings. The man played the piano and was much older than the young girl who played the violin. Apparently the man virtually kept her a prisoner in the house and she had told a friend that she was going to leave him and break up their partnership. When she told him her plans, he furiously hit out at her and when she tried to escape, he strangled her then shot himself.

After Rina's experience the girls were afraid to be left alone in the house. Rina moved out of the basement into another dormitory and the others were in constant dread of being haunted by the same apparition. A few months later a new student went into the basement to collect a folder. While she was down there, she felt a cold shadow pass over her and heard screams rolling down the wall. She dropped everything and never went down

Return: To the Land of Durga

there again. Rina thought that the girl's screams were locked inside the wall and that when she tried to scream, the wall also sucked in her voice. I think it is possible that records of our emotional state can be stored in the fabric of our houses, homes and workspaces and that at times, when our mind frequency is in line with the recorded emotional vibration, we can tune into the hidden sounds. The same applies to memories of people who appear as ghosts, especially if a person dies in shock or terror or torment, their emotion runs into high frequency levels and seeps into the fabric of the walls, where it remains until someone tunes into it and it is replayed as a past record of events.

A short while after that event, in my second year, I lived around the corner in a small ground floor flat in a large, prestigious Edwardian house. The bathroom was situated along a dark hallway outside the main flat. I woke up around two in the early hours of the morning and sleepily dragged myself out of the flat to walk down the cold corridor. As I rubbed my eyes, I bumped into someone standing in the hall. I politely apologised and half-asleep, I yawned my way to the bathroom. It was only when I sat down on the lavatory that I suddenly realized that I had bumped into a grey thing. It was an amorphous grey blob undulating by the stairs and I had accidentally banged into it. I felt its body as though it were a living being. Its presence seemed to fuse inside a grey fog and had no real form. When I inspected the memory of what I had seen, I was terrified to go back down the corridor. I knew I couldn't sit on the lavatory all night, so I plucked up the courage to run down the hall, shielding my eyes in case it was still there, but the thing had disappeared. However, the next day a whole series of unfortunate things happened, and I dread ever bumping into a grey blob again.

As I got up in the dark bedroom in Diana's house, I wondered whether the atmosphere lingering in the room was caused by a memory locked in the walls. Perhaps something had happened to Diana's family. Certainly the story of Shri Baba was intriguing and the fact that ash fell from his photograph was incredible. Whatever it was, I didn't feel brave enough to face the night without the help of the sleeping tablet. In the scariness of nowhere, with phantoms wandering in the shadows past midnight, you wade through the place where smothered screams are diluted in icy fear and you cannot turn back; all you can do is ride out the moment and wait for the light of the morning to dispel all in a flood of dawn pink, as you are left wondering if it really happened. As the morning brightened through the chink in the curtain, I sauntered to my little bathroom, always on the lookout for spiders and stray creepy crawlies hiding in corners. The old-fashioned shower taps were difficult to control and I never managed to get the right temperature—it was either too cold or too hot. I chose to grit my teeth and take a cold shower, being careful not to swallow any water that splashed my face as Granny had always warned me not to let the water go down my nose or in my mouth and always to use boiled water to clean my teeth.

Our plan for the morning was to visit the John Sullivan memorial house in Kotagiri. Sullivan was given the post of Collector of Coimbatore between 1815 and 1830. He founded Ooty and brought British style, social etiquette and architecture to the Nilgiris, together with agricultural crops such as potatoes, barley and other English grains. Granny's house had been a typical English country bungalow, part of the John Sullivan style legacy. When I first encountered Granny's bungalow, it was like stepping into a time warp where a little piece of eighteenth century England lay cocooned in the countryside preserved in the pristine decorum of a Jane Austen novel. With my eighties miniskirt and hippy-style long hair, I had dared to challenge the security of the little potted plot of distilled Britain and rock Granny's impression of the new youth of my day. The visit to the John Sullivan house would be interesting from a historical viewpoint, to see the photos and records of the past and study the social background that had influenced Granny's generation.

The ride out to Kotagiri in Diana's little car was bumpy but pleasant, the landscape altered from clutches of houses and shops perched on hillside ledges, to rural farms and fields growing English produce. The agricultural life-style gave it a different atmosphere, where the people toiled to follow the crop cycle, working the seasons and separating their fields into neat sections. We passed a school with a large, red, earthen, excavated playground where the children in their navy blue blazers and light blue shirts were playing. The navy blazers jogged another memory—I saw myself momentarily in a navy blazer with a light blue and white striped dress wearing a straw boater hat.

I was standing in the playground looking towards the sky feeling the "beyondness" of the moment, feeling older than my twelve years, knowing that the present would fade, that the battle of school days would die, and that sometime in the future I would travel beyond my routine little world out to unimaginable places. My love of travel had been encouraged when I became a member of the Mountaineering Club and revelled in the challenge of the climbing and the time away from home, especially being with a group of girls who were like sisters. Watching myself looking skywards I recalled my trip in the wilderness of North Wales, where our group was taken by our leader and his wife to stay in two small, tin caravans in a tiny Welsh valley, snugly hidden between two impressive mountains.

Five of us staying in one tiny caravan were squashed together like sardines in a can, but it was part of the fun. We spent the day climbing mountains and in the evening we partied around a campfire and sang songs. I was the storyteller elect, and every night I entertained the girls with a ghost story. They loved to be scared and it was easy for me to plug into nightmare scenes that I had lived out in reality. Little did the girls know, when they curled under their sleeping bags, frightened, yet feeling safe knowing it was just a story, that I was actually recounting my own experiences. I never shared this with them as it was too unbelievable and I valued their friendship too much to allow them to think I was crazy.

One day while we were climbing, I began to plan the story for the night. We were inching our way up a grassy verge, just beneath a rocky ledge, when the idea of something hidden under the earth waiting to be unlocked, like an Aladdin's cave genii, popped into my head. Pausing for a few moments to recoup my breath, I used my fingernails to scrape away some moist earth compacted under pale boulders. The smell of damp soil in the clear mountain atmosphere momentarily made me dizzy. Whirling in the heady earthiness, I felt the presence of a creature lurking underground. It was locked in a dark cave. I let it out. Without fear or thought, I just allowed the thing to use my energy and climb on my back. Somehow the trace of soil under my fingernails gave me a connection with the troll-like creature. I wasn't afraid because I thought I had imagined it and I was busy weaving my story in readiness for the evening's performance. I had no idea of the strength of my psychic energy or of the power of the unearthly being, and I never thought for one moment that the thing could be evil or wish anyone any harm. It was innocently a part of my story.

 I thought I was imagining carrying a monster-like goblin on my back. I thought I had invented it. Lost in the grip of the thing, I became quiet and introverted, arousing my friend's suspicion of something awry. I told them I had a headache and strangely, I did have an odd kind of headache, different from anything I had previously experienced. Back at the turning to the camping ground, it jumped off my back and hid behind a wall. I didn't question its behaviour, but my gloomy mood miraculously dissolved and my sense of humour recovered as we dumped our things in the caravan.

 I soon forgot everything as we set about cooking. We rustled up a good hearty meal and left a large tin of treacle sponge pudding to boil in a saucepan. The caravan was heated and lit by Calor gas, which was also used to fuel a small cooking stove, but the smell of the gas was nauseating, so we ate outside leaving the pudding to simmer. While we were eating, an almighty bang exploded inside the caravan. The water in the saucepan had dried and the tin exploded covering the walls, floor and ceiling in a hot treacle grunge. It was so disgusting that we found it hilarious and burst into fits of giggles as we set about clearing up the mess. It took ages as the explosion had fired treacle pellets into the tiniest nooks and crannies and they were difficult to remove, sticking to the tin walls like super glue.

Finally, when we were sure we had detreaclised the caravan, we were so tired that we flopped into our sleeping bags. Kathleen was the last one left standing, so she locked the door and climbed over sleeping bodies to get to her bunk. She left the gas lamps burning so we could talk for a while. When we'd finished gossiping about the science teacher's affair with the new maths teacher, it was decided that it was time for a "Lesley story." Until that moment I had forgotten about the creature, and I sat up with a jolt. It was hiding behind a pile of stones.

"What's the matter?" urged Mary.

"Nothing!" I whispered. I closed my eyes and plugged into the story about a troll-like monster which had been tricked to go inside a dark underground cave where it was imprisoned until it would one day be released by a child's smile. I described how I had found it lurking below where we climbed and how it was curled up on a rock with its hideous face slumped between its naked legs and its curved body crusty with barnacles. I explained how it was easy to set it free and how it jumped on my back all the way to the campsite.

"Where is it now?" shivered Elsie half-hidden under her sleeping bag.

"It's waiting to come in!" I replied with a voice that didn't belong to me. I mentally wandered outside to find the thing, but it had changed into a dark mass of blackness, bubbling and seething like a scalding cauldron, hovering to unleash its deadly power over us.

I described the evil mass blubbering towards us in the dark. I was part of it. It was using my energy to hurl forwards and I couldn't break free. I saw the thing encompass the tiny caravan in a black bubble squeezing its way in through a crack in the door. Suddenly a freak thunderstorm tore the door open. Everyone screamed, including me. The shock shook me out of the spell. Thunder cracked and rain pelted the tin roof like gunshot fired from a short distance. Lightning streaked across the cabin and a tornado wind gushed inside blowing out the gas lamps. A noxious smell polluted the air and we were plunged into a bleak blackness. Everyone cried and screamed. I forced myself to get up to close the door. I tugged and pulled until it almost blew off its hinges, but I couldn't move it. The leader and his wife came rushing to our aid. They calmed us down and relit the lamps.

"It's only a storm!" they said.

We all knew in our hearts, however, that it was something much more sinister. I knew that it was the troll and when all was quiet in the camp, I surrounded everyone in a protective balloon of white energy and sent it far away. I will never forget it and I learnt a lesson from my carelessness. It was like the tree spirits in India, the *Bhutas*, which, we are told by the locals, can latch onto humans. If you dare to go through the forest at twilight, they will follow you home appearing in the guise of another human.

"How will we know they are *Bhutas*?" I once asked a wise old man.

"Because they wear their feet backwards!" he whispered.

Leaving the playground and my memories, we rounded a corner and drove up a small incline towards a vivid, terra cotta-red building, square and flat-fronted like a doll's house with a white castellated roof edge. The bright white window frames leapt out of the ordinary surroundings and were incongruous with the farm buildings close by.

We went inside and were warmly greeted by two female attendants. The atmosphere was reminiscent of a Sunday school hush, in an old, abandoned Presbyterian church and the wooden floor was just as dusty. Pictures and photos were displayed in the style of my infant classroom sixty years ago, and silence echoed the emptiness of time wasted waiting for visitors. I felt uncomfortable and wanted to go immediately, but Branden went ahead with Diana to explore upstairs. I glanced at the sepia photographs showing rows of faces upon faces wearing masks of pretence. The smiles looked false and reeked of Victorian duality—of stiff, cardboard etiquette hiding forbidden desires and brutality. It had been a society that covered up piano legs, deeming them too provocative in public, while dealing in slavery and corruption on every level. Something of the injustice of the era stirred indignation in me and something hidden under the floorboards and in the walls, whispered cries of abuse, while the law hid the guilty ones, who roamed free to commit other crimes. A vision flashed across my mind, but I pushed it away. The acrid smell of cruelty and fear overwhelmed me when I saw in my mind a forgotten white shawl stained with black dry blood and the floor dented with a dead body decomposing underneath. I heard a voice crying: "Beyond the creaking portals of brooding masks, there is a stray ghost that must be tracked down and slashed. Don't move the dreams within me. Don't nudge the mechanism into firing unwarranted shots into the dark." I didn't understand what it meant and had difficulty in controlling the rising nausea in my stomach. I made myself go up the stairs as a powerful overriding sense of injustice and exploitation overwhelmed me. At the top of the stairs I looked across the room to a large empty chair facing away from me; but the figure of a large man with a bald head sat in the seat, and I dashed out.

Back in the car I shared my experience with Branden and Diana who explained that a friend of hers who was doing some research on the area, had unearthed some evidence from the locals that might shed some light on my vision from the past, because they had stories to tell about what really happened. Needing to escape the depressing apparition, I asked Diana if we could visit the Coonoor Club as I had many memories of staying there with my two little daughters when we had visited Granny for the last time before she died.

Will and I had made the long, tedious journey to visit Granny with our two little daughters, Sarena and Mina. Mina had nearly died before we reached Coonoor. She was nearly two years old and became ill in Bombay. Her sickness caught us by surprise and her rapid deterioration was terrible. On the dreadful night when she slipped into an unconscious sleep, I watched over her, praying she wouldn't be taken away. A doctor was called and he begrudgingly came. His stale, alcoholic breath polluted the bedroom and he wrote out a prescription whilst swaying against the wall. There wasn't a chemist open so we couldn't get the medicine. In the early hours of the morning she was barely breathing. I carried her to a waiting taxi. Her little, limp body was so frail, and I was helpless as she deteriorated into a shell hour by hour. I thought of the English women who had brought their children to India to settle into army life, where many had died after only a few days of arrival and I understood how quickly death could swoop. Sarena, who was nearly five years old, was quiet, understanding something was dreadfully wrong and she held her little teddy bear, Charliebear, close to her chest, imitating the way I was carrying her sick sister.

The "Black Hole of Calcutta" was a phrase I had heard in a history lesson when I was at junior school- it was used to describe a despicable prison, a hole in the ground where many people had been incarcerated, but I never dreamt I would experience a similar situation in which I would describe the train station at Bombay as a despicable "black hole." We had to take a short train journey to where our little commercial plane was going to fly us to Coimbatore and the moment we stepped out of the taxi into the suffocating heat the nightmare began. I clutched my sick baby to my chest and was swamped by a tide of bodies surging forwards to the main ticket office. I couldn't breathe as the air was polluted and heavy with bad breath, the smell of stale spices, sweat and coal dust. People pushed, cramming together like fat pork sausages packed tightly in a sealed packet. Carrying Mina made it difficult to hold onto Sarena's hand and I feared she would be crushed in the swelling mass. I was angry with Will because he should have organised our tickets well in advance. We were pushed forwards by the crowd from behind in their eagerness to get their tickets in time to take the early morning train. Helpless to counteract the assault, we were shoved inside a small office, where bodies, heedless of my situation with two small children, pressed and pushed me from all sides. We were crammed together tighter and tighter as people pulsed forwards. Poor Sarena was besieged by the heat and deluge of bodies towering over her. Sheer terror washed across her pretty eyes. I piled Mina over my shoulder like a sack of potatoes and lifted up Sarena out of the flood of bodies, flailing my arms angrily as I shoved people out of the way. Sarena clung to my neck and hinged her little legs around my thighs. I couldn't breath. I needed air space. Inside I was panicking, urging Mina to breathe second by second waiting to feel her hot breath on my shoulder. She was so pale with the life force slowly trickling away. Bodies heaved and smashed against my front and back. There was no room to turn to protect my little ones; all I could do was stand and take the battering. My body was lathered in sweat and my cotton dress clung to my clammy, sticky body. Sarena hid her head in my ear as she pressed her beloved bear into my chest. Will was a few feet ahead fighting to get to the ticket booth, struggling with our luggage. All I could do was push down the rising panic flaring inside and pray for help; pray to be delivered from the hellhole, the black hole of Bombay. My heart pounded fighting confusion and resentment and I thought I was going to faint, but the pressure from the crowd held me up and I floated forwards on the tide of the surging throng, on and on in the dark cell, until I was thrown ashore out of the mayhem into the sour early morning dawn.

I heaved a sigh of relief on the station platform, but my head throbbed and my vision was blurred. The battering was shocking as I tried to walk my legs buckled but followed Will down the aisle towards the steaming train. The engine exhaled short gushes of smoke that hissed intermittently, blasting the baking air with steam. A flurry of porters took the bulk of the luggage and as always, little Sarena drew attention from the crowds with her rosy English complexion, her fair hair and bright blue eyes. Little Mina, with her pure white skin, jet-black hair and green eyes, also pulled focus. People wanted to stop to talk, but all I wanted to do was run away and make my sick child better. The hotel in Bombay, where we had stayed, had warned us to keep an eye on Mina as children her age and colouring were often stolen and sold into sex slavery. We also were warned to be on our guard against a little girl who was positioned at the main gate of our hotel, whose sole purpose was to take any opportunity to steal Mina. A member of the staff at the hotel cautioned us and pointed out the child, who remained at the gate day and night. I was glad to have been given that piece of inside information;

otherwise, I might have been beguiled by the little girl's smile and her eager arms reaching out to hold Mina.

In the rush to get the train there was no time to go to the chemist and I tried to tip little drops of water into Mina's mouth, but she was too ill to respond. I think our mistake was allowing the children to swim in the outdoor swimming pool at the hotel, as later we learnt that there was a cholera outbreak in the city and that places like open-air swimming pools were to be avoided, but at the time we were not aware of the danger. On the train I held onto her little body, lifeless like a rag doll. Her breath was faint and the veins in her arms showed through her pale skin. All the time I prayed and clutched onto the thought of her regaining consciousness. The train journey was hell, but Sarena slept quietly. Eventually we boarded the small commercial plane where the attendant looked at Mina and whispered: "That child is very sick." When he uttered those words, I burst into tears and sobbed uncontrollably. The few passengers on the small aircraft were silent and distantly shared my anguish. I kept my mind fixed on arriving safely in Coonoor where we could get a doctor. Throughout the tedious journey Mina was unconscious, and I kept her close to my chest willing my heart to keep hers beating.

When we finally arrived in the hills, Prudence was called to greet us. She had arranged for us to stay at the club in one of their little bungalows in the grounds, as she didn't think it would be wise to stay with Granny, who, she said, she was too frail to deal with the added noise. Prudence had taken over the running of the house and Will and I suspected that she didn't want the fuss of having us there. We thought Granny was disappointed by her decision, but nothing was said. When Prudence saw the state of Mina, she immediately contacted her friend, the military doctor, who came straight out. We handed him the prescription and he looked at us warily. We told him we thought the doctor was drunk. He didn't say anything and took Mina. When he returned, he assured us that she was going to be fine, but he added: "I am so glad you were not able to get this prescription because I tell you, my friends, if you had, this child would be dead." We all fell silent and I cried again.

"This doctor is mad!" he added angrily. "You see, he not only gave the wrong prescription but an adult dosage as well, which would have been lethal. I will look into this matter, my friends; rest assured he will not get away with this and the little one is going to make a speedy recovery. She has an infection that we can treat!"

His words were all I needed to hear and I knew she was in safe hands. The tiny bungalow was no more than a holiday hut with a small sitting room, one bedroom and a bathroom, but it was adequate. Behind the hut was a large green, square building, which was a school and with Mina responding to the medicine and sleeping peacefully watched by Will, I took Sarena for a walk. She was secure knowing we were all happy again, and she was delighted to see a long row of children sitting on the grass, eating their lunch from banana leaves and eating with their fingers.

"Don't they have plates?" she whispered. I explained it was their way of eating and she commented, "Does it taste better without knives and forks?" I said they didn't have any. I gleaned what was brewing in her mind. None of the children wore shoes and she noted it saying, "Have they left their shoes inside to keep them clean?" I smiled and said that they didn't have any. "They could wear their slippers!" she stated with authority. I explained they probably didn't have any of those either. Sarena noted everything she saw and when we returned, she insisted on throwing her shoes away. We had to explain to her that she needed to protect her feet from a tiny worm that lived in the soil, which might burrow into her feet and grow inside her tummy. Bilharzias, was very unpleasant and prevalent in that area, and we had been warned not to allow our children or ourselves to go barefoot.

We had a wonderful old man as our bearer and he took great care of the children, serving their meals in the sitting room and waiting on them with Grandfatherly care. When he served Sarena scrambled egg on toast, she refused to eat it, as it was not served on a banana leaf. Mikie laughed and told her there weren't any left. She said the children in the school had plenty and he could go and borrow some. She refused to eat with her knife and fork, but somehow Mikie managed to persuade her to use her cutlery. The wear and tear of the journey had been terrible and when Mina finally opened her eyes and managed to drink a little milk, I was relieved beyond measure.

I wanted to have a little time to myself to give thanks, so I decided to take a walk across the lovely luscious, well-kept golf course and commune with the Great Spirits. Freed from the anxiety of Mina's sickness, I revelled in the vastness of the fields and the beauty of the hills and the tranquillity of the moment. My baby was out of danger and responding to the medicine; thank goodness we had not been able to find a chemist to make up the prescription. In the distance I could just make out a holy shrine and decided to say my thanksgiving prayers by the holy place. In my mind I prepared a prayer. As I neared the shrine in the middle of the golf course, I spied a statue of a black Madonna and child and another that was a strange amalgam of Jesus with a beard and Buddha. There was a Hindi script underneath which I couldn't read because of my poor eyesight and I was thinking of a holy salutation to say when I was directly in front of the statues. When I was close enough to read the Hindu inscription, I was shocked- it stated "PLEASE KEEP THE FOURTH HOLE CLEAR!" I burst out laughing in the silence of the reverential moment and could not think of anything appropriate to say, so I walked away smiling.

Mina grew better each day and was soon able to run around with her big sister chasing tiny frogs in the grass, hiding them in their pockets and making them ride little cars and jump over bridges. Mikie was wonderfully attentive to the whole family fetching the children milk whenever they were thirsty. He arrived on our doorstep early every morning with the children's breakfast and every day there was a fresh rose next to my bed. In the evening he always chose my dress from a choice in the wardrobe and laid it out on the bed. Each day Mina grew stronger, but her little cot had a straw mattress and was full of horse fly eggs. One morning I was shocked to find her bitten to shreds and everything had to be changed and the mattress burnt. She had so much to contend with and fortunately she was strong enough to withstand it all.

After a few days we were allowed to visit Granny. At the time I did not know that she had made a special effort to get up out of bed to sit in a basket chair on the veranda. She was so happy to see us and she loved the girls. Sarena had practised a little piano piece that delighted her and she clapped with pride as Sarena jumped down off the high stool and handed Granny a mohair shawl. "Mummy said this will keep you warm, but I think it's scratchy!" stated Sarena with confidence. Momentarily, I saw myself in church with Granny's old mohair shawl covering my legs, and I remembered how I too thought it was itchy!

"Thank you so much!" crooned Granny; "when I wear it and you are far away across the sea, I will blow you a kiss and you will feel it like a soft breath of wind on your little rosy face." She tugged Sarena's cheek as she spoke, and I thought what a beautiful thing to say. Precious moments are remembered forever, as are moments of terror: moments when visions appear and reappear and will not go away no matter how hard you focus on mindless routine. My mind wandered back to Pear Tree Cottage, I was washing up at the sink…

Directly opposite my kitchen, in Apple Tree Cottage, was a small, squat, electricity sub-station, which dealt with high voltage power for the village. Every time I stood at the sink doing the washing up, I would read the warnings and the voltage printed on the side of the bricks. I couldn't help it. If words were printed in front of me, I was compelled to read them, no matter how many times I saw them; but every time I read the words my mind meandered to another level. It was like being hypnotised. When I entered a deeper level of consciousness, I saw a young girl wrapped in a duvet, perched on a ledge in an underground sewer. Her name was my name and I was terrified for her. She lay in the dark, shivering in fear, visited by rats, fed only when her kidnapper appeared with his guns. She was dying in that godforsaken hole. On entering the vision while hazily swishing my hands around in the hot soap suds, I felt her pain and I would quickly pull myself out of the vision. I thought I had been daydreaming, but one day while I was clearing away the pots, I caught the radio news. A young girl had been kidnapped from her home and taken from her bedroom. A huge ransom was demanded for her return. Her name was Lesley. The kidnapper called himself the Black Panther and threatened to kill the young teenager if his demands were not met. A cold shock ran through my body and I glanced over at the electricity substation. I knew she was the girl in my trance vision, but I did not know where she was or how I could reach her. The situation was dire, like watching a horror movie unfold from behind a mirror; but it was real, and I saw it and I couldn't smash it to reach in to help her. I wondered if she heard my thoughts or could feel my presence as I felt hers. I tried talking to her, but all I heard was my voice echoing down a black hole. Weeks passed and I couldn't tell anyone what I was seeing. Who would believe me? What could I do? The police had already been down the sewer, but missed her. She could not cry out because she was gagged.

One morning I knew she was dead. I did not feel her energy. She had slipped away. The sad news was relayed on the evening news. The man was eventually caught and he coldly, almost casually, described how he had crept up to his victim's bedroom and seized her while her parents were downstairs. He coldly recalled how he had taken her to a sewer where he chained her to a ledge, wrapping her in a duvet, leaving her to die. It was shocking to think that a child was not even safe at home and hard to come to terms with the nightmare that the parents faced, reliving the horror of their child's torture. I shared a brief glimpse and have never forgotten it and could not envisage a worse situation. I did not know that the Black Panther episode was a warm-up to something far worse.

As Diana's little car bounced into the Club parking plot, I held my breath with anticipation. I had to go inside; I had to roll back the years and see if the young woman at the great dining table was still there where I left her, waiting for herself to return from the future to set herself free.

CHAPTER II

Postcard Back from the Future

Do not demand to live; do not demand to die—for in the blink of an eye you have already left and already arrived, arrived and left, left and arrived and—gone, but are yet to come.

It is impossible to hold onto time and to tie it down and hold it in your hands forever, or to preserve it like pickles; or hunt it down to own and brand it like a struggling steer, for at some inauspicious moment, the lid will fly off the pickle jar in a fermenting explosion or kick loose like a bucking bronco and send you hurtling into a different dimension. Just when you think you know it all, time coils around you and squeezes out your last breath. However, amidst the time bomb ticking away from the moment of birth, there are instants along life's journey when action is frozen and time briefly wears a different mantle. I experienced such a happening when I was staying at the clubhouse with Will and the children, where Mina was making a speedy recovery after her dreadful illness.

Our children's meals were organized by Mikie, and served in the bungalow. Adult meals were taken in the great, grand dining hall where children were not allowed, so Will and I took turns to have our meals alone. Unfortunately, at the time, there was only one other person staying at the clubhouse and he never ventured into the dining room, so each meal was a strange, solo affair. It was there that part of me became locked in a fairy-tale sleep and where a tiny fragment became frozen in a time zone, waiting to be released at a future date. The dining hall was situated through a massive lounge bar where tigers, deer, antelope and buffalo heads peered down with glassy, glazed eyes. You could almost hear the voices from the past of colonels and army officers discussing military affairs with the atmosphere of the British Raj military tradition, reeking of vintage cigars and mothballed Harris Tweed jackets, lingering in the fabric of the old chairs. Inside the long hall, which was encased by heavy, mahogany wooden walls, was a long, highly polished dining table running the whole length of the room. At the head, a place was precisely set for one with a white, crisply starched linen napkin wrapped in a glistening silver ring, shiny cutlery, crystal glasses and china cups. Three bearers stood to attention awaiting orders. Like royalty I sat alone. If only they had known my background. I was a farm girl and a tomboy at heart. I was used to milking goats and climbing haystacks, but to them I appeared rich and glamorous, bringing a taste of a faraway country into their underprivileged lives.

Sitting alone at the head of the vast table, silence was interrupted only by the regimental ticking of the grandfather clock beating each second with a baritone bass echoing around the empty walls—TICK TICK TOCK. The bearers stood motionless quietly awaiting their commands. They were used to being ordered around, but I was not used to giving orders. I felt awkward while they attentively watched. TICK TICK TOCK—as I spooned each mouthful of delicious mango into my mouth, the clock marched on regardless. Another mouthful and the bearers were immediately at my elbow ready to take away my plate and replace it promptly with an overwhelming full English breakfast, including mountains of toast, jam, marmalade, butter and endless cups of coffee. I wanted to dance around and shout: "For goodness sake, please talk amongst yourselves"; but I couldn't. TICK TICK TOCK I sat in the stillness, in the enforced silence and played my majestic part while the deep empty tones of the grandfather clock echoed like a metronome keeping time for the old timers long gone, whose ghostly vestiges were all that remained of their gracious living. Outside the long windows, endless stretches of beautifully tended lawns undulated at the foot of the mountains and were part of the golf course that kept the dense jungle at bay. Trickles of villagers passed along the small footpath to collect water; beautiful women in their elegant saris carried pots on their heads, strolling with the gait of super-models shifting their weight from hip to hip as though dancing a slow rumba. They floated along the grass not at all impeded by the heavy weight on their heads. I watched the struggle of their daily routine outside my world where theirs played before me like a distant film. Inside the great hall I guiltily ate my fill and had a life-style that was beyond their reach.

Lunch was not so formal and sometimes, when Mikie had the children, Will and I were able to dine together. Usually there was only one bearer and the whole affair was less ostentatious; however, the evening meal was another matter—it was an event. I don't remember how it came about that Mikie always chose my dress but from the first evening he took it upon himself to choose what I should wear. He said the bearers always looked forward to the spectacle of what I wore as I brought the latest fashion from England, explaining that "for them, Madam, it is like show. You are dancer, they are audience!"

So every night I dressed up just for them and unlike my previous student times in India, I had come prepared with lovely long evening gowns and jewellery. One evening Mikie insisted that I wear my best dress that I was saving in case we got invited to a special dinner and I wore it just to please him, tying up my hair with sparkly pins and wearing my best necklace and earrings. The bearers all lined up to greet me, and the servant girls came running from the kitchen to take a peep. They all applauded and cheered as I took my lonely place at the head of the table. The silence filtered through the routine, and the sound of the clock took command—TICK TOCK TICK, I drowned in my thoughts as the clock routinely kept strict watch over the proceedings.

It usually took around an hour to eat in the evening and afterwards, in my finery, I would walk back to the bungalow where the children were sleeping. Will would then go out to visit his mother's friends and I would sit by myself in my lovely clothes and wait to go to bed with the sound of wolves and wild dingoes howling through the night. It was a strange and lonely time. I had thought that our trip to India might bring us closer together, but it was too late. Will and I were friends, but not lovers, companions and not husband and wife. His secretary at work was closer to him and had been for a long time, while I had fallen deeply for someone else and kept it a close secret. It was an impossible situation and one in which we struggled to maintain a false front.

One morning at breakfast while I was watching the women on their way to the well with their flowing hips swaying rhythmically in the early morning breeze, as they carried their water pots on their heads, I drifted effortlessly towards them in spirit and hovered along the footpath. I longed to escape my situation and felt heavy with a deep sadness and depression. I wasn't sure how I could go on living a lie with unhappiness and fear around every corner. It was easy to drift out of my body to escape my inner turmoil.

Looking back at the clubhouse dining room I could see myself seated at the great table. It was an odd feeling watching myself viewing the world outside, while I was outside of myself surveying the world inside. It was easy to drift out of my body to escape my inner turmoil. Floating high above myself, I swirled out into the gentle breeze and marvelled how I could see myself still seated at the great table. It was odd watching my body from afar, whilst roaming freely, but after a short interlude where time held its breath and I could no longer sidestep my anxieties, I was sucked back inside my body into the quiet world of the grandfather clock's monotone ticking and the grave silence of the bearers. There for a while, I stood outside of time trapped, sitting in a lonely dining room in an unreal world, while another part of me cried for the beautiful times and the lovely moments of golden treasures. Once I had had a love; once I had known passion—two people entwined body and soul; but perhaps love was too young and we loved so much that we drank each other dry of all emotion. A stray tear escaped over the edge of my eyelashes and rolled down my cheek. I had lost love. I tried surreptitiously to brush away my sorrow, but I knew the bearers missed nothing. They saw me cry silently. As the moment of forgetting and remembering faded, I withdrew and left the young woman staring out of the window, promising one day to return to set her free when she would finally escape the chains of her regret and retrieve hope to wipe away the past.

In that moment when I left her, something in me died; I realized that my marriage could never be rescued and the spark of life that had once ignited our union was lost in the ashes of nowhere. That evening, as I walked back to the bungalow in the yellow glow of the night lights, I was lost, like tumbleweed sweeping aimlessly from door to door with no fixed roots but blown endlessly at the mercy of the wind. Only emptiness loitered beyond the path. Anger sprouted new shoots shouting in my head: "Don't tell me love is shining both ways!" Through the grey mist lurking in the foot of the forest the wolves ran howling. (Together they are fierce, but alone they cower.) Watching the moon peep through a cloudy night, I was knocked off balance by a shiver of fear, but I was not going to cower like the wolves. I wanted to run through the forest and climb to the top of the mountain shouting: "I will fly. I will sail. I will rise above my panic and doubts." The night gave me courage, and I vowed that I would achieve my goals. Through a silver strand of moonlight I had a brief vision of me standing in the same place in the future having fought my way through a knotted path and looking back, remembering what it took along the way to arrive there. I knew what destiny would scratch from my soul and tear from my heart to reach my goals. I already knew that I had poured my spirit into yesterday but that I would find more strength for myself from the light of beyond.

Standing in the grounds of the club with my son was a powerful moment. I had kept my promise. I had returned. Outwardly the place had not changed; the gardens with the little row of bungalows were still the same. I was impatient, however, to go inside and find the long dining room where the ghost of the young woman still waited patiently to be set free. I raced inside regardless of not having permission to enter. The long bar was almost as I remembered, but it was smaller and less grand. The wooden floor had been refurbished and a few of the old wild trophies still held pride of place on the high white walls. Gone was the wonderful old lounge with its comfy cigar stained cushions, instead, it was replaced by ordinary, middle-class, uncomfortable and characterless high backed chairs. The long dining room no longer existed. In its place was a restaurant with small tables set at angles decorated with pink tablecloths. The clock had vanished, but the view outside the long windows was still the same. Alone, I stood envisaging the dining room as I had known it and there she was—the young woman sitting at the head of the table gazing out of the window. I swept her up like a child into my being and wrapped her in the newness of me. I was her, but from the future and she melted into my psyche bridging the gap that had been left by all those years. At last a part of me was reunited with myself and I felt whole again.

My son followed me into the dining room and all I could say was, "This is not how it used to be; it's not it at all!" We didn't loiter inside as I had seen all I needed to see. The bungalows outside were still the same and were occupied, so I couldn't tell whether they had been modernised, but I caught a glimpse of myself through the window and smiled. The woman I was had certainly changed, and I was glad that I had not given in to my deep depression all those years ago. It made me realise how easy it is sometimes to wallow in despair dragging our spirits beyond the darkness to an even bleaker level of desolation. Sometimes the easy answer will end the misery, but it is not the answer; it is much better to trawl through the bad times and come out the other end a wiser and hopefully better person. I was glad I had lived my life and had hung on through the rough times.

Remembering those years when I was depressed, uncertain and lost, I recalled the terror that invaded my life at Pear Tree Cottage with the whisperings, the sound of footsteps, the lights clicking on and off and the feeling of being watched by an unknown presence. When Serena was nearly two years old, I thought it would be a good idea to move her from her little nursery into a small bedroom with her own little bed and girlie furniture. Will and I chose lovely wallpaper with happy smiling faces of rabbits, cats, dogs and other farmyard animals. When we had finished decorating and moving furniture around from room to room, everything was complete and looked beautiful. As night approached, the sun shed a warm pink glow over the faces of the animals and as we put her to bed, she was happy. As twilight spilt colours of mauves and purples onto the wallpaper, however, the smiles of loving animals dissolved into leering eyes of creatures stealing through the gloom highlighted by the street lamp shadows rocking menacingly. As the sun sank low behind the clouds, strange noises bounded through the ceiling as though furniture was being moved and things thrown around. Sarena began to howl and I ran upstairs to see what was wrong.

Eyes everywhere stared. Slant eyes, sideways eyes, glared in the half-light. I picked her up and took her downstairs. I had no idea that the innocent faces of the creatures would transform into monsters with glaring stares from every angle of the room. Downstairs I comforted her, but the sounds upstairs continued. It was as though someone was looking for something and was moving furniture in order to find it. Then it suddenly dawned on me that the "thing" didn't like the change of the furniture and was showing its disapproval. As I sat cuddling Sarena, a neighbour knocked on the door and I was relieved to see a friendly face. She accepted my offer of coffee and she took Sarena as I boiled the kettle. Above us the scraping and banging continued.

Suki looked up and asked if Will was moving furniture, but I told her there was no one up there. She thought I was joking and laughed as something crashed down in the bedroom above us.

"You're not going to tell me that's nothing!" she snapped.

I didn't reply.

"Here!" she handed me Sarena, "I'm going to take a look for myself!" She stormed upstairs and I waited while I heard her investigating each room. The noise stopped. When she came down, she looked pale.

"How long has this been going on?" she inquired in a quiet, serious tone.

"A long time." Another bang and a scraping echoed through the hallway.

"You've got to get help!" She sat down and attempted to sip her coffee with shaking hands while above us the "thing" continued to vent its anger. Eventually it calmed down and Suki left, but I knew I had lost a reliable baby sitter and that she would never dare to be alone in the house again.

Back in the present yellow roses smile and a large green sign with bold, black letters proclaims "Do not pluck." The sign had not been there when my little ones had played on the grass, but then it was out of the question to interfere with the mali's beautiful work and no one would have dared to pick the flowers. I could hear Granny's voice:

"Give back to nature the beauty of the spirit which withers on the bough for the bloom, which was once vibrant, will sag and fade and the red rose and the yellow will fall to the ground to be swallowed by the earth and will come again in the spring—such is the surety of life. Rejoice, for all will be as it should be in the true rhythm of life."

I understood her message knowing that her love was still around. I turned and laughed at the high hedges shaped into fat doves nesting in uneven broken waves. (Perhaps a new mali was practising his topiary skills.) Two fat, black, squat cannons still guarded the main entrance, but there was no Mikie- no familiar face. It was a Sunday and people were beginning to arrive for a special event and the Management personnel began to appear questioning our presence. It was time for us to move on and with a sigh of relief I climbed into the back of Diana's car, happy to have revisited the past.

As we drove up and down the tiny, winding roads on our way to Sim's Park, a Sunday reverence hovered through the hills accompanied by a quiet serenade of birdsong, which chanted through the eucalyptus trees and chirped through a myriad of rays falling into clouds. The faint knell of church bells peeling through the forest wove a lethal combination of religion and grey sobriety appropriate for the Lord's Day, reminding everyone that it was a day of rest. I remembered the boring, long, tedious Sundays spent with Granny and how we had to attend Church twice on the same day and keep a low profile so as not to suggest that we were in any way enjoying ourselves. I hadn't visited Sims Park for forty years and was curious to see how it had changed. When I was last there, it was a natural space full of herbs, flowers and strange plants used for healing tropical diseases. This time, unlike our visit to the Thread Needle Garden, both Branden and I wanted to visit the park, so we alighted from the car in good spirits leaving Diana to drive on agreeing to collect us later.

There was a token entrance fee and as Branden and I strolled through the tollgate, families gathered to take their Sunday constitution through neat rows of flowers planted in strict patterns like seaside public gardens with brightly coloured iron railings. Long stone stairways through luscious plants and foliage lead to a boating lake, and next to it a playground was equipped with climbing frames and various kindergarten adventure apparatus. Children were dressed in their Sunday best, the girls with their long hair plaited and tied with multicoloured ribbons and the boys with theirs plastered neatly to their heads. As we passed by, they stared inquisitively. For me the park had lost some of its primitive charm being coated in a candy, seaside rock opulence and although there were still some untainted long walkways, the general ambience of the park had been spoilt. Branden had similar feelings and we decided not to linger but to hurry back. As we forged our way through a large family, poised to have their photograph taken on a runway of stone steps, an old granny, who was perched on the highest step, broke wind just as we passed and the sound reverberated through the trees cutting the sweet silence with a rude blast. Branden and I had great difficulty in keeping our composure and hurried out of sight where we burst into uncontrollable fits of giggles behind some yellow bushes.

When we had regained our composure, we set off to wait for Diana. The midday heat cut through the low cloud and as we made our way to our meeting point, the dry, dusty earth caked my feet in a thin layer of grime. It was arduous walking up a small incline, and I was glad when Diana pulled up to collect us. A blue bus chugged by, and written on the back in bold, black letters was: "Jesus is my Daddy." I had a flash vision of the missionary school where Will was sent before being hauled off to England to begin his aristocratic education in a series of private schools. The missionaries were well meaning but taught with very little insight and understanding of children's needs. They had no idea that Will had very poor eyesight, so that when he was asked to draw a picture of Jesus on the blackboard and he drew a fire engine instead, he was beaten for blasphemy and after that he had no faith in Jesus whatsoever!

As we drove past Sunday strollers, I reflected on Sim's park and its transformation. The park in the past had produced amazing herbs and plants used in the process of finding cures for many diseases, and I remembered a time in Pear Tree cottage when I made an assortment of lotions and potions to help heal newfound friends in the village. Once they had gotten to know me, they trusted me and often came with minor ailments, which I cured with my homemade remedies. One woman in particular, Frances, who was curious about me, visited purely to pry as she had been a nurse and couldn't quite understand my gifts. She had a son Sarena's age, and eventually I predicted she would have a second child, a daughter. She was delighted. When I also predicted the date of birth, she was astounded since it was her deceased mother's birthday. I had forgotten my prediction and was not surprised when Frances became pregnant.

One morning I was bending down to take something out of the oven when a terrific pain shot through my uterus. It was intense and I had to sit down. Suddenly I realized it was a simulated childbirth. I looked at the date and remembered predicting the same for the birth of Frances's second child. I rode out the pains; at 12:15 they subsided, and I knew she had given birth to a baby girl. An hour later the phone rang and her husband phoned but before he could tell me the news, I told him he had a baby daughter and the time she had been born. He was astounded and didn't know how I knew all the details. I was never doubted again and as my psychic gift developed, I was able to help many people. I could not, however, evict the evil presence in my cottage; it continued to watch and wait and terrify me.

By the third year of living in Pear Tree Cottage, I had become accustomed to the "thing," and although it didn't manifest itself all the time, I was always conscious of something lurking. On the night before my second daughter was born, I heard a child crying and footsteps sneaking towards my bedroom and low masculine voices echoing down the hallway. Later, while walking through the village, the night sky was charged with pink sparkling light as a star fell across the sky and vanished beyond the horizon. When the wind picked up through the trees, and whinnied in a low minor key like a gentle lullaby, I knew it was time for her birth. It was wonderful to have two daughters. They were so different. Sarena had white blonde hair and deep blue eyes, while Mina was born with a shock of shiny black hair, sticking out like bristles on a coconut, and hazel green eyes.

Mina was born on a beautiful morning in September when the trees were resplendent in their autumn glory and the sun gave no hint of leaving, but when, a few days later, I left the hospital, the trees were black and skeletal reaching out under a grey lidded sky and a winter wind whistled warnings of the bleakness to come. Back in the cold cottage with my new baby and busy toddler, I decided that I was not going to spend another bleak winter without heating, so I went against Will's wishes and turned on the central heating. The pipes clanged into action and creaked, groaning against the labour of heating the house. For a few hours it was cosy and the cold world outside didn't matter, but then without warning, the house became a war zone of sounds, clashing, crashing and smashing iron against iron like steel broadswords fighting in a medieval battle. Mina began to cry and Sarena huddled against my legs. A malevolent invader surrounded us and I hurried to get out of the house. I bundled Sarena into her boots and coat and wrapped Mina up in a warm blanket and snuggled her into her pram. I turned off the heating and took cover in a friend's house.

    I refused to go home until Will arrived, and I made a fuss until he called someone to service the heating. After a few days it was mended and Will agreed to let me keep the heating on. Things settled down, but when I was outside in the garden just a week later, as the sun was sinking below the conifer trees, in the dim light I saw a bat fly from the garage and edge its way under the eves. For some reason the sight of the creature disturbed me. Should it have hibernated by that time? Did we have a bat colony? What should I do? I told Will about it, but he didn't seem to think it was anything to worry about. Later that night after I had put the children to bed, I went to draw the curtains in my bedroom, but something outside fluttered against the windowpane flapping its black wings against the glass. When I rushed towards the window, it vanished. Something silly came into my head- a few nights previously, Will and I had watched an old horror movie in black and white and the scene where Dracula turns into a vampire bat raging at the window trying to get to his sleeping victim, alarmed me. I laughed at myself. How stupid to even think of such a thing. It wasn't the idea that was ridiculous, however, rather it was a feeling of something evil forcing its way into my home that unnerved me.

    I stood at the window feeling the malevolence outside malingering. It wasn't the blackness of night calmly transforming the day—it was something else that spied and waited. I quickly drew the curtains. I tried to shake off the ridiculous images of the Dracula bat, but the picture was lodged in my mind. When I heard a fluttering against the window again, I hurriedly swished open the curtains, but all I saw was my own reflection. I went downstairs to watch television to empty my brain of the asinine worries fluttering in my imagination, but when I went to bed, the heavy silence of the night drew unwanted images inside my head, and I became rigid listening for something. Fears of the unknown and the dark from when I was a child returned. I was afraid the entity lurking outside the window had the power to invade. I lay still, hardly able to breathe and unable to move, as I spied a black shadow slide from under the curtains and cross over from the window to poise beside my bed. Its presence was sickeningly evil. I could not move and lay motionless for about two hours, terrified to even breathe. In my head I repeated Granny's mantra and fought the entity with goodness energy. Then for some reason it disappeared and I mustered the strength to sit up, but it was not over. Across from the bed a face sneered through my dressing table mirror. It was monstrous. It was demonic, with black, slanting eyes and an elongated head with luminescent, flashing colours in mosaic designs hovering around its head. I froze in terror, not believing the hideous face and a flashback from when I was four years old jerked my memory.

    I was playing outside in the sunshine but wanted to go to the toilet, and I hated the outside lavatory because it was dark and dank and spiders lurked in the corners. I could hardly perch on the seat, as it was so high and I was afraid I would fall in the deep bowl and the spiders would attack me. That day, however, it was necessary to use it. I didn't close the door as I was afraid of the dark, but it was ajar enough to let in a streak of light, which lit up the dark green wooden door where a face suddenly appeared. I thought it was the devil because being brought up a strict Catholic, we were threatened with hellfire damnation and the devil's torture and were shown pictures of tormented souls in hell where the devil roasted the screaming souls on a spit.

The face was similar to the devil in the picture and it seemed to leer at me. A cocktail mixture of muddled understanding confused me. I was shocked and afraid, and I was ashamed for being caught on the toilet, but I was made to feel special all at the same time. I ran out of the lavatory fearful of the face. In the quiet of the flowerbed I struggled to come to terms with the vision. It was horrid, yet I felt I had been chosen for something. I never forgot it but could never explain it or understand it. In the bedroom the face smiled and I suddenly found my scream. Will woke up and told me to go back to sleep, as it was "only a nightmare." But I knew it was not.

Back at Diana's house we sat under the shade of the trees and listened to the sound of Sunday, with neighbours cooking for their families and music from different cultures blending into the background hubbub. I was pleased that my return to the clubhouse had brought me closer to the person I had been, and I mused how wonderful it would be if we could send ourselves postcards from the future to reassure ourselves in the present. Past experiences had proved the possibility of projecting forwards into the future, and others who have experienced the same of "quantum jumping" into the future claim they can alter their lives through the process. I recalled a time when I was fifteen years old studying music in a quiet classroom listening to Vaughn Williams's *Fantasia on a Theme by Thomas Tallis*, which I had never heard before. I closed my eyes and through the symphonic grandeur of the beautiful medieval melody I was transported to an ancient castle, where I stood looking up into the decaying battlements. High above the turrets and broken walls, one large window remained in the debris looking out across a typical Yorkshire landscape of fields, hedgerows, meadows and leafy glades, where curling streams bubbled over timeworn rocks. I knew the castle from another life, yet it was being shown to me from the future. The grasses quivered beneath my feet in a sweet, summer sigh and I knew I belonged there. Thirty years later I stood on the very same spot I had seen when I was fifteen while listening to the music. The grasses moved like a green sea beneath my feet, and the summer sun shone over the battlements. High above the rubble, the window was slowly crumbling where the rooks still nested, swooping in and out of the ancient bricks, cawing in the stillness and crying in the peaceful graveyard of past battles. It had been the scene of skirmishes lost or won for King Richard III. I had no idea how important my time spent living alone in the little cottage by the castle would prove to be.

So-called coincidences can be comfortable explanations for those who do not dare to explore beyond the realms of "possibility" and while I accept that many things in life can be explained in this way, I prefer to believe in the greater synchronicity of the universe; even simple signposts along the rocky path of life's routine drudge can indicate to us that we are heading in the right direction. All we have to do is read and interpret the signals. While I was living in the little cottage by the castle, I was driving once a week down to London to study for my Master's degree in choreography, and I chose Isadora Duncan as my subject to research for my first paper. At the time I was also looking for new premises for my dance school in York. Eventually I found a suitable space and stood wondering if I could make it work as a dance studio. Then I spied in the corner, an old, broken desk with a scrolled piece of paper lodged inside. Being curious, I unravelled it and found an old newspaper photograph of Isadora Duncan leading many children in a dance around her garden. I knew immediately that the dance space would work and that I too would lead many children in the dance. It was like receiving a post card from the past projected to the future, to let me know that the decision I was about to make was the right one!

CHAPTER 12

Infinity Tea, Nonesuch Tea

The Nilgiris produces wonderful tea and although I do not drink it, I appreciate the amazing diversity of flavours grown in the mountains. Diana arranged for us to visit a tea plantation and sample the various types grown in the area and as we tackled the bumpy roads out to the rendezvous, I remembered the first time I visited a tea plantation to see the factory process and to sample different blends. It was just Will and I and we were shown around the factory as though the two of us were on a royal visit. It was interesting to see the mounds of tea on the factory floor being swept into piles ready to packet and ship to different countries. The unmistakable aroma compacted into one room was overwhelming, making me feel sick. I couldn't stay inside the enclosed area, so our guide, dressed in a white coat, took us to a clinical, almost scientific, room where rows of teas were ready for our tasting.

"This Madam, you try, and you will like tea too much!" urged our guide. I declined explaining that I never drank tea and the poor little man was flabbergasted.

"Oh Madam, you cannot be English—all English peoples loves tea!" I politely refused and turned his attention to the best quality tea, enquiring who bought the most expensive.

"Oh it is always the Russian peoples; they always buys the very best."

"And what about the British?"

"Oh, the sweepings off the floor, Madam. You see, they do not know any better!"

I laughed to myself remembering the conversation and wondered what the tea tasting would be like this time.

We did not drive to where I thought the plantations were situated but out farther in deeply forested areas where the mountain air was crystal sharp and Tolkien-mossy glades shaded thickets of jungle scrub. The rain had left dewy patches on the trees and through a cloudy mist the sun was beginning to cast long shadows across the tea bushes, which snugly covered the hills in a thick, verdant green carpet. We chugged along a small track until we came to a lovely house set in the crook of the hillside and were greeted by a lovely woman who took us into her house, where her son waited to give us a talk about tea growing and life on the plantation—it was very different from my visit to the factory. This was a more informal affair given in the owner's home, and we sat at a table next to a vast window overlooking a fantastic panoramic view of the valley. The talk was very interesting and it was lovely to hear a young man speak so passionately about his family's business, as well as to share his vast knowledge on tea. I asked the same question as before, "Who bought the most expensive teas?"

"Arab states and China and of course Russia also," stated our young host, who asked his mother to lay before us samples of the tea. She set six large glass jars before us in a row. The first was white, which appeared like misty water; the second was fawn; the third was a light gold; the fifth was amber and the sixth was a light green. I agreed to try the different types and was pleasantly surprised to find that none of them made me gag. We bought some of the teas to take home for presents and paid the young man for his time.

Walking out into the bright, startling sunshine, we said goodbye and made our bumpy way to the station to buy our tickets in advance but found that this was not possible. The man behind the counter wrote our names on a chit along with many others piled together on the side of his desk. It was a matter of first come, first served. It was necessary to get to the station very early the morning before the train was due in order to secure a ticket so Diana said she would send her housekeeper on the errand to make sure we got them, in the meantime, Branden thought it would be a good idea to get a cup of "real" coffee from one of the few American cafés.

Back in the car we chugged up the hill to the parking lot. I had never seen anything like it before. The car park looked like a scrap yard, with all kinds of vehicles parked so closely together, bumper-to-bumper and door-to-door, that there was no room to manoeuvre in or out. A little man appeared from nowhere. Diana gave him the keys and we watched in sheer amazement how he squeezed it into a tiny space without scratching any body parts.

"He's okay!" reassured Diana, as we walked to the bank. The humidity was increasing as storm clouds gathered and I was relieved to be in the cool of the cash cubicle. I needed to pay Diana a lump sum and was in a hurry to complete the transaction. The bank accepted my card and I was happy to go ahead with the operation. Suddenly a crack of thunder exploded and the computers in the bank crashed, but not before the statement had shown that I had very little money in my account. A wave of panic overwhelmed me as shouts echoed across the hall: "Computers are down, everything's down, won't get it back till five this evening!" I stood motionless, shocked and dazed. I had to have money in my account—I couldn't understand what had happened.

I slumped wearily towards my son and told him the terrifying news. I had lost my appetite for cake and coffee, but we strolled towards the café nonetheless. How could I face Diana if there was no money to pay her? How would we get back? How would we survive? Numbness held my reason ransom. I was worthless. I was nothing without financial identity. I had promised myself never to be in that debilitating state ever again after having once feared losing everything from a tax investigation and I was ashamed to feel all the horror of the insecurity returning. The whole world collapses when finances dry, and I had just enough to pay for the coffee treat but felt sick with worry that it drained any enjoyment. In desperation, I texted a friend to ask for money to be put into my account, feeling demoralised at having to throw myself on the mercy of someone else, pleading for help. After coffee I dejectedly wracked my brain to determine what might have happened. I could only think that it was a total mistake and that the computer had misread my account before it crashed. I tried to console myself with that thought throughout the rest of the day. I reassured my son that I would have money and not to worry, but underneath my calm exterior I was quaking.

When you have enough money to take care of your needs, life takes on a different hue and when you don't, despair is a constant, malingering shadow. I remembered the plight of Mikie's family, our bearer, who had looked after us so well at the club bungalow when we stayed there and how he worked long hours everyday and was only paid by the club around five pounds a month. He told me of his struggle to keep his family together and how his daughter had suffered miscarriage after miscarriage until eventually she was on the brink of giving birth. Two days later he proudly announced that he had a baby granddaughter. Tears welled in his old eyes and I was moved by his love. I asked him if I could go and visit his daughter in hospital and take a gift for the child. He was shocked by my request but agreed and bowed his head very low and held his hands in prayer as a gesture of gratitude. I was naïve and had no idea what I was about to encounter.

I made a special trip to a jeweler's shop to buy a beautiful silver bangle for the baby and held it tightly as I stepped out of the taxi into a dirty, concrete compound. Mikie opened the car door and showed me the way inside the swing doors, parting beggars and sick people in rags strewn across the steps as we made our way through the noise and commotion. I had expected a hospital, but I was shocked to find a dumping ground for sick bodies. I appeared a wealthy, white woman dressed in fine clothes and jewellery and all around plaintive eyes questioned my presence. There were no doctors or nurses in sight, only rows of uneven beds with all kinds of bedding and old blankets strewn over sick bodies. Mikie guided me to a long room full of small beds all different, uneven and falling apart. Women were screaming in labour; but the awful thing was that as soon as I entered, all the crying and shouting stopped. Everyone glared. It was as though the women were afraid of me and embarrassed to make a sound, so they bit their lips and buried their heads under filthy blankets to scream in silence.

Mikie's daughter, Maheera, was lying in a bed near the door and her poor face was awash with embarrassment. She would have blushed bright pink had she not been dark ebony. Her chicken-legged baby girl lay next to her and I gave Maheera the present. She took it as though I was handing her the crown jewels. She gasped when she saw the silver bracelet. I asked politely if I could hold the baby and she handed her to me naked, wrapped in an old, grubby shawl, while the whole ward looked on in astonishment. In a deathly hush I placed the bracelet on the thin bony wrist of the wriggling baby. I held her for a few moments making all the right cooing noises and then handed her back making my excuses to leave. I left quickly, much to everyone's relief. After I pushed through the door, the women continued screaming in peace.

The memory returned to show me that poverty was much more than the rising panic that was invading my mind and as we drove back to Diana's house, I prayed to the great ones for help. The computer read-out had to be a big mistake and I tried to push my fears to one side and trust in the goodness energy to help me. I was reminded of the same kind of feeling I had experienced when I was alone struggling in Pear Tree Cottage day after day dealing with an evil force that was sucking out my life blood.

It seemed there were two entities in the cottage—one was a small child struggling to be heard, needing help fighting to communicate through the piano and other methods to attract my attention, while the other was purely evil with a destructive, malevolent agenda. Often I heard a child's voice crying upstairs when there was no one there. Sometimes I heard a child singing a plaintive song in a faraway tone but when I would go to investigate the sound, it would always stop. The piano playing stopped, but sounds of breathing, sighing and calling continued. I knew I would have to eventually learn what was causing the upheaval and try to help the soul find peace. I would also have to fight the evil force and lay it to rest, but I was afraid to lay myself open to the dangers involved with such a mission, especially when I had my two little girls to protect. They were growing and developing their own little personalities and I rejoiced daily in their new skills and all the fun and laughter we shared.

I remembered one morning when the autumn sunshine gleamed through Mina's nursery. She was nearly one year old, and a cool breeze wafted through the open window warning of cruel weather to come. I was changing her and she lay happily kicking her legs in the air, reaching up towards the mobile dangling teasingly above her head when Sarena, who was four years old, marched in heftily kicking open the little wooden door.

"Who's done this?" she screamed.

I screamed back in horror at the little dead mouse she was holding by the tail.

"Who's done this?" she howled.

"Well, I expect Daddy set the trap; you see we can't have lots of mice in the house, now can we?"

"But someone killed it?" she sobbed.

I was horrified at the rigor mortised body dangling from her fingers. I stealthily picked up Mina and gingerly coaxed Sarena to carry the dead mouse outside where we gave it a dignified burial among the dahlias. We had a litter of Shi Tzu puppies and I turned Sarena's attention to them snuggled in their basket in the conservatory. I left her stroking them while I put Mina to sleep in her pram in the kitchen. I turned my back for a few moments, but shot a glance backwards when I heard strangled gurgling from Mina. Sarena had woken her up and was trying to spoon strawberry yogurt into her mouth.

"She needs it!" stamped Sarena. I reprimanded her and set her to play with toys in the garden.

Back inside the house a strange hush descended and I sat down in the kitchen watching Mina sleep. I closed my eyes and saw in my mind the Victorian pregnant lady who had sailed past my bed before Sarena's birth and watched a fragment of her life strangely unfold. She was the wife of the eccentric explorer who had brought the beautiful bathroom tiles from his travels in the Far East. She was a sweet and sensitive person and played the piano. Being of a delicate disposition, she never accompanied her husband on his adventures. I felt her fear brush past me like a hushed whisper and linger for a few moments before dispelling into the cosmos. I wondered what that vision meant and was about to explore it further when an unusual smell made me sit up and sniff the air like a hunted fox. I suddenly realised it was burning newspaper and ran to where I kept a pile in the conservatory. A little face hid behind the door. I dashed to fetch water in the nearest pan lying in the sink and quickly quashed the small flames fighting to take hold. Sarena, bored with her toys had found some matches in Will's shed and decided to make a bonfire in the conservatory. I was very angry and sent her to her room as a punishment but not before she had vented her own anger and frustration on the kitchen floor by banging her head and flaying her arms and legs on the tiles. She soon found the floor a little hard, and she removed herself to the dining room where the carpet was softer and staged her temper tantrum until she made herself sick, by which time Mina was howling in her pram having been woken by the commotion.

When all was quiet again and Sarena was asleep on my lap and Mina happily cooing in her pram, I closed my eyes and the lady appeared again. I do not know her name, but I will call her Marianna. It was as though I were viewing her through a misty veil while eavesdropping on a private conversation. I couldn't see another person but imagined another lady who had become a close confidante of hers listening in secret. Her speech betrayed a slight French accent as her dulcet tones whispered through a tunnel-like vacuum: "You see it is as though I am a prisoner in my own house. He will not let me go out to see friends or even contact my family. What am I going to do?"

I knew exactly how she felt as I had experienced the very same emotions during the early months of living in the house and particularly afterwards, when Sarena was tiny. It seemed that I had picked up her malaise and was reliving it for her. It was as though her memory had fixated into the walls and worked on my subconscious.

"He has been acting so strange since his return and has a secret box, which he keeps locked in the small room upstairs. He is, how shall I say, changed. When we married, he was gentle and caring; but now his demands are rough and unloving. I don't know what to think. He wants me only as his slave and now that I am with child, he is like a bear with a sore head."

I felt sorry for her and knew what it was like to live in a loveless marriage.

"He sleeps in the small room, which he locks, and many nights I hear voices and strange sounds and footsteps on the stairs and crying, a child's crying."

Her words made my heart skip a beat. I often heard footsteps and voices and a child crying. What was she trying to tell me? At that moment Sarena stirred and looked up at me with such loving eyes and said, "Sorry, Mummy!" and I melted within as only a mother can. We got up to play hide and seek in the garden and to enjoy the last rays of afternoon sunshine. As I bounced Mina on my hip, I looked towards the upstairs window and fleetingly saw a little white face with dark hair like Mina's. The little girl stared blankly as though from another world and then disappeared.

Back at Diana's house my inner turmoil bubbled, and I tried desperately to tell myself that all would be well, but the thought of not having any money to pay bills or get us back to the airport was frightening. I was reminded again of the feeling of having nothing, being no one, being judged by what you have rather than who you are. I argued with myself that I was still myself without money, but was I? Take away the support ladder and you find yourself hanging in the air, lost and unable to keep suspended and you know without that prop you will crash down into the unknown. Fear drains, drowns and degrades and is a low vibration that drags you into the mud.

As I sat alone in my room a voice spoke from afar: "Fear keeps the masses downtrodden and unable to lift themselves up to glimpse the world beyond the world. Rulers ride on the back of fear. What stops you from finding joy which should be a natural state and part of humanity's heritage? Exuberance should be your daily bread, but fear starves your life force. Fear drives out your confidence and leaves you in a state of panic, where those in power can easily manipulate you and lead you to accept anything, even that which is contrary to your beliefs."

I listened and resolved to be stronger and learn to rise above the fear. The voice continued in a lifeless monotone. "Keeping people in poverty ties them to fear. They are afraid to speak; instead, they endure what they think is their destiny. Believe me the world is becoming dark and bleaker times will come. Why are you worried needlessly about a small matter when you should be aware of greater threats to your liberty? Listen to these words, for you will be required to teach what you know: *It will not be easy!*"

The voice faded. I wondered about the heaviness of the words and how I could help.

I told myself there was nothing I could do at that moment. The reality of having nothing was hard to shake off and dismiss lightly, but realising that I must not let the fear interfere with my enjoyment of the present, I knew that I had to trust to the universe to make everything right. I had to shake myself and not wallow in self-pity.

The voice momentarily returned breaking through my thoughts with calm surety: "There is nothing to feel upset about. Remember all you are given is given for you and as the eagle falls through the sky tumbling and twirling at will, he does not hit the ground but soars high when the earth seers near. Don't take things *en masse;* you will be swamped, like being under water in a muddy pool where you cannot even see your own footprints. Just breathe and take a few steps at a time. That is all."

I heeded the lesson and told myself all would be well; besides, after lunch we were going to visit a local school. Branden and I had raised money for a project to help schools and we wanted to see for future developments what was needed to help the children. We drove up through a small, winding road, up through a copse of eucalyptus trees and through bright blue gates, where a small, concrete building, like a signal box, was beautifully painted with luscious scenes of trees and elephants, with a warm welcome to the "Children's Home" painted on the side. It was not just a school, but also an orphanage, where children were looked after and given opportunities to cope with life and older teen-agers were taught skills for jobs to prepare them for a life outside the institution.

As we got out of the car, I noted that almost every wall was decorated with paintings of flowers and birds with signs in Hindi and English. A large sign over the entrance read "Peace and Prosperity Dwell in This House"; it was delightfully amusing as paintings of babies with grown-up faces stared through a maze of unrelated scenes. More signs, such as "God Cares for Us,"; "God Bless Our Efforts" and Please Mind Your Head," were boldly emblazoned on the walls. It was strangely silent except for the drone of crickets and the birds twittering through the trees. Monkeys perched in corners amidst the crumbling paintwork by the main entrance dared to stare, like old men with tufts of grey hair sticking out behind their large pointed ears. One monkey with only one arm scratched its head with his left arm and screeched as we approached the main door.

The Headmaster came out to greet us and told us that most of the children were in classes and that it was not possible to see them but he fetched two lovely children to take us to view their handiwork, which they sold to visitors. We were shown to a small squat building where the finished articles were stored in an assortment of cupboards. The two young girls aged twelve and thirteen years, were well dressed and polite. Their hair was neatly plaited away from their faces and they shyly smiled as they produced wonderful embroidery and batik work. I fell in love with a bold batik picture of an elephant designed in black and red with burnt orange features. The girls were delighted that I bought it and giggled as they tidied up the rest of the articles.

"Come, come, we show you where our young girls have sewing lesson," the head master stated with pride. We were escorted to a tin classroom that was buzzing and whirring with treadle sewing machines deftly handled by fifteen young girls aged fifteen to seventeen. They looked up in amazement and stopped sewing as we entered.

The teacher, a small, rotund lady, smiled enthusiastically as I greeted the class and told them that my son and I were from England. They asked some questions about our weather and I luckily had photos on my camera of the snowfall that had lasted for over a month at Christmas time. They were amazed at the whiteness covering everything and were very interested to see my home, which was so different from the houses in India. They invited Branden and me to have a go at the machines. I was reminded of my sewing lessons with a similar machine worked by pedalling the tread and manoeuvring the material with one hand while the other guided the wheel. The girls laughed when I found it difficult. The heat of the afternoon seeped in through the lattice windows, while outside the door the monkeys played tag.

The girls were being prepared to go into factories to earn a living as none of them had homes or families and had been brought up in the orphanage. It was good that they were not on the streets and looked healthy and well cared for. Back outside in the burning brightness we were introduced to six housemothers, who were only very young, themselves. They took us to another building with an amazing ceiling where the children had made cutout paper flags and trails of waves in multicoloured tissue paper that fluttered and glowed under an electric light. The housemothers sat at a desk while I was given a chair in front of them and Branden stood beside me. We politely opened the conversation, then, out of the blue, they asked me to sing a song! I was dumbfounded and looked at Branden, who appeared sheepish.

"You sing a song, Branden!"

"No, you sing a song!"

"No, you're much better at it than me; remember how you used to sing songs in French and Spanish? Oh come on?"

"No, you sing a song!"

The girls listened to our banter and I embarrassingly realised we must have sounded rude. So there was nothing for it but for me to sing a song! There was no escape. Hurriedly in my head I wondered what to sing. It was a Christian school and heavily religious, so a music hall song was out of the question—not that I knew many, but one or two came to mind. I didn't know many pop songs, so the only viable candidate that was acceptable was a Gregorian chant, which I had learnt when I was eleven years old receiving voice training in a choir. In fact, as a choir we won a song festival with our rendition of the beautiful undulating melody in *Salve Regina*. So I took a deep breath and thought-here goes, throwing myself into the chant. I heard my voice from afar ring through the rafters and resound across the ceiling. I remembered how to crescendo and decrescendo in the right place until I held the last note squeezing out the breath until it faded into the silent room. They applauded, and my son even said it was good. Then the girls, at the slightest encouragement, got up and sang and danced for us. It was a very special time; we loved their engaging smiles, quaint moves and controlled, little leg kicks from beneath their saris. After the interchange of entertainment, it was time to track back and the girls waved cheerily as we trundled out of the main gates. I was disappointed not to have seen the children but was satisfied that there was a tremendous amount of good work inside the institution.

As we drove back, the holiday mood of a Friday late afternoon was spreading through the hills making for a relaxed atmosphere. Diana had shopping to attend to and drove us to a supermarket store, which sold everything from furniture, food, clothes, gardening equipment and works of art. Branden wandered around and found an amazing picture and decided to buy it. We spent a long time in the store, as Diana was busy ordering things and was looking specifically for some bedroom furniture so we were taken to a strange warehouse by a lake. Mosquitoes excitedly buzzed, spying juicy victims as we got out of the car. Grey twilight was descending over the strange warehouse and I wanted to escape the mosquitoes inside the old, flat, decaying building, where the smell of damp and mildewed furniture was overpowering. Congeries of furniture were piled high to the ceiling, some made up of the most beautiful and exquisite antique pieces I had ever seen, but sadly left lying in a dump. A sense of Tibet and the Himalayas where the British Consulate lived and where Granny had grown up in the lavish, royal life-style of the era was in evidence through the luxurious sofas and chairs left to rot in the dank humidity. I wanted to free some of the delicate pieces and buy them, but, of course, it was impossible. The light was dimming and the noisy mosquitoes were growing more agitated, itching to feast on our exposed limbs. Diana did not make a deal and Branden and I were again tired of waiting for her to make up her mind and were relieved when we got back into the car. As we were driving up the hill on our way back home, a gaggle of girls enthusiastically waved and called out a jubilant greeting and I waved back recognising the housemothers who were relieved of their duties for the weekend. It was lovely to see them so happy.

Damp, cold, clamminess was closing in the day, filling the air with dank-scented pine and eucalyptus balm. Driving back to Diana's house, the thought of Pear Tree Cottage and the sense of isolation drifted back. I needed to know what happened to the child who had been making herself known increasingly through little sounds and sighs and faraway singing. The evil entity was forever in the background, and I suspected it kept the spirit child imprisoned.

One day, when Sarena was at play school and Mina was asleep, I heard a child's voice, barely audible, drifting down through the old beams from upstairs and the face of the child I had seen in the bedroom window came to mind. Trancelike, I drifted up the stairs following the sound. It was like a mantra. From my periphery vision I thought I saw a man in a black cape glide past me; his footsteps echoed near my bedroom door and then he disappeared, while the child was chanting. I paused outside my bedroom while the little voice was still repeating the words. Then a deathly hush descended before spiralling me into a cave of emptiness. It was the heavy absence of sound that dipped underneath my feet like an underground cave where no sound bleeds through the dense rock yet the sound of no sound is deafening. Then screaming and crying exploded around me and I fought to crash through the bedroom door, where the yells instantly stopped. As I entered the room, only the sun cast shadows of the trees over the walls and all was calm. I dissolved into a heap on the bed sobbing.

Horribly, I confess I wanted to quit the world and was thrown down a tunnel (one which I have experienced a few times since then) with light terra cotta walls, made out of what looked like the substance of sweet candy shrimps. Dizzily, I spun down the channel and came out into a courtyard heavily cobbled with grey stones where I stood underneath a medieval archway with a long dark room in the background, just vaguely visible in the gloom. Strangely, Edward appeared. He had been a boyfriend, my first heartthrob, who had died on the motorbike given to him on his sixteenth birthday. I was overjoyed to see him and a very odd event took place. He told me I had to go back and that it wasn't right for me to be there, but he said that he was with me. Then he stood behind me, and we held out our arms together like the Vitruvian Man in the painting by Leonardo de Vinci. We were fused, like a quick-flash photograph where the negative in black and white remains, bonding the image of us together against the dark medieval walls. Suddenly Edward dissolved and I rolled back down the tunnel. It was a strange experience, and I shook myself out of the depression knowing that Edward was right; I must not be affected by the evil energy—I had to fight it. I rushed down the stairs, glad to be alive to hold my sleeping baby.

As we arrived back at Diana's house, the light disappeared over the hills, yet the trees exuded a parade of colour. A twinge of sadness drifted through my mind knowing the spectacular, epic journey was reaching its finale. A rush of navy and silver flashed across the sky washing away the day, and a trickle of fear returned.

A faint voice spoke as I paused in the garden: "You are consciousness and the same being with or without material acquisitions. Wealth is an external illusion. It is not where reality lies. Your reality lies beyond."

I listened to the voice and reasoned with myself, returning to my concerns about the money situation. The voice returned: "Imagine a day where every moment is filled with exquisite luxury. Shift your thoughts and your perception, and you can change everything around you. Reshaping your mind creates a new dimension to your being. You can strengthen, enrich and gain knowledge about yourself to develop your energy. Your energy is like a muscle that you can train to respond to your input. Keep targeting the input, and strive to maintain a constant level of inner vibration. Keep spiralling upwards and outwards beyond what you know, see and feel. Take on the eagle's eyes, see through the clouds and soar high above the mundane, out into the fresh world. Listen to the wind. Listen to the sigh of the trees and take time to see."

The voice faded and I knew the words to be right. The money situation would be sorted out. I had glimpsed through a tiny hole into infinity where time has never existed, to a "place" that always has been and always will be and where being my true self is all that mattered. I smiled remembering the name of the tea plantation we had visited that day—"Infinity Tea"; further down the hill was "Nonesuch Tea," and it was comforting to think that the tea planting, growing and drinking would go on for as long as the world exists and that as long as the world exists, man will strive to solve eternal problems but the real truth of existence is beyond infinity where there is 'nonesuch tea'.

CHAPTER 13

Night Terror

The next morning we drove to the bank, and I was feeling positive, convinced that all would be well. Branden was anxious while he waited for me to type in my code number. A trickle of sweat rolled down my back before the information appeared on the screen. Luckily there had been a terrible mistake; not only did I have enough money in my account to cover costs, but a friend's money had been posted and we had more than enough to pay for everything. I was so relieved that I jumped up and down with joy- strange how it only takes a number on a screen to change the whole world? One minute I was in the depths of despair and in another elated, all because of paper money.

As we walked over to Diana, who was smiling at our relief, I argued with myself that being with or without something should not affect inner stability. It was a similar situation regarding my night fears. I was not afraid during the day, but I hated the dark at night. When I was terrified, I tried to convince myself that the absence of light was only an illusion and that I was still the same person in the dark as in the light. But it is hard to take that leap of faith when you are in the grips of uncontrollable fear.

Lesley Ann Eden

I remembered the phase in Pear Tree Cottage when the mere sight of a certain person on television used to send me into a cold sweat. It is hard to explain to people who have never experienced the gift of psychic insight- but believe me, sometimes it is hard to cope with the visions and the sounds and the feelings and emotions that bombard your mind and thoughts unwillingly. It was a time when my children were old enough to watch a children's programme, "Play school" and we would sit together on the sofa to enjoy a half-hour's educational entertainment. It was during the awful period when the "Yorkshire Ripper" was claiming many lives, victimising the county and terrorising women and it was unsafe to go anywhere at night alone. Sometimes a man would present the programme, and I would have a terrible reaction to his appearance. I couldn't look at him. Visions appeared of the Ripper's horrific butchery and sadistic cruelty to his victims, so that I had to shoot off the sofa and be sick in the kitchen sink. This happened often where the presenter stirred up the real murderer's face, and I knew that he was plotting another killing. I also knew he had been in the police station, but they had let him go. My husband, newly qualified from York University, as a Probation Officer and dealt with the police daily, so I felt I could ask him to speak to someone in authority about my visions but he was reticent to do so. I grew more and more distressed with the visions and the disgusting details of the murders that I witnessed in my head, that I begged him to let me speak to an officer on the case.

I remembered only too well how the case of the Black Panther had affected me and how I saw the young girl who had been murdered lying in the underground sewer and was helpless to do anything about it. Similarly, the Ripper victims were invading my everyday consciousness so that I couldn't think of anything else. A telephone conversation was arranged with the officer in charge of the case, and he listened very politely and carefully to everything I had to say, but I had the awful feeling that he didn't really believe me. I felt better having passed on all the information that I had filed in my head, but I still couldn't watch the presenter of the programme without getting horrific pictures in my mind. Time passed and eventually the Ripper was caught. His photo in the newspaper was very similar to the presenter of the children's programme. All the information released was the same as that I had disclosed to the police officer even to the details of him being taken into the police station but not arrested. Everyone was relieved to be able to live normal lives again without the lingering fear of being attacked, and I was happy that the right man had finally been locked away in prison so that my visions ceased.

Fear of any kind is terrible for the victim, and there are many different levels of this negative emotion. Fear that derives from lack of money is not the same as that perpetrated on a psychic level. All my life, I have dipped in and out of the psychic realm and have struggled to live half in and half out of two realms at the same time so that life at times can be very confusing. I have known both kinds of fear and how they can affect daily living. As in the African dance where there is always a falling to the floor it's not the fall that is important—it's how you get up and recover that affects your destiny.

As Diana, Branden and I walked joyously towards the coffee shop, I was overcome with relief; but a voice entered my head as I stared down at the dusty road: "All is well and will be so. The two sides of the coin can be flipped so easily from one side to the other. All it takes is one little nudge and you react to the toss of the coin. How much better it would be to remain in a state of constant happiness. You are in charge of your emotional domain and if all it takes to unseat you is a very small slant on perception of your reality, then surely you must learn to be stronger. You can adjust your emotional energy to realize that you have the reins and can control your feelings regardless of the outside stimulus. Remember, heaven and hell remain the same and are two sides of the same coin."

I understood the lesson very well, but it is hard not to be affected by everything happening around you. I guess the answer is to try to climb out of depression by changing things inwardly, appreciating that a positive attitude will affect everything outwardly. I recalled the saying, "As above, so below." I realized that through the momentary loss of financial support, I had learnt a lesson and had to try to put into practice keeping positive, no matter what was happening on the outside. In the café, I danced down the aisle feeling relieved that a huge weight had been lifted from my shoulders. I thanked the universe for the lesson and enjoyed a large latte. But questions arose from my brain: "It's all very well changing your outlook, but what if you can't?"

Almost immediately the voice from afar answered the doubting question. "It is true some people cannot drag themselves out of the quagmire of depression and must seek further help, but you need to know that the weight given each person to bear is never more than he or she can take. Help is always closer than the air you breathe. Never lose sight of three things: hope, trust and belief- the tables will always turn and there is a solution to every problem, for no problem exists in your world without its counterpart. There is no disease that has no medicine to cure it. Everything has a balance and man must seek it."

The voice faded and I was grateful to be comforted by the teaching. Our last day in the hills was strange. Goodbyes on any level, at any time, anywhere can be painful and having accomplished what we set out to do, Branden and I were sad to leave. I had made new friends and had caught up with the past forging links with old family friends of Granny's and experiencing a roller coaster ride of emotions in exploring the truth. As we drove to the club for the last time, I knew that my purpose in the Nilgiris had finished and that there would never be a reason to travel back. I took one last glance at the tennis courts remembering my final goodbye to Mikie, our wonderful loyal bearer. It was a wish of his to own a wristwatch, having desired one all his life and on my departure, I handed him a small package gift wrapped in gold paper. He looked at it in disbelief and held it up to his forehead giving thanks.

"Open it!" I urged, swallowing my tears. He obeyed quickly manoeuvring the paper without tearing it or dropping any pieces on the floor. He paused as he looked at the decorative box then slowly opened it. His eyes glistened with pride and a smile spread from his toothless mouth from ear to ear.

"Mem Sahib, I thank you from my gracious heart, and I thank you every day and in my dying breath I remember you always!" It was very moving and I had to quickly climb into the waiting car. I had hoped to meet him again this time, but perhaps he was better left in my memory.

As we drove past Granny's house for the last time, I swallowed back a tear recalling our final farewell. On our last night at Diana's we had a barbecue but it was a forced affair as she had invited two friends to join us, but hadn't heard from them, so she decided to drive us to collect them. Branden and I weren't sure about arriving unannounced. As we drove up the dark driveway I felt weary and not really in the mood to party with people I didn't know. Diana blatantly beeped the horn in the quiet while Branden and I feared that the couple had gone to bed. Sure enough after we woke them with our knocking, they appeared in their pyjamas. Branden and I were embarrassed for the couple, for no matter how hard they tried to wriggle out of the invitation, Diana had them on the end of her hook and she wasn't letting go. After much discussion and tug of war between them all, they decided to come with us. After Diana cheekily asked them if they had anything to drink, they produced a bottle of whiskey. Branden and I exchanged glances feeling sorry for the poor coerced couple.

When we returned, Diana's housekeeper had lit the charcoal fire on a special spit and the flames sparked into the night like a fifth of November firework display. Diana as usual created the most wonderful food and we did enjoy the feast, but I was exhausted and my patience was beginning to crack; I needed to go to sleep. The people were polite and played their part, but I felt sorry for them as we trundled into Diana's car to take them home. On our way back my eyes began to close and all I wanted was to drift into slumber; when we returned, I went straight to bed. I had packed my things earlier for the journey the next day which gave the room a different feel. I was so tired that I didn't bother taking a sleeping tablet but I assured myself that I would soon fall asleep. I turned onto my stomach on the hard, uncomfortable bed and drifted off. I am not sure how long I slept, but I was woken by something shaking my feet and lower legs.

Energy in waves rocked my body from my feet upwards. As I woke into conscious thought, I wondered- is this is really happening? My legs are quivering like soft jelly and the bed is shaking!

The juddering pulsation worked its way up through my legs, through my pelvis and up my spine; when it reached my shoulders, music cascaded into the air. A full symphonic orchestra vibrated through the ceiling accompanied by a beautiful haunting piano playing a romantic melody, which lingered above the swaying violins. Whoever or whatever was responsible knew I loved the sound of the piano. I wondered whether the music was a decoy to stop me from feeling what was really happening to the lower half of my body or whether the music was part of a mystical experience. I knew horrifically that I wasn't dreaming. I was fully awake. My body was being shaken by something that I had no control over and I lay in shock. The physical attack was torture, but the music was heavenly; my mind and body were confused. Then I was aware of a masculine energy superimposing itself on top of me, and I was afraid the lower part of my pelvis was being forced to acquiesce in sexual manipulation. His hand lay over the top of my left hand and I felt his energy pressing down on me. I couldn't breathe as my face was pushed into the hard mattress. I struggled against the unseen force, fighting to lift myself up; but the energy was too strong. I mustered up all my inner strength and screamed in my head: I hate you! I hate you! Leave me!

The presence responded in a surprising manner. It paused and ceased its attack as though it was hurt by my anger, hatred and rejection, and the music stopped. Then the rotating energy shrivelled high into the corner above the door, spinning in a glowing mass, and disappeared down a vortex, leaving the room ringing with a heavy silence. I was unable to move a muscle, scared at the thought of its coming back. I went through the happening repeatedly in my head testing the truth of the horrific attack. I definitely hadn't imagined it. When eventually I dared to twitch a muscle, I tried to shake my legs as though someone was shaking them; but there was a definite difference between an outside force ruffling the covers and vibrating my legs to my causing the motion myself.

I began to assimilate what had happened and as I lay pondering the attack, my senses became very sharp. I could hear far away the smallest detail of insects flitting, clocks ticking, people talking, dogs barking, droplets of water dripping into a pail and someone whistling down the road. Normally I had poor hearing, but it seemed the whole world opened up a swell of sound that swept into my head. My body tingled with awareness that had been driven by terror and I was aware of my spirit lighter and more alive than ever. Was the experience some kind of blessing that I had messed up? Was it a spiritual awakening from Shri BaBa whose holy presence had been witnessed in the house? I couldn't comprehend the method or the meaning of the experience because for me it had been invasive and had made me terrified. The music was glorious, but I couldn't fathom what had occurred.

For a long time I lay in a stupefied daze until the light streamed through the curtains; then I shot out of bed to find Diana still asleep and woke her to relay my experience. We both cried at the strangeness of it all, but neither of us could understand the motive nor the action. It was to remain a mystery and we had very little time to sit and ponder the incident as we had to get ready to leave by late afternoon. Throughout the day and no matter how hard I tried to immerse myself into my ordinary activities, it was hard to stay focussed; for at the back of my mind all the time, I was replaying the terrifying happening. I wondered whether I had done the right thing in sending it away. What would have happened if I had allowed the spirit to continue? Had I missed out on an amazing spiritual initiation? Question after question muddled my mind; I knew that something was not right and that the hint of a sexual invasion was not a spiritual blessing. I assured myself that I had done the right thing.

Sitting in the garden pondering the attack, I thought of other events in my life that had involved evil spirits and Pear Tree Cottage came to mind. I had lived under a cloud of being terrorised for five years and had not managed to solve the mystery of the cause of the assaults or lay to rest the child spirit that wandered aimlessly through the house. I think it was because I was too afraid to face the truth of the matter and too cautious to cause further disturbance that might affect my children. Sarena was five and I knew it was time to move on. By that time Granny had died and her daughter, Prudence, was returning to England to live with us. We had bought an amazing mansion; it included its own lake with a little island in the middle, which we could row to in the summer, and it had massive grounds with orchards and rhododendron walkways. Prudence was going to live in a flat at the top of the grand mansion, and I had space to create my own dance studio. I felt confident, as we were moving, to try to solve the mystery through a concentrated meditation and allow myself to be used as a conduit in which the spirit could channel a message.

    I had spoken to a neighbour who had lived in the cottage, and she said that the lights were always being switched on by themselves and strange sounds, plus other noises were often heard. She had no idea what caused these events, but she was glad when they moved, adding: "Some things are better left alone!" So there was no clue from her. I knew the cottage had once been two small farm houses renovated into one large house in the late 1800s and that a gentleman explorer had bought it. There was a mystery surrounding his background and no one seemed to know much about his disappearance or that of his wife and child. The house was later sold to a banker.

    I had very little to go on except my visions. So I set aside one afternoon not long before we were to leave the house, when I was alone, to try to delve into the mystery and stood in the dining room where the piano had first played by itself. I prayed for guidance creating a bubble of protection around myself by using Granny's mantra as a shield against any evil intent. I relaxed into my meditation, using a special breathing technique to allow myself to drift into a whirlpool of bright light, where I saw Marianna running as she had when I saw her the first time escaping across my bedroom, holding a candle and wearing a long, white nightdress. Her face was pale and gaunt and she was heavily pregnant. She passed straight through me followed by a man I presumed was her husband. I will call him Jake. He was wearing a long black cloak and a satanic mask, like the awful face I had seen in the mirror in the middle of the night with a demonic glare, staring through black eyes. Others appeared from the shadows dressed in satanic robes with similar ugly masks. A fire crackled nearby and the group chanted in rhythmic bursts as Marianna was pushed into the centre.

Momentarily I gasped and shot out of the vision. It was too much to witness. I sat down and bowed my head, but the pictures returned like watching a film unfold. I saw a box and the lid lifted by Jake, who was wearing his robes, a mask and long, black gloves. Inside the box was a shiny knife with jewels sealed in the handle. I watched him lay it down in readiness for a ritualistic killing. My mind was telling me what I had already suspected, but I couldn't watch. I brought myself out of the meditation, but the cold-blooded horror of the child sacrifice made me sick. The energy had hung around in the house like a cancer decaying the fabric of the bricks. No wonder when I had first seen the house, the satanic energy had lured me to it, intent on sacrificing the unborn child in my womb. I hadn't seen the "For Sale" sign with my eyes, but with my mind. I had fallen under the spell of the house and the first night I had spent there alone, the evil energy had tried to suck the life force of my baby from me. The person in the window in the black cloak and my fear of a vampire attack made sense after I saw the vision of Jake in his black cloak and the way the presence lurked next to my bed one night, waiting for me to make a move while I was paralysed with fear. The constant battle between it and me had almost become a part of my life during the five years in the cottage and whether it had won or not, I was going to leave.

I was concerned for the spirit of the murdered child, as I knew it was crying out for peace and calling for help. I understood how Jake was the satanic leader, who had slaughtered and sacrificed children; no wonder I had heard the cries of children and the noises and the invasion of evil intent. I believed the piano playing was a plea for help from a child locked in lower earth vibration and needing to be freed. I set about sending the child love and giving it peace so that it was at rest. I believed that I had freed the child through sending her love but the evil energy was too strong to fight and I was glad to be leaving it.

The next few days were spent packing; all was quiet, the house was at ease with itself and I was relieved to close the door on that chapter of my life. Living in the mansion was at first a novelty and the children loved the lake and the small boat and they had two pet ducks to rear, but I was not happy in my marriage and Prudence was a very difficult person to live with, especially as she and Will collaborated on things for the house without consulting me. Walking in the grounds one morning while the children were at school, I looked up at their bedroom window. Sitting in the window well, staring back with her faraway look, was the child from Pear Tree Cottage—she had followed me and a new chapter was about to begin!

Back in the present of the quiet garden, I heard Branden moving his luggage into the hall and Diana issuing orders to her caretakers. Our taxi driver arrived to take us to the station. The afternoon had dulled and the end of the day was drawing in like the end of our journey. I took a long last look at the little hill station town and the faces of the people gathering in their huts and compounds to prepare their evening meal. On our way, we pulled up at a bakery where Diana bought goodies for the journey, and she handed Branden a little box of pasties. The driver, who was scruffy and not very talkative, had tied our bags precariously on the roof rack and as we wound up and down and around the winding streets, we could feel the pull of the bags swaying on top. Branden and I kept our concern to ourselves as the driver honked his horn heedlessly around corners blasting others out of his way. Behind the mist the sun broke out, momentarily streaking across the dusty streets, where the dogs gathered to lick piles of decaying rubbish and the woman beggar, whom I had seen in the town when I first arrived, was still sitting, begging and scratching her matted hair aimlessly watching the world drift by through glazed eyes. Evening smoke curled into the dampening air as the clouds sailed like night sea mists from the ocean sucking out the heat of the day and the chill of the evening breeze wafted on a trail of spices. We bounced up and down through an assault course of potholes and out towards the snaking pass leading to the heat of the plains. A brief gap in the trees gave a shocking view down the mountain. I had forgotten that we were so high in the sky and that we had been living at such a high altitude. When my ears began to pop, it was like the descent in an aeroplane with an enforced, cotton-wool silence engulfing everything as we dropped into a lower zone.

All too quickly we caught up with Sunday evening traffic, travelling back to the plains after a weekend break, with a barrage of horns and impatient drivers stationed along the narrow road. A car ahead had broken down and a tyre change was in process. We could not afford to miss our train and the delay was worrying. There was no room to overtake, no room for oncoming traffic, so the situation was dire from every angle. A troupe of monkeys sat on a low wall opposite our car watching in case someone threw them some scraps, delighting in the mayhem that provided great entertainment as they sat eating fleas from each other's backs. A waterfall on the other side spouted brown rivulets in dancing cascades down the impressive rocks, and the occasional distant call of a peacock cut through the pandemonium of sirens and car horns.

Suddenly the cars were on the move and our driver was keen to make up for lost time so kept vying for a position to overtake, especially around blind corners. It was frightening in the dimming light as the tiny road became a racetrack for headstrong drivers. I closed my eyes as we scrambled around hairpin bends just missing lorries head-on around the blind spots and Diana had to caution the driver to be more careful. Large boulders half blocked other sharp bends, having fallen recently during heavy rains, causing our driver to slam on the breaks and skid sideways as he fought to control the wheel. In the back I made notes of my final glimpse of the Blue Mountains feeling the paper in my diary becoming limp and damp in the humid atmosphere. As we sped further down and down, I closed the book and sighed. I would never come back.

I closed my eyes and allowed the memories of past decades to flood back. I remembered the first time I went to the bazaar, when I was living with Will and his mother in West Bengal, just after his father had died. I was dressed in a short mini skirt. My driver was my guard, armed with a pistol and as I walked through the thoroughfare, the villagers gathered in estranged silence. They had never seen a young white girl dressed in a miniskirt strolling down their marketplace. In the peculiar quiet I asked for some nimbus (limes) from the woman behind the stall, who shyly gave me some in a bag and smiled when I gave her the money as though she was on television filming an advert. Little did I know that the whole village had sprung from nowhere to view the new Missy Sahib and when I looked back, there was an organised gathering of villagers as though posing for a school photograph. I felt uncomfortable and became acutely aware of my bare legs; I didn't know that it was not appropriate for females to show their legs. In the few silent moments during which they stared, I wasn't sure what to do, but then I began to laugh, and they laughed with me and together we laughed as they followed me back to the car, giggling and waving. It was an unnerving experience for a naïve farm girl and from that point on I decided to wear a sari or long skirts in public.

I remembered the young sweeper girl who had helped me to tie a sari and the fun we had dressing up exchanging roles. When I went to teach in school full time, I never saw her again, but by then I had learnt to tie my own saris and wore them with pride to teach at the convent school run by Irish nuns. The children were lovely, always obedient and smiling, never unruly or rude. While I taught them Western music and dancing, next door in the other classroom the drums beat, pounding out intoxicating rhythms, which I found difficult not to succumb to and I had to force my feet not to obey the pulsation of the exciting vibration. Under duress I managed to keep my mind focussed on Bach and ballet.

The days were hot and the school food fiery. A burning curry was made everyday in a large dustbin and dished out to all the hungry children. Guiltily, I managed only to pick at mine. I stayed at the school for a short while, since I had to hurry back to London to take my coveted university place. I had no idea that the return journey would be a life changing experience. When I left the school, the children painted my face and hands with intricate, sandalwood designs, which shocked Prudence and she accused me of "turning native" and made me scrub it off until my skin was sore because I was not to be seen in public with her or her son, appearing to be like "one of them!"

The car suddenly turned off the main road and onto an avenue of trees- within seconds we were bouncing along an uneven road into a noisy, jostling station with trains hooting and whistling as though the great beasts were becoming impatient to speed off into the night. The air was humid and smelt of cooking and unwashed bodies. The moment to say good-bye to Diana had come, and we hurriedly hugged as our bags were unloaded from the top of the car. Branden, as usual, took care of everything and was eager to find our train and get settled on board. I thanked Diana profusely for taking care of us and hurriedly followed Branden. My stomach churned as I hadn't travelled on an Indian train for many years and felt apprehensive. Gone were the days when Prudence used to travel with a loaded pistol in her bag. It had been a necessity in those days to be able to use a gun and her husband, a young officer in the Indian Police, had to deal with riots and rebellious outbreaks in the cities, so was well equipped to deal with emergencies.

In the days of the British Raj, things were taken seriously, with a "stiff-upper-lip" attitude and with a "grin and bear it" mentality. Prudence told me once that when she was with Jeremy and newly married, they toured outlying villages to help keep the peace. They camped wherever they could; however, setting up camp in those days meant taking a cook, a bearer and a maidservant to cope with all the chores. It entailed having all the upper-class comforts of indoors, outdoors. The table would always be set with a pristine, white, linen cloth, polished silver cutlery, numerous china plates and dishes needed for three course meals with wine and all the trimmings to be served in the middle of the jungle. They would always change for dinner, no matter what, as life went on as though they were living in a mansion in a country house in Britain.

She recalled that one evening when they had gone to bed, she heard a strange noise outside the tent and a horrid smell wafted in. She quickly sat up when something nudged its head underneath the canvass and she was alarmed to see a tiger emerge. Before Jeremy could get his gun, she fired at it with her hairspray, which was conveniently by her bed, and the shocked creature retreated back in great fear of the Mem Sahib with the spray solution. Not many people can claim to have been face to face with a tiger, disarming it with hairspray!

Jeremy also had a terrifying experience with a tiger, which nearly cost him his life. He was sent to kill a man-eating tiger that was terrorising a village, and he set a trap one night by a cluster of trees, where he and his bearer tied a young goat as bait. The plan was to wait in the branches above the tree and shoot the tiger when it attacked; but while Jeremy was busy with the goat, the tiger leapt at him. The bearer was cowardly, afraid to shoot and ran away screaming, leaving Jeremy pinned to the floor by his arms with the tiger's claws digging through his skin into the raw earth. A villager came to his rescue and shot the tiger, but Jeremy was very badly injured. He had to spend six months in hospital with his arms in a special solution. The tiger having clawed him to the floor, attempted to eat his shoulder; but he was saved just in time. His wounds eventually healed, but not many people would have survived such a gruelling attack. He must have been petrified at the time, but he said everything happened so quickly and all that he could do was succumb to the attack. I knew to some extent what that felt like; for in the horrific minutes of the strange ordeal the previous night, when an entity held me captive, pinning me to the bed, my only way out was to muster up all my inner energy and force it away with sheer hatred. Jeremy was a brave survivor and lived to endure many more terrifying events, and I never cease to marvel at his resilience and acceptance of life's challenges.

As Branden and I hurried down the platform to find our places, in the noise and the heat of the night, I said a quiet farewell to the Blue Mountains and a loving goodbye to Granny. I knew I would never return- there was no need for she would always be near.

CHAPTER 14

Uranus Ureignus

As Branden and I stepped onto the waiting train, officials in blue uniforms pompously patrolled the carriages. The idea of travelling through the night and arriving somewhere different in the morning was exciting, but I hated the thought of sharing a tiny sleeping space with strangers and remembered my first experience on an Indian sleeper with cockroaches crawling from behind the seats. I shuddered and hoped things had drastically improved. When we found our bunks, I sat precariously on the edge, wary in case any creepy crawlies would emerge from the blankets. Branden opened the bag of pasties that Diana had given us, and I attempted to eat one but wasn't hungry. There was no one in the carriage, and I felt relieved to be with my son having safely travelled around India, knowing we were on schedule for the first part of our return.

"I'm so glad you're with me," I said as I hugged Branden, "I don't think I could have done it by myself, not this time. It's so strange to think that after all these years I returned with my son to look after me."

"That's all right, Mum—we had fun!"

"It's so different from the very first time I returned to England by myself; I never dreamt I'd get locked up in Moscow!"

Branden clicked his tongue and shook his head, "Trust you, Mum!"

"I know; well, I was so young and naive that I didn't realize the danger of the situation."

"What happened?"

"Oh I'm sure I've told you before and it's a long story; I can't just tell you a snippet—it has to be savoured in full!"

"We've got plenty of time before we leave—come on." Branden laughed knowing full well that it wouldn't take much to nudge me into recalling the story.

"Well, I suppose. You see, it's difficult to explain and what you have to remember is that things were very different in those days. The root of the problem was at the airport. Nowadays the rules are more stringent so that you can't even take your make-up through customs, let alone a whole case of antique guns, as Will and I did once. Mind you, we had the help of the Head of Police since they were family friends of his father and the guns were priceless antiques."

"You mean the police helped you smuggle guns out of India?"

"Yes, well, as I said, that was a long time ago and it was all Will's doing, not mine. My problem started when we went to Dum Dum Airport, Calcutta, to see if we could find a cheap flight back to London. I only had £180 in British sterling, which, I suppose, in those days was worth a lot more than today; still, it wasn't a great deal and it was all I had. Will managed to track down a cheap flight through a friend and as we sat in the Aeroflot office, I couldn't help feeling that the young man organising the flight was not altogether honest. When he asked how much money I had in cash and I told him the amount, he said that it would be enough to secure a place on the plane. He said there was a slight problem though with a connection from Moscow to London, as there wasn't a flight for three nights and a day. At first I wasn't certain about the long wait, but Will said I had no choice and that I could while away the time in the airport, reading and catching up on my studies.

"It seemed a reasonable idea at the time and so I agreed and gave him every penny I owned. Then the smarmy little man told me that part of the bargain was to say that I had acquired my ticket from Singapore; when I asked why, he said it was easer that way! I wasn't sure what he meant, but Will was eager to secure the deal, so I didn't press further for answers. I asked if I needed a visa, but he shrugged his shoulders and said, "'You are only going to be in the airport, so you don't need a visa.' I should have followed my instincts, but I thought that he knew best."

"Mum, everyone needs a visa!"

"Yes, I know now, but I didn't then and besides it seemed feasible if I was in transit!"

At that moment a large officious man with a moustache entered our carriage and asked for our tickets. Branden handed them over and they were duly checked. Doors opening and shutting echoed into our carriage and the sound of scraping bags and attendants banging heavy parcels on the floor juddered through the walls. Intermittent coughing and shouting breached the peace, and the engine juddered into a low humming while we waited for other passengers.

"So did you buy your ticket from Aeroflot?"

"Yes, I had no choice; it was the only way I could get back quickly to claim my place, as there was only one space available for the B.Ed. course from my college and I had unexpectedly won it. You had to get A's in all your subjects, and I was almost certain that I wasn't good enough; so I had gone to India with Will. When the results came out, I was shocked and the pressure from everyone to get back was fierce."

"Yes, I suppose!"

"No 'suppose' about it; I had to do it! Anyway, before I left I stayed with my great friends Mony and Sorarb Mamajee, since their house in Calcutta was convenient to get to the airport. The odd thing was the night before I left, I was sitting playing chess with Sorarb, who was very ill, and he said to me, 'Don't go. Don't go; they will lock you up!' I laughed not knowing that his words were prophetic. Mony was concerned for my welfare making me a pack-up, like a school child with fruit and vegetable samosas to keep me going during the long wait, as I had no money to buy food. When I said good-bye to Sorarb, I knew

I would never see him again and he whispered in my ear, 'I will come and see you when I go!' I knew what he meant, but I didn't want to acknowledge it. It was nonetheless true. When I eventually returned home, he had died and one night before sleeping he came to me and we shared the joke of it all. He said, 'I told you so!' Ah, dear, dear Sorarb!"

"Weren't you scared, travelling alone without a visa or money?"

"I was nervous but not scared. It never entered my head that it might be dangerous. I didn't really question the situation on the plane; but looking back, I realize that I had been sold a spare seat on a military jet as there were only Vietnamese and Russian soldiers on board."

"Oh Mum!"

"Well, I know—it did seem odd when I boarded, as it wasn't like a normal flight, but the soldiers were very pleasant, especially when I began to cry as the plane left the runway and Will stood on the top of the building waving."

"I can imagine!"

"I suppose I did appear strange to them in my hippy Indian clothes overloaded with bangles, beads and jewelry with my long, hair loose over my shoulders and my floppy, open sandals worn to shreds. It was September and I hadn't thought about being prepared for the cold weather."

"Didn't you even have a coat?"

"No, everything was arranged in such a rush and it didn't cross my mind to take something warm. Inside the plane was fine and the soldiers, feeling sorry for me, gave me a huge glass of fiery vodka and motioned me to down it in one! I didn't like it and only took small sips to please them. They couldn't speak much English, and I certainly couldn't speak Russian; but they taught me a few basic words, like "please" and "thank you"; and we whiled away the journey with mimed conversation and laughter."

The carriages began to fill up, and an elderly gentleman across the passage began to get his bunk bed ready and drew the curtains. I wondered how long it would be before our carriage filled up and who would be our companions for the night.

"So what happened next?" enquired Branden, finishing the last pasty.

"Well, as I said, the journey to the first port in Russia, Tashkent, was entertaining because I made friends with the soldiers. We arrived late afternoon and as soon as we touched down, I was sent to an office to report to the officials. The woman behind the counter asked for my passport, which I duly handed over. Then she dictatorially held out her hand and demanded: 'Visa?'

"I said I didn't have one and had been advised that I didn't need one. A flash of anger crossed her face, and she didn't know how to respond. In my eyes I had done nothing wrong, but in hers I was already a criminal. She made a phone call to her superiors. Then she asked in a deep guttural voice, 'Do you 'ave anyzing to declare?'

"I said, 'No,' as she rummaged through my rucksack disregarding a few silver pieces of jewelry and some antique ornaments, until she came to my food.

"She teased my goodies out the bags suspiciously and pompously counted out in a loud voice, each piece of fruit, placing each item carefully on the desk as if handling guns: 'Four apples, six bananas, two oranges, and zree pears.' She turned and banged her fists on the counter shouting: 'YOU ARE SMUGGLING FOREIGN FRUIT INTO RUSSIA—ZIS IS VERY BAD!'"

I imitated the woman, using a phony Russian accent and making Branden laugh, "That's not very Russian, Mum!"

"I know, but you get the drift. Honestly, it was like a Monty Python sketch where the character uses a banana as a gun; I really thought the comedy team would appear any moment, especially as she proceeded mechanically to place all the pieces of fruit one by one into a large safe behind her."

"Really? I bet that was comical?"

"It was, but the situation was just beginning to get serious and more so, when an armed guard appeared and escorted me into a corridor where some of the other soldiers were waiting. They saw that I was upset and through mime, asked me what was wrong. In a charade way, I mimed that the officials had taken all my fruit. 'Ahhh!' said one soldier and translated to his friends my predicament. They laughed and barged into the closed restaurant and took a piece of fruit from each table, graciously handing me the spoils. I was amazed and delighted by their kind action and placed the fruit gratefully into my rucksack."

"Well, it just goes to show there were some good people," stated Branden lifting his bags onto the top bunk.

"Yes, it seemed that the normal Russian people were extremely kind, but the officious, bureaucratic ones were like automatons, who could not think for themselves. This observation became increasingly prevalent the longer I was in Russia and I became affected by the sharp difference in treatment from the two factions. In fact, this difference became the basis for my first play, *Uranus, Ureignus*, but I'll tell you more about that later."

At that moment a man came into our compartment, searched around for seat numbers and then quickly marched out again. Sounds of the engine whirring into action began to reverberate through the compartment, and in an instant we juddered forwards and backwards as the brakes were tested. I hoped that we didn't have to share our little space with others, but the chances of that were slim, especially as more people were boarding.

"So what happened next?" urged Branden as he sat next to me to listen to the saga.

"Travelling on an army plane without the correct papers, little money and no visa to enter the country obviously made me a suspicious person. I needed to be watched, particularly as I had been caught importing foreign fruit into Russia. After all, I could be a spy? Unfortunately, at that time, fifty Russian diplomats had been expelled from Britain and Anglo-Russian relations were very strained, so that made things doubly awkward for me.

"I did not know that an armed guard had been planted on the plane in Tashkent to keep an eye on me, so when the plane landed and I followed everyone to get off, a pokerfaced, severe guard with a gun stepped forwards. It was alarming but comical at the same time as he looked like a replica of Strelnakov, a character from *Dr. Zhivago,* who organised a revolutionary army in the film. The young man wore the same metal-rimmed glasses, through which he squinted at me, pointing his gun with trained precision and ordering: 'You vill stay here!' I obeyed and stood by his side as everyone filed passed, not daring to look up because they didn't want to be associated with me. When everyone had gone, "Strelnakov" stood in front of me and demanded my passport. I gave it to him and he pointed his gun to the door. I felt at that point I was definitely in a spy film and would soon be rescued by a handsome agent."

Branden laughed, "Mum . . .!"

"Well, that's the way it was—oh and this will make you laugh—as we stepped off the plane, the tarmac glistened with a hard frost. I hadn't seen frost for a long time and bent down to look at it closely and to feel its cold, glossy texture. Strelnakov thought I was crazy or on drugs and made me move on."

"What? You bent down on the ground to examine it?"

"Yes, it was so pretty and magical!"

"He would definitely think you were on drugs!"

"I didn't care what he thought and I began to shiver in the frosty air as I was only wearing very thin Indian clothes. It was an odd feeling because I hadn't felt frozen for a long time. Anyway, I was taken to a small office where an attractive woman sat behind a desk. All the clichés of a spy film unravelled when she turned a small lamp into my face. I half expected to be tortured. She asked me questions directly and expected me to answer them honestly. She asked: 'Vere did you get your ticket?' I had been told to say Singapore, but I knew my passport was stamped Dum Dum Airport, so I immediately told the truth, as there was no point in messing around. You see I wouldn't make a very good spy, as I would spill the beans at the first opportunity; anyway, I told her that I had given the young man all my money and that he had said I didn't need a visa. She nodded with a certain knowing, having worked out that I was a naïve, young student and that the man had taken advantage of my situation and wangled all my money from me for his own profit. 'You will be our guest for the next few days!' she stated sarcastically smiling, but I didn't catch the sarcasm and stupidly thanked her profusely for the hospitality, as I was beginning to get increasingly worried about waiting in the airport as things were turning out to be very serious."

"Well, all that wouldn't happen today because you wouldn't be allowed to leave the country without a visa."

"I know, but then it was different. As I was escorted out by Strelnakov, whose face had remained fixed like a wax dummy, I couldn't help but look at the frost up close again; I mean it was spectacular with the biggest formation of sparkling crystals I'd ever seen, but Strelnakov was impatient to move me on. I paused to look around for the neon lights of the promised hotel, but I couldn't see anything that resembled a hotel, not even a mere suspicion of a bed and breakfast. It seemed we were heading towards a small concrete building sectioned off from the rest of the compound."

"Was it a prison?"

"Yes, it was a detention centre for people the Government was unsure of, as it was safer to detain them until they were certain what to do with them. I didn't realize where I was being taken until the guard opened a door in the squat concrete block and at the top of a steep flight of steps was a woman waiting in a black skirt and jumper with her hair pulled severely from her face coiled in a bun at the nape of her neck with a large bunch of keys jangling at her waist. She had thick-rimmed, small glasses through which she disapprovingly peered at me, saying something about "Russian Hospitality." Then the penny dropped and the shock made me remove myself from the situation by viewing the scene from above, watching as events unfolded as though I were the heroine in my own reality movie. It was the only way I could deal with the truth of the circumstances and not worry about being lost or the fear of never being found, as no one knew where I was, and the bureaucrats had my only means of identity—my passport which was the only evidence that I existed."

"That must have been quite frightening."

"It was, but what happened next made me forget my own fear!"

At that point a young woman entered the compartment smelling of Vick's vapour rub, and Branden and I watched as she unloaded her bags and unravelled the blanket on the bottom bunk. She snivelled and sniffed, blowing her nose loudly. We continued to stare as she took out a jar of Vick's vapour rub and smoothed it over her nose and neck. Almost immediately the whole carriage was filled with medicinal fumes, which weren't unpleasant but a little overpowering in the heat of the night. As she settled herself down, Branden and I snuggled closer to continue our conversation so as not to disturb her.

"What was it that made you forget you were scared?"

"Oh well, you'll never believe it. It's hard for me to even think it happened, but I was shown to a room where the door was locked firmly behind me."

"You mean you were imprisoned?"

"Well, yes, but it wasn't a disagreeable room. It had two beds and a sink, a wardrobe and curtained windows, which concealed black, iron bars. As I put my bag down on the bed, I heard a noise, like teeth chattering. I turned around and cowering in a corner by the other bed was an Indian woman dressed in a sari, clutching the bedcovers and shaking. I looked in horror at her poor body quaking. I didn't know whether she was quivering with the cold or whether it was sheer fright. I moved towards her to help, but she flinched as though I was going to hurt her; so I stepped back and tried to stay calm. My guess was that she and her family had been prey to a similar plot as myself and had given all their savings to a crook in order to travel to the UK; they probably didn't have the correct papers and were detained pending a flight back to India. From her clothes, I gleaned that she was from a poor family and she had no concept of what an ordinary bedroom was like, as many of the poor families slept on mattresses on the floor or futons laid out on verandas, and in the heat they didn't need bedclothes; so the whole arrangement was foreign to her. I tried to smile but the more I smiled, the more she looked uncomfortable."

"Poor thing—she probably thought you were going to do something awful to her!"

"I know; that's why I tried to behave normally. I washed my face, cleaned my teeth and changed swiftly into my pyjamas. Then I got into bed and motioned her to do the same. She understood and somehow comically jumped onto the bed in one leap. It was so amusing I wanted to burst out laughing, but I curbed my reaction. Then the poor woman didn't know how to get into bed through the layers so I got out of my bed and showed her how to climb in between the covers. She scrabbled at the eiderdown and sheets until she found the entrance and dived in. As she lay down, she was still shaking. I felt so sorry for her that I didn't worry about my own situation. I turned off the light and in the dark silence, all I could hear was her teeth chattering. Somehow I went to sleep and when I woke in the morning, she was gone. I had no idea what had happened to her."

"Didn't you wake when she left?"

"No, I didn't hear a thing and that was quite unusual for me. I suppose I must have been very tired. Anyway, the next morning there was a really nice woman on duty. The old hag had gone, and the new woman told me that she was a teacher. She explained that citizens took turns to do their duty in the detention centre and it was her turn that day; unfortunately, it was her daughter's thirteenth birthday and she wanted to get her something really special. She explained that the ordinary people were not allowed to buy anything from the airport and her daughter desired some sweets in the shape of strawberries that were sold in the airport lounge. There were four strawberries in a little carton glazed with pink sugar and it was a simple matter for me to buy them for her so when she said- 'You could buy them for me. I will give you the money. When you go for breakfast, you can ask to be escorted to the shop and they will let you buy them. If you do this for me, I will arrange for you to have a guided tour around Moscow on our airport bus. Would you like that?' The idea appealed to me, particularly when I had so much time to waste and it wouldn't be difficult to accomplish the task. She slipped me some money and called the on-duty guard."

At that moment another young woman came bustling into the carriage and climbed to the top bunk. Branden and I moved our feet as she edged her bags past. The woman opposite, having filled the air with Vicks vapour rub, proceeded to rub some more on her neck and then speak loudly on her mobile phone. The woman on top looked down and without saying a word closed the curtains around her. There was more movement on board with shouting and calls from passengers to onlookers on the platform and as the train prepared to set off, last-minute boarders hurled their bags into the passage and hurriedly searched for their compartments. Branden and I were not sleepy and he wanted to know how it all ended, so we continued to speak softly.

"So you were going to buy the sweets for her?"

"Oh yes, it was planned that after taking breakfast in the transit dining room I would ask to be taken to the lounge. Well, getting to the transit canteen was a real laugh. The first guard took me about a hundred yards from the detention centre and then halted, where he had to make a call on his walkie-talkie to another guard who checked my details and came to collect me and walked me on for about another two hundred yards, where he did exactly the same as the first guard; then another came to take his place. I thought the whole rigmarole was ridiculous. The airport was only a short distance away and to have three guards in total to escort me to the dining room was ludicrous. Anyway, when I got there the breakfast was civilised and I was allowed to take my time choosing what I wanted and didn't have to hurry to eat it. The guard stood patiently by the door and I wondered whether all the people eating knew that the armed guard was guarding me? It was an odd feeling and amused me to think that over a short period I had become a criminal—what would people back home think?"

"That's silly!"

"I know; but when you're in that situation where you are nothing and are floating in limbo, all kinds of different ideas infiltrate your mind. You can't imagine what it feels like to suddenly have all your freedom taken away; to have your life as you know it, altered from one sphere to another in the blink of an eye. Also to be viewed and judged as a criminal if you are different and where you have to guard everything you say, because free expression is forbidden and ideas are squashed unless they are in accordance with the Government's. I had been used to my own personal freedom and to have it snatched away was hard. I wondered how the ordinary, everyday people coped with the harsh Communist law and how they viewed other noncommunist countries."

"They wouldn't get a chance to vocalize their feelings!"

"No, that's true. We don't know how lucky we are. When I was allowed to go to the shop accompanied by the guard, he scrutinised my every move and watched closely as I bought the sweets. I felt as if I had achieved a great feat and held the prize possession with great care. I also felt like a spy who had successfully completed their first mission. Escorted by two guards at different checkpoints was a tedious affair and when I got back to the detention centre, the lovely woman was thrilled with the present and quickly hid it in her bag. She said she had arranged for the bus ride and I would be called later, in the meantime, I had to go back to the room where I was locked up once more."

At that moment the ticket collector popped his head round the door to check the new arrivals' tickets. The Vick's vapour woman fumbled in her purse for hers and eventually found it, while the woman in the top bunk had fallen asleep and had to be woken to have hers stamped. Branden and I watched the procedure as though somehow it had to be performed in silence and when the ticket collector disappeared, we continued.

"What did you do while you were locked up?"

"Well, I had a lot of time to think and began to formulate information for my play, but it wasn't just ideas slipping into my mind as I was experiencing a form of meditation where I was shown a world to come, which was very different and very frightening."

"What do you mean?"

"I was shown a kind of 'brave new world,' the likes of which you can't imagine!"

"That's a bit far-fetched?"

"Not really, Branden—you've no idea the shocking truth behind what's to come."

"I think that's pushing it a bit. People living in a democracy wouldn't allow any kind of dictatorship."

"Branden, it's already happening—"

"Mum, you're exaggerating you don't know—"

"Look, for now let's just agree to disagree; anyway, all kinds of odd things happened while I was supposed to be locked up."

"What kind of things?"

"Well, you've got to remember that at that point in my life I was not worldly-wise and had no idea about the devious methods people used to manipulate someone, so that when another woman on duty came to my room and said that I was given permission to go to the lounge where there were magazines and books to read, I was very grateful. I had been in the lounge for only a few minutes when a young girl came in and began a conversation. We were alone together in the room and she made polite conversation wanting to know about my life. Then she said her brother was studying at Moscow University. She explained they were from a royal family from the Middle East and that their father had sent them to Russia to expand their education. I thought it was fascinating as she described their privileged lives and how they seemed to have whatever they wanted.

She then said that her brother would be very pleased to meet me and asked if he could come to visit me. I had no idea what lay behind the request or the fact that people in the detention centre could be singled out and used, so I politely agreed. She then excused herself, and I was taken back to my room and locked up again. The usual rigmarole of routine checking and escorting occurred when it was time for lunch; by that time I was getting used to the atmosphere. I could imagine how easy it would be to slip into oblivion and numbly obey a code of law and that was only after one night and half a day! I decided to hold fast against losing my identity, which may sound silly at this point, but when you lose contact with the outside world, even for a short while, the mind has nothing to cling to and I could see how simple techniques can be applied to a human being to alter their thoughts and control their behaviour. My voices began to give me all kinds of information about 'mind control' and the major role it would play in what was to come!"

"Mum, just get on with the story!"

"Branden, you've got to understand how I felt and what I was told."

I paused to look out into the night. Branden excused himself to go to the lavatory and a cold shiver ran through my spine at the same time as a tickle of hot sweat dribbled down my back, as I remembered the visions and the information I was given by my voices about the "brave new world" to come. Forty years ago, when I was locked up in Moscow, I felt isolated in my ideas; I thought I was the only one glimpsing under the veil a horrific state, which was cascading headlong into focus under everyone's noses. The first lines of my play, *Uranus Ureignus*, drifted back to me and inwardly I viewed the opening scene, where beings, no longer fully human, had been brainwashed into accepting the New World Order. Zombielike, they repeatedly spoke a mantra: "There is no self—self has no identity. There is no self—self has no identity."

I recalled an image I was shown of the future, where a secret society changed our planet to such a degree that the ordinary person in the street had no personal rights, no belongings and no control over his life. Everything was directed from a central bureau and unless you were one of the elite, you lived a vegetative existence. Forty years on, my visions and voices are urging me to look more closely at what is really happening, not only in my country and society, but also in the whole world, where everything I saw in my visions is becoming reality.

I recalled other lines from my play where a central character declares: "Your planet Earth was slowly revolutionised by our people from the sky and the moon, which is another satellite, and not what you think—it was merely part of the process."

I shuddered when I remembered those words because I had been reading recent documents, which accorded with my own belief that the moon is not what we think it is. Ever since I was a small child, I have said, "The moon is my home" and recent developments are revealing that this may not be such a fantasy.

Another quirky idea that I brought into the play forty years ago was that not everyone we see is a human being. As a child I could see people as energy. Not all energies were the same—some were stranger than others, that is, not fixed to the earth. By that I mean human energy is earthbound, but non-humans are not and in the play one character describes how non-humans from another planet learnt how to wear the form of human beings and so disguised, set about implanting new knowledge into the general consciousness to prepare everyone for their eventual takeover. I have always known that there are many strains of humanity on earth and that here among us now are beings both good and evil who are not entirely human and who only wear the outer form as a skin to hide their true identity. I also know that there will come a time when these beings will not wear a disguise and will walk the earth freely among people, for they will be the keepers.

As I looked out into the Indian night watching the evening fires glow in the villages while people settled in for the night, I remembered the lines: "It is necessary to force humankind into a readily receptive state of somnambulant acceptance." Those words I wrote forty years ago struck a chord. My voices make me aware of mind control techniques today that are being secretly fed to the population in order to sedate the masses into accepting all kinds of unacceptable things.

I remember my voices telling me: "Your reality is a canvass, on which your world is painted and portrayed just the way the artist wants you to view it. You look at the painting and accept what you see, but you do not see behind the canvass and the deception in which your world is coloured." To me our planet is beautiful, and I fear what is to become of our wondrous world. During my life I have lived a dual existence dipping in and out of two worlds. One is the reality that is painted for us, which I have tried so hard to accept and live by and the other is a higher consciousness, which I wish to share with others to help them understand how to live in greater awareness of their true identity. I have hidden behind a seal of routine living for too long, and I cannot run away anymore. I have to speak what I know, regardless of the cost.

The train juddered as it crossed lines and the black night cloaked the countryside in a deep velvet curtain. In my own family I had always felt like a cuckoo in the nest and was never fully accepted, always being told to shut up and not speak about what I was told or what I saw, so I learnt how to hide everything inside myself. As a small child I was shown many things that did not make sense, yet I now realise that the future I saw is now. It is so easy to distract the masses and feed information to the world that everyone accepts, even though it blatantly screams deception. In our holographic life, world leaders with power and money can manipulate anything. Hitler, I was told, did not die in a fire, even though his remains were found; he lived on in America and helped to formulate new "mind control" techniques. Sadam Hussein did not die. He lives on. It is easy when you have many look-alikes to take your place. Everything is easy when you have lorry loads of money and easier still to have a face-lift so that you can slip into oblivion. Anyone with knowledge of stage magic knows how easy it is to create the drama of a hanging. It is easy to create a scapegoat in the form of Osama Bin Laden to shoulder the blame of the sins of the elite, and to televise a public murder and throw his body in the sea where it cannot be traced. The killing of Gaddafi was finely timed so that he wouldn't be able to scream to the world what he knew about all the underhanded deals the world leaders are involved in, because if we knew the truth about the new world order, everyone would be shocked into rising up against the invisible cowards running the show. Similarly, two years before Princess Diana's murder, I predicted that she would be killed; again, when you have control, it is easy to stage one of the biggest lies the world has witnessed. Her body does not rest where you have been told, for sadly when the powerful had finished with her body, there was not too much left to bury.

Lesley Ann Eden

My voices—then, as now,—are clear in what they teach and I realise, shamefully, that I have sat back and listened all my life while the real Uranus has stolen the reins and is reigning. Continually I am told shocking information that I cannot withhold any longer, regardless of what others think I must speak out.

CHAPTER 15

Russian Dolls

As the night train sped through miles of open countryside, smells of food infiltrated our carriage with people settling down to their supper before retiring to their bunks. Branden returned from his visit to the lavatory and since my former experiences on Indian trains had been disgusting, I dared to ask if the facilities were clean. He assured me that they were fine.

As we had already eaten, I continued my Russian saga explaining that when I was escorted to the canteen for lunch, there was no choice—only typically Russian food with a kind of red cabbage stew and stodgy pudding, neither of which I liked.

"Well, what did you expect, Mum? It was after all a Russian restaurant."

"I know, but I was hungry, and there was nothing I really fancied; the stew had congealed grease floating on the top. Anyway, when I returned to the centre, I was locked up again and the hours dwindled. Nothing happened and I thought that I was not going to get my promised ride around Moscow; but just when I had given up hope, the door was unlocked by the horrid Helga, the woman on duty the first night I arrived, stating begrudgingly, 'You vill ride on bus.' She motioned me to follow the guard and I was taken to a waiting bus, where two men sat—one an American and the other an Australian.

"As I took a seat behind them, we exchanged greetings. The American was the editor of the *National Geographic* magazine and complained that he had been detained by the state for having arrived later than scheduled and was not allowed by the government to proceed until things were sorted out. The Australian, on the other hand, had arrived earlier than planned and likewise was detained. When I explained why I was locked up, they felt sorry for me and were concerned that I had no money. The American pushed some notes into my hand saying, 'You might need this—go on; take it!' I was extremely grateful but had no idea how much trouble the money would cause later."

"Well, that was kind," interjected Branden.

"Yes, he was a lovely man. He took a photo of me in Red Square and promised to send it to me and he kept his word."

"Have you still got it?"

"Yes, I think so—somewhere; anyway, a few more passengers got on board. They were a group of Chinese businessmen. A large woman with a man's face climbed into the driver's seat, and another large woman with dyed blonde hair stood at the front of the bus. As we set off, she didn't need a microphone as her voice penetrated the sound of the engine. The American, Australian and I were used to chatting freely in that kind of situation, but she became angry and shouted; 'Be quiet! Pay attention! Zis is Moscow. You vill learn about Moscow!' We were shocked by her ranting and immediately obeyed like school children.

"The trip was quite pleasant and an unexpected treat, especially as I had not expected to take one step out of the airport. In the couple of hours that we toured around the city, we saw all the main sites and even got out at particular locations where we were allowed to walk freely, though watched by our strict courier. During that time I managed to talk to the American and exchange addresses so that we could trade experiences. As we drove around the city I was amazed how uniform all the buildings appeared and how the few shops had long queues of people straggling along the pavements, all queuing for the same items. They had no brand choice; there was only one brand of toothpaste, one brand of soap, one brand of flour and one brand of almost everything. I wondered how the ordinary citizen would view our way of life, with endless choices of almost everything.

"It was wonderful to be away from the compound. We experienced a joyous sense of freedom, like a caged animal being allowed out for a short playtime and then packed back in the cage until the next short excursion. After another night in the compound, the next morning a different woman was on duty; as usual I was taken for breakfast in the tedious manner of having three guards to escort me to the restaurant. By that time, even though it was a short period, I was used to the routine and I understood how easy it was to become institutionalised, accepting the situation as the norm and blending inconspicuously into the regime. However, because I had been given a little slice of identity—the money that the magazine editor had given me, I felt rebellious and wanted to use it just for the hell of it!

"Inside the restaurant was a lavatory, and alongside it, was a long staircase. As I sat sipping my coffee, a streak of rebellion flashed through my mind, tempting me to find out where the stairs would lead and daring me to try a new adventure. If the stairs lead to a shop, I could spend my money—how glorious it would be to have such freedom. Feeling brave, I motioned to the guard that I was going to the lavatory and he nodded. I went inside and waited a short while and slipped out when the guard was busy talking to another soldier. I quickly merged into a group of people walking down the stairs and found myself inside another restaurant where many of the airport workers were queuing for their breakfast, so I daringly nudged my way into the queue to get myself a cup of coffee with my money. It was a simple idea and such a simple plan which gave me much pleasure; even queuing was a delight. However, when I got to the check-out with my coffee and handed the woman my money, she stood back and began to shout. It was the worst thing that could have happened. I intended to buy my coffee, drink it and then return inconspicuously to the restaurant, but the woman had drawn attention to me in the most dramatic way, and I couldn't understand what she was saying. I wanted to curl up on the spot and die. A man in a uniform approached and smiled. He asked if I was French, or Swedish or German. Then he said; 'Ah, you are English. This restaurant is for our workers and you have given the woman a note that is worth in your money about fifty pounds. She cannot change this. None of our workers have this kind of money. Please come with me; I will get you a cup of coffee, if that is all you want?' I nodded and followed him. The woman returned my money, and I put it in my pocket. Half of me was afraid, but the other half revelled in the unexpected situation. "'Come, you will have coffee with me and my friend.' We all introduced ourselves and settled down to have coffee. The men were both airline pilots and looked quite handsome in their uniforms. There are times when being psychic has its benefits, for I knew I could turn the situation to my advantage, as it became quite clear what their real intentions were when they offered to buy me all kinds of things and the cup of coffee was frilled with extras such as cakes and a shot of vodka. There was a small gift shop next to the canteen, which was duty free to visitors and obviously to pilots, and they asked me if I would like to choose a gift. I graciously accepted their offer, and they bought me something I had always admired—a real Russian doll with stacks of other little dolls inside. They also bought me sweets and perfume. When we returned to our table, they ordered another drink. They were not on duty and were about to take time off in Moscow. We had another round of shots and then they invited me to go into the city with them.

It was crunch time. I innocently looked sad and told them that I had to get back to the 'place over there!' pointing towards the window where the compound was just in view. They exchanged horrified glances. 'Over there?' they echoed.

"'Yes,' I replied innocently fluttering my eyelashes. I wanted to teach them a lesson. I knew they had wives and a family, and I hated the idea that they would cheat on them and that they felt they could just take advantage of me for the price of a few gifts. They quickly got up from the table looking guilty and uncomfortable, especially when two guards appeared to take me away. It had only been about half an hour that I had gone missing, but it was enough for me to have had an adventure, acquire a few gifts and create a nuisance of myself. When I was escorted by two guards, one on either side of my shoulder, to the compound, Helga, back on duty, was furious with me. She shouted, ranted and raved, screaming: 'YOU HAVE ABUSED RUSSIAN HOSPITALITY—ZIS IS VERY BAD!' So I was locked up immediately and no one came near. Not even tea was allowed; I was in solitary isolation without food or drink for the rest of the evening.

It was at that point that I became frightened, realising that it wasn't a game and that my little adventure had to be paid for; but I did like my Russian doll and enjoyed lining up all the different sizes on the windowsill. I had never seen so many dolls, one inside the other, as the rest I had seen were only replicas of the real product and this gave me a little comfort. The night passed away without anyone visiting me and in the morning another woman unlocked the door. I was allowed to go to breakfast but this time closely watched in the restaurant. I felt like a true criminal, but it wasn't the end of my adventure; little did I know what had been conjured up for me. When I returned to the compound, I was locked up again, and then let out halfway through the morning to be taken to the lounge where the young woman I had met the previous day was waiting. She asked me if I was all right and told me that she had spoken about me to her brother, the prince, who was interested in meeting me. She said that if I agreed he would visit. I accepted but had the feeling that I didn't have much choice in the matter.

"The day passed in regulation, uniform routine, and it wasn't until late afternoon that the door was unlocked and a young man entered. He was dark skinned with black hair swept back from his face and black eyes that darted around the room. He introduced himself and sat down on a chair. He asked me to sit on his knee as he patted his right leg, crisply indicating where I was to sit. I was shocked by his intimate approach and cautiously sat on the edge of the bed. At first he ignored my disobedience and entered a more formal conversation, as though to while away the time. Then he demanded me to sit on his knee again. I timidly did, feeling extremely uncomfortable, and he attempted to kiss me. I didn't respond and he grew angry, shouting: 'You are not a woman! You are a child, a child!' I didn't mind his response as it gave me a way out of the situation. 'Do you want to love me?' he questioned.

"'No!' I replied sternly. He was obviously not used to being refused anything because he turned around and pushed me onto the bed, threw himself on top of me and tried to kiss me again, but I found it abhorrent and he rolled away in a rage, claiming again that I was 'a child, not a woman, just a child' and left the room in a frenzied fury. As the door banged shut and locked, I was left in a strangled silence. I couldn't believe what had happened. Many things crossed my mind. How dare they use me! How could they think that I was an easy target? Was it because I had dared to have coffee with the pilots that they thought I would comply with a sexual liaison with a stranger? Did they do this kind of thing often? Did they watch out for a likely subject to use in this way? I looked around the room to see if there were hidden cameras, as I suddenly felt exposed. I sat there for a long time as the afternoon wore to a grey dim before I lay down to lock out the grim reality.

"The next day passed without anything untoward happening and I grew excited and anxious about leaving. I kept asking about my flight, but no one would tell me whether it was on time or even worse whether I was allowed to board it. I grew fearful and tearful about what might happen, for I realised that they had my passport and were in control. The morning wore on and I had no news. I banged on my door, but no one came. I sat in the austere silence feeling the walls close in on me. Lunchtime came and I was not allowed out. No one visited. The afternoon wore on and no one came. The heaviness of every minute stacked on my shoulders until I felt weary from the worry. By three o'clock in the afternoon, the door was unlocked. I was asked to follow the guard. I was lead through several offices and asked questions at each point until I was allowed onto the next. It became a kind of ritual until I reached a different part of the airport, where things began to feel more natural and there was an air and an atmosphere of something I recognised as normality.

"I was handed over to an official who said: 'You do not have a seat on this flight!' He pointed to a piece of paper. At first I was shocked. I felt as though someone had punched me in the stomach and my breath stolen.

"When I regained my composure, the words tumbled from my mouth in a flurry: 'You are wrong! I do have a seat on the plane. Everyone knows—my friends and family are waiting for me in London. My parents know I am on this flight and if I do not appear, there will be trouble!' I was on the verge of crying, but just stopped myself as he glared at me as though I were dirt.

"'Wait here!' he commanded and stormed off. A short while later another official appeared and said: 'It is correct that there is not a place for you on the plane; but if you wait here, we will see if there is a space for you.' He showed me to a spot just outside the line where people were free to catch their scheduled flights. He made me wait just outside the barrier where I could see people coming and going. I stood on the spot for three hours, waiting in anxious desperation. I felt they were making me sweat, punishing me for my misdemeanours.

"Eventually a woman came with my passport and told me I was free to go. I fled through the barrier like a caged bird soaring to freedom. I dared not look behind but kept moving forwards in case someone tapped me on the shoulder to take me back. All it took was crossing a simple line and I was myself again. I almost skipped to the boarding gate, flooded with a sense of joy and realizing that freedom is everything. I boarded the plane as though I were climbing a stairway to heaven and when I sat down at the front of the aircraft and was served a drink; I really knew I was finally on my way home.

"I was so traumatised by the whole experience that I wrote my first play, *Uranus Ureignus,* which was accepted by London University as my degree examination production. It was the first time a student was allowed to produce their own work, as normally the candidate had to direct a well-known piece. It was filmed for posterity. Strangely I had dusted off the script and read it again before our current journey to India; I was amazed at the accuracy of what I predicted forty years ago, especially my reference to the 'twin destruction' that would take place."

"That's amazing" said Branden, who was ready to bed down after our long session. I watched him climb to his bunk. The lady opposite, who was smothered in the Vick's vapour rub, was already snoring. I lay down with my coat over my head to lock out the noise, but the Russian saga was still playing like a film in my head, and it was difficult to get into sleep mode. Remembering what I wrote forty years ago made my mind buzz.

Uranus Ureingus is set way in the future and the action occurs when the whole world has been taken over by a singular power. The main character, Major 244, explains to an uninitiated group what happened to the earth when he says: "The earth, your planet, became completely united under one organised unit. Uranus, our leader—Uranus, our thought is all that we are and all that we need. Each night we are lulled to sleep by the soft, swift voice of our leader transmitting his thoughts to each of us, and we wake each morning all thinking the same thoughts."

I was alarmed to think that my play, my words, had pre-empted what was happening today with warnings of hypnotic trance vibrations used through music, television, film and radio in order to brainwash the masses into thinking and believing propaganda sold to the public by the few in power. The warnings of the earth being taken over by the New World Order are becoming louder as more people fear world economic collapse. It was frightening and I marvelled how I had merely tuned into a vein of knowledge that fed information to me. It was like taking dictation—I transposed what I heard onto paper. Similarly, I thought about how my voices were growing stronger, and I was being fed more information. It pointed to the reality behind the charade that was being played out by the government, introducing laws to sap peoples' freedom and free speech. Many would consider the information outrageous, and even I find it hard to believe; yet I know I have a duty to speak out.

I tried to block out the night and the noise of the shaking undercarriage, but every time I closed my eyes thoughts poked me awake. I was pensive about the previous night and the peculiar visitation from an unknown energy. It scared me. I was afraid it might happen again. I knew in the train compartment I was safe, but what about when I returned home and was alone in my bedroom? It was a terrifying idea, which I didn't want to acknowledge; so I thought about the terrible journey home with my children after we had said our last good-byes to Granny. It was easier to exchange one horrific thought for a less gross memory.

I recalled that just as we were about to leave India to return home, Mina had become ill again. Travelling with a sick child was terrible. I had nearly lost her once on the journey there, and I was afraid of losing her again on our return. She began to vomit and suffered from bouts of diarrhea. I was covered with vomit. I ran out of nappies and diarrhea leaked into my clothes. It was impossible on the plane to cope with the mess, and the long hours travelling half way across the world under those circumstances were a nightmare. I kept forcing her to drink water to prevent her from dehydrating, but the more I did so, the more I was coated with mess. I had very little help from the air hostesses since they were busy with other passengers. By the time we reached Heathrow airport, I stank like a sewer and little Mina was feverish.

I was so relieved to get her to Will's aunt's house where I could reach a doctor, but he was reluctant to give her any medicine until I sought the help of my own doctor. By the time we returned to our cottage in Yorkshire, little Mina was so weak that she couldn't walk. My doctor was very helpful and kept a strict observance over her, but she didn't walk for six weeks. She became debilitated and so thin that her tiny arms were just sticks. I began to despair; but one morning when her Godmother came to visit, she got up and walked to her and that was the beginning of her recovery. Each day she became stronger and put on weight until her illness became a distant memory. I thought of Mina as a grown woman with her own children and successful teaching career and was grateful to the Great Ones for restoring her health.

At that moment I drifted a little and thought sleep would come, but loud snoring and throat gurgling from the woman opposite interrupted the peace and threw my mind back into wakefulness.

For some reason the word "turbulence" came to mind, and in a flash I was inside a memory from my first visit to India. It brought back a very turbulent time both physically and emotionally. I had never sailed before let alone taken part in the sport and had no experience of crewing a dingy, understanding the specific nautical terminology used by sailors or any knowledge of how to use the equipment on board; therefore, when it was suggested that I take part in a sailing race on the Hooghly River in Calcutta, I declined. Will, on the other hand, was a keen, experienced sailor, like his mother; and he had no one to crew for him, so his mother insisted that I do it. Not wanting to cause a family row, I acquiesced.

I was wearing shorts and was dressed for the heat in a cotton tee shirt and thought that my attire was appropriate for the task; but having no knowledge of the sport or weather, I didn't realize how inappropriate my clothes were for the occasion. I clambered into the small boat as though it were a Sunday outing and even managed a smile at Will who was sitting with a serious face in the Captain's corner. He briefly explained what I was to do and how to do it when he called out certain commands, such as, "turn about," "jam in the cleats," "boom across" and others that I couldn't remember. We set off peacefully under the grey sky in the muggy heat cruising towards the start line.

My attention was caught by something floating next to the boat. I stared hard at the object, which I instantly recognised but couldn't place in the unusual setting. As my brain clicked into gear, however, I was shocked when I realised I was staring at a severed hand. The fingernails were pale and the hand muddy brown like the river. "There's a . . . there's a hand in the water!" I gasped.

"Oh you'll get used to it! There are lots of bits of bodies around, junk that doesn't get burnt in burial pyres!" stated Will nonchalantly, gearing himself for the start of the race. I gulped and looked away, afraid to see more.

Just as we were nearing the start line, the sky cracked and a monsoon storm drenched everything. I was enthralled by the heat of the water—it was hot rain! It was just like taking a shower fully clothed. It was the first time I had ever experienced such phenomena; and when the gun went off signalling the start of the race, I was not concentrating but looking skywards and didn't catch Will's first command, which he bellowed at me angrily. I looked blankly at him, and he shouted the order shoving me from one side of the boat to the other. A wooden post was in the middle, which kept catching my bare legs, grazing and cutting into my shins as he bundled me across the boat in an attempt to swing it around quickly. I had never seen that side of him before and was alarmed at his violent competitive streak. His mother had taught him to win at all costs and I was part of the price.

I panicked in the downpour and the shock of Will's behaviour. I couldn't understand what he was saying through the blast of the storm. All was muddled—the commands, the grey water, the bits of bodies, the heat, the rain, my wet tee shirt—everything spun around in a dizzy haze; the more I became confused, the more angry and frustrated Will became, and the more he threw me around in the small space. My legs were bleeding and bruised, like my feelings. I was dumbfounded that he could treat me so badly. I was amazed that by the end of the race we came fourth out of eleven boats; but as I climbed out, I was furious with Will and didn't speak to him for three days afterwards. That unfortunate incident was not the end of my sailing misadventures, as I had to crew for Will once more on a hydraulic dam in Hydrobad.

After my first introduction to sailing sport, I never wanted to race again; but once more Will had no one to crew for him and I was coerced into the job. It was a special cup race held annually on a dam, and the prize was highly coveted. As we rounded the corner in the car, I spied a delightful sailing club beautifully decked out with bunting across the restaurant and bar. The boats merrily waited for their owners bobbing up and down on the blue rippling water like playful steeds waiting to gallop out into the open blue prairie, decorated in brightly coloured flags quivering in the light breeze. It was a charming, chocolate box picture of peaceful utopia. I wondered why my stomach was churning anxiously? Will had promised not to be so severe, but I doubted his intentions as I had seen him turn into a monster under competition conditions. As the sailors took their boats out into the bright water, Will was calm; but underneath I could see the stressed determination to win the race in his mother's boat, rising to the surface as he chewed his cheek.

I remembered most commands as Will had instructed and felt nervous as I swung from side to side, wearing trousers to protect my knees and a windproof jacket in case of rain. As we set off, the weather was beautiful and the playful breeze set us dancing out towards the starting post. I was determined that this time I was going to concentrate and listen for the gun. The atmosphere among the contestants was friendly and lighthearted on the surface, but underneath the smile was a grim determination to win. The gun flared into the sky and everyone buzzed into action chasing the will of the wind. For a short while we were busy "about turning" and jibing not noticing the changing sky. The wind grew stronger, and Will shouted to sit up on the edge of the boat and lean over into the choppy waves. I was afraid of the water and was not a good swimmer and to bend backwards into it was terrifying. I had to "jam in the cleats" (jam the rope into a tight vice on the side of the boat and hold on tight and lean backwards); but what I didn't know was that once the rope was in the vice, it was secure. I thought I had to hold onto the rope for dear life and the coarse hair cut into my soft hands.

After a short while, leaning backwards wasn't so scary. Once I realised that the boat wasn't going to tip over, I strangely enjoyed the sensation; but when the storm clouds gathered overhead and the bright sky turned black and the deep foaming water heaved up and down in crashing waves that smashed into the centre of the boat, I began to quake. Storm conditions required every move to be speeded up a hundred times faster than normal; and as I wasn't familiar with the equipment in the best of circumstances, so I struggled to keep up with the commands. One minute the boat was up and the next we were down in a deep blue cave coming up and crashing down again. My poor hands clinging onto the rope were bleeding; the water continually washed away the blood, but I was so afraid that I didn't notice the pain. Fighting to keep afloat, we didn't realize that we had strayed far away from the others and were heading straight for the edge of the hydraulic dam.

On the drive to the dam I had seen the spectacular site with white foam spraying over the fall as the water cascaded below in deep rivulets, like white wavy hair shimmering in the sunshine. I knew that we would never survive crashing over the edge and as we fought to steer away from the danger zone, the storm drew us closer and closer. I was vaguely aware of the rising fear from onlookers far in the distance, as I could just make out figures frantically waving flags and jumping up and down warning us of the danger ahead; but I didn't have time to think, only to hold onto the ropes and lean out. Farther and farther we were swept towards the gushing dam and the deafening sound of the crashing water grew louder, while the storm lashed the boat in a raging tempest. Lightning like a flashing sword cut across the bow, momentarily lighting up the sail in an electric pink glow, and thunder rolled through the bleak black clouds reverberating with an eerie echo as it hit the gaping dam. Closer and closer we were sucked into the undercurrent and I prayed so hard and thought of Granny, imploring her help.

Just as we were on the verge of entering the perilous zone, a strange thing happened—the wind changed. It was simple. The wind changed direction and almost with a gentle hand, it guided us away from the edge of the dam back towards the safety area of the yacht club. By the time we navigated the boat safely back into the harbour, the race was well and truly over; but everyone was so relieved to see us that we were cheered and given an amazing welcome. As we climbed out of the boat, I began to shake uncontrollably and pain cut through my hands where blood was trickling down in rivulets. A doctor bandaged them; and in the warm, party atmosphere we celebrated being alive.

I have never sailed again because that experience shattered my confidence in boats and when I think of the terror of the moment, I am flooded with wonderment and gratitude to the Great Ones for having saved my life. In the warmth of that feeling my eyes began to close. I mused that I was like a Russian doll—on the outside full of bravado, appearing to the outside world strong and confident; but digging deeper and further in, sifting through each smaller image of me, I realised how infinitesimally small I am in the great cosmic ocean beyond knowing.

CHAPTER 16

Invader

Through the hypnotic drone of the train, I managed to sleep for a while; and when the evening stars drifted behind a hazy, pink veil and cracks of blue leaked across the new day, I stirred my stiff limbs and swallowed through a dry mouth. Branden climbed down and stood in front of me saying, "Oh Mum, you were making such a noise snoring all night!"

I made a face and tried to motion him to stop speaking. "Honestly, it was so loud!"

He persisted as though admonishing me; but I whispered, "It wasn't me, it was her!" He quickly glanced behind at the Vick's vapour rub lady staring blankly out of the window and stifled a giggle as the train drew to a holt; whereupon all the passengers catapulted into action, jumping off the train, slamming doors and calling for attendants. Branden collected his bag from the top bunk and pointed to the awful brown smears next to his bed.

"I had to sleep next to that last night!" he grimaced. I was shocked and asked why he hadn't said anything, but he explained that he hadn't wanted to upset me. I was so sorry that he had to put up with the unsanitary mess, but we didn't have time to stand and discuss it.

As we clambered off the train, a clutch of porters dressed in red tee shirts and khaki shorts scurried to our assistance, and one in particular drew my attention fighting to take our bags. He only had one leg and supported himself with a crutch whilst carrying bags on his head. I gave him an extra tip as I was moved by his bravery. Outside the station, the atmosphere was nauseating—a blend of toxic fumes from early morning traffic and the smell of spices. Branden had booked us into a basic hotel in order to get some rest and change our clothes in readiness for the final haul back to England. Our taxi took us to a small hotel squeezed beside a similar hotel packed into a small courtyard. It was a quick stopover place for business people and handy to get to the centre of Chennai.

We were both exhausted from the journey, and our room was situated right at the top of the building where we had to step over wires and mounds of rubble as the hotel was still in the process of being built. We both collapsed onto our narrow beds and fell asleep in our clothes. A few hours later, I woke and crept around so as not to disturb Branden. Although the bathroom was basic, it was wonderful to have a shower and wash the grime out of my hair and get dressed into clean clothes. When Branden woke, he did the same and by the time we were ready to face the day, it was too late for breakfast; besides, we didn't relish eating there, so we went in search of a clean place to have coffee.

Outside the heat was intense and just walking along the noisy, polluted thoroughfare was debilitating. We found a place that was sanitary; as usual it took ages to produce two lattes by two attendants with no other customers to serve, but it gave us time to work out the day's itinerary and count our remaining money. I wanted us to have a good meal in a lovely restaurant as a farewell lunch, and we decided to search for such a place after coffee. In the evening we had been invited to dine with Martin, a friend who was going to take us to his favourite restaurant and allow us to leave our bags at his house until our departure in the early hours the next morning.

After coffee we walked out into the blistering heat on our quest to seek a special place for lunch. Branden had an idea about a particular café, but when we got there, I couldn't even go inside because it was so drab and dirty. We continued walking through piles of plaster and concrete clusters littering the pavements. Gnarled tree roots at certain intervals jutted out through the cracked slabs, like wrinkled knuckles on an old man's hand, and were difficult to walk over causing me to stop and stumble a few times, while Branden, as usual, lead the way fearlessly like a young Crusader on a victorious quest. The walk seemed endless, and as we had no idea where we were going, we ploughed on. Eventually we came to a wonderful hotel with an exclusive restaurant set in beautiful grounds, and we both agreed that it was just what we needed—a slice of luxury to end our journey.

The restaurant was refreshingly cool with only two other people dining, and we took a table near the window where we could view the luscious gardens. I was so proud of Branden for having navigated us successfully through the trip and having brought us safely back to Chennai. It was the last leg of the journey and as always, that part of an adventure is a waiting game, where it is important to play out the last scene in style. The meal was wonderful, and we had all kinds of treats and delights to reward ourselves before trekking back to the grim hotel; but my stomach began to complain about all the rich food I had imbibed and I hoped I wouldn't be ill on the plane.

By the time we had packed all our bags back at the grimy hotel and ordered a taxi, it was time to head out to the city centre to find Martin's house. It wasn't far from the Radisson hotel, where we had begun our trip in fantastic luxury, and as the evening traffic built up smothering the roads in a congested fog, the long pauses in the endless queues were tiring and tedious. I glanced down at my mobile phone, which had lit up in my bag, and read the message: "Sorry to tell you, but can't see you tonight as I am very ill with a stomach upset. Hope you are fine. See you another time, Martin." I read the message again and relayed the content to Branden, who wasn't surprised that we had been let down. We were almost at Martin's house, and I was angry that we were stranded with nowhere to go.

"I know—let's go to the Radisson; it's not far from here!" I suggested eagerly, trying to alleviate the situation.

"It's really expensive!" added Branden.

"I know, but it's an emergency; and I can pay on my card; and well, let's face it, we have very little choice. Besides it's a great way to end our trip."

Branden agreed, and we asked the driver to change direction and take us to the magnificent hotel, where we were given a warm welcome and a great business deal from the management. We were allowed all the added extras, even though we were only staying for half a night, such as an amazing foot massage and free drinks in the bar and luxury cookies in the bedroom. In fact, it was the best thing that could have happened to us, as we spent our last hours in Chennai in the lap of luxury. As we left, in the early hours of the morning, we waved good-bye to the porters and swept out into the quiet roads. When we arrived at the airport, it was flooded with bright lights and early morning activity, even at three in the morning. We settled ourselves in the uncomfortable seats ready for the long wait, but we were dismayed to find that our plane had been delayed for several hours. The time went by slowly and although we attempted sleep, it was virtually impossible in the endless racket of the airport traffic. Eventually when we boarded the plane, we slumped into an exhausted slumber and managed a few hours respite.

The flight back didn't seem so long; the hours quickly passed, so that when we were standing in Heathrow Airport waiting for our bags to appear on the carousel, we knew our journey had finally ended. After all the planning and the months of preparation, it was over. It was hard to say goodbye to Branden after being together for so long and experiencing many things. With a lump in my throat, I kissed him and heaved my bag onto the train bound for King's Cross. I was aware that I probably smelt of spices, garlic and curry and tried to keep myself closed off from everyone on the crowded train. I just wanted to get back as quickly as possible to my cottage and to my daughter, who would be waiting for me with my little wild cat Sheba; I wondered if Greta had managed to tame her.

It was odd racing back through the English countryside with not a water buffalo in sight or a cluster of children congregating by their water tank, or outrageously bright shrines placed on roadsides or clusters of goats tended by young boys waving eagerly at passing cars. I longed for a bath and a change of clothes and to sleep again in my own bed. Every journey forges new beginnings; I felt satisfied that I had accomplished all that I had set out to achieve and was ready to face the next phase of my life. As the Yorkshire countryside came into view, I felt a tinge of excitement urging the train to go faster. As I flung my bags into the back of the waiting taxi, I glanced towards the city walls, strong and impenetrable. The familiar pale stone glinted in the late afternoon sunshine after a refreshing rain shower; the air was scented with the smell of wet soil and old English roses and I knew I was back home in York.

Home at last! I opened the door, and my daughter shouted from the sitting room. I was surprised to see my cat strewn across her knees, lying upside down having her tummy tickled. I hugged Greta and naughty kitty sloped off to find her food bowl; Greta assured me the willful, wild thing had become a little more docile, but I believed it was only for her. When I was alone with Sheba later that evening, she was just as wayward as before, sparking out when I tried to stroke her. It was odd being back in my cottage alone again after another adventure. From my conservatory I watched the evening fade until dark circled nightriders shadowed the moon.

Emptiness echoed in the hallway and "gone" was the only word that crept resolutely into my mind. The smell of loneliness tinged the air mingling with lavender from my bedroom, and I fought the sour taste of "missing" with a glass of wine. I missed Branden. I missed Greta, especially as the sound of my key in the lock before going to bed was a finality. I realised she was living with friends and not coming back, but it didn't stop me listening for strains of music drifting from her room. My single pad of one pair of feet up the stairs echoed a solitary existence. Suddenly Sheba swept past, brushing my legs with her soft fur. I was happy that she was around as fear of the unknown and the black night began to pinch my confidence. I had pushed away all thoughts of the "invader" from the last night in the Nilgiris, and the thought of it happening again was terrifying. I was relieved that Sheba was sleeping on my bed. Strangely she seemed to guard me; and I felt safe feeling her warm body on my feet as I pulled the covers up over my head blocking out the shadows.

The next day, September nerves jangled in the blaze of a renegade autumn sun as I drove on my first morning back to school. The heavy rain during the night had washed all the trees and left them with a fresh, green sheen and across the sky a distant rainbow arched a bridge to nowhere. The news on the radio was doom and gloom with rising discontent across the country as many people were losing their jobs. Economic cutbacks were causing severe threats to industries and closures of major companies. The picture was bleak. As I switched off the engine in the school car park, a voice in my head momentarily warned of darker things to come. It suggested that the early rumbling of rebellion, like the voice of distant thunder, would gather momentum and the storm of outrage would spark and singe the country in a flaming fury that would shock the world.

I shuddered to come to terms with the pictures in my head and pushed my fears away swapping them for other, more immediate anxieties, such as what my new classes were going to be like. As I walked up the steps to the entrance hall, I glanced back at the playing fields to see the sun break through a grey cloud, appreciating that autumn in the last dregs of glory, was struggling to maintain a semblance of beauty; but I knew each consecutive day would take a step nearer to the long, dark sleep. How I dreaded the winter! I paused on the steps and a voice spoke softly: "Winter is part of life's cycle. There are winters in a life span, moments when all seems to lie in darkness; but under the earth it is not barren—the pulse still beats, waiting to rise and live anew. Winter is a necessary vein in the earth's nervous system bringing fresh blood after sleep." I smiled. I heeded the gentle encouragement and walked to my first class.

The days passed in routine order with Sheba and me settling into our ways. I had feared letting her out in case she wandered near the busy road, but one day I left a tiny window open in my bedroom and somehow she had managed to spring up and jump through the tiny crevice onto a ledge and fly through the air onto my conservatory roof. I searched the house and realised that the only way she could have escaped was through a small gap in the top window. I ran outside to see her worried little face peering down with her beautiful green eyes pleading for help. For a few brief moments we bonded in our united anxiety. I coaxed her down and she leapt to safety, where I scooped her up and held her to my chest for a few precious seconds before she realised she was being loved and then she scrambled to freedom to find her food bowl. I was relieved she was back as I had grown used to her company, especially at night, as she seemed to ward off any spirit intruders; and I was still afraid of the energy that had invaded the room in India. I worried that it would return.

Soon the autumn days folded into winter gloom bringing the early morning frost settling like a layer of sugar icing across the fallow fields; the sharp air, smelling of peppermint and washing powder, cut the back of my throat as I scraped the frost from my car. Joining the early morning traffic queue, I huddled over the car heater to warm my frozen hands and watched my breath steam up the windscreen. Farther down the road the black, ploughed earth sparkled in the watery sunshine like brittle sugar spun on top of an over-baked chocolate pudding; my thoughts meandered to the hot days in India.

I longed to be back in Pondecherry by the sea secretly dreaming hidden thoughts locked in the soft lining of my heart, where days were coloured with warm memories and I was free from the prison walls of noisy classrooms. I thought of Che and my emotional farewell to him in Cuba and of how time had lapsed and no more visions had appeared. While driving, I remembered the anniversary of his death, and a voice drifted into my head stating calmly: "I do not have an anniversary of death, for I am always living!" The message had jerked me out of my contemplation, and I marvelled at the quick response from beyond and the poignancy of the words. I drove on in the icy veil and knew that he was somewhere in the cosmos gathering strength for a rebirth.

Where is the now? I am sitting in my kitchen at my tiny table watching the Sunday afternoon sky turn purple. My cat has grown in confidence and deigns to sit next to my computer and wash herself. She has to be part of everything and watches me strike the keys with my fingers. I feel at any moment she might pounce, but she seems mesmerized by the words appearing on the screen. It is as though she is reading the content with teacher-like scorn. Does she know I am writing about her? She pushes her grey/blue head on my screen demanding attention. It is cosy next to the computer where a rush of air gushes out spontaneously, and she bathes in the heat as if it were a hot-air shower, because it is cold in the kitchen and I cannot afford the heating. I wonder if Sheba is cross with me for not providing her with better accommodation.

She meows to be let out seeking adventure from my boring activity, and I give in to her demands. I watch her stalk across the lawn as she sneaks a second glance at me with a strange air of finality. I walk back into the kitchen feeling uneasy. Perhaps I shouldn't have let her out. I watch the black sky cloud over with a white mantle as snow begins to fall gently over the landscape. I panic and go outside calling her in the white stillness, but there is no response. I can't settle. All night on and off I search the garden, calling her name and rattling her bowl but she does not return. Eventually I climb the stairs alone missing her naughty face waiting for me at the top. The winter wonderland outside is a transformed white landscape with which she is unfamiliar and I worry for her safety. I leave food in the conservatory for her in case she slips through the cat flap and is hungry. I hate going to bed alone without the comfort of her warm body on my feet. I struggle to sleep in the emptiness of the white light that drifts in through the curtains from the snowdrifts outside, and I wish I hadn't given in to her demands.

Through a strained silence I fall asleep but am disturbed by the cat jumping on my shoulder near the top of my head. She doesn't usually do that; in fact, she never does that; she always lands near my feet. I struggle to find my reasoning as I suddenly realise that she is missing and that something is tapping my shoulder like Sheba when she gently paws and pummels the bedclothes. My heart races and I stop breathing. In rising alarm

I know it isn't Sheba. My body falls rigid as I feel pressure moving down my back onto my buttocks. The terror of the last night in India returns and I relive the horror. The sensation of the pressure grows stronger and my heart almost cracks through my ribcage. I fight inwardly to face the unknown and with a sudden burst of strength, I sit up. In the gloom there is nothing. The room is quiet, but I feel eyes watching, like the eyes in the room in Diana's house. I had feared the entity would return and without the protection of my little cat, I am vulnerable; or perhaps it is the turmoil of my emotions that it feeds upon using the negative energy to gain a foothold in my consciousness.

Downstairs the house is strangely quiet and the white glare from the outside draws an icy, eerie stillness into the kitchen. There is no sign of Sheba having touched her food in the conservatory. Outside in the soft snow there are no tiny cat tracks and my hopes sink. Pink luminescence shimmers from the east in a grey opaque sky. Much of the country is plunged in snow and the trees have become white candy sticks. I resolve when I am dressed to search the neighbourhood to see if I can find her. I push back the horror of the visitation from the invader and make coffee.

A day passes and neighbours report that they have seen Sheba cavorting in the fields chasing birds and that she is being fed by a neighbour, who leaves large bowls of food out for her. When I visit the house, I am dismayed to see the evidence. I feel I have let her down. I tried my best to make her happy, but at heart she is wild and needs her freedom; and if she is safe and happy, then I have to be content with that. I miss her mostly at bedtime and in my lonely fear, I dread the return of the invasive entity. I research all kinds of related matter on what happened, and I am comforted to find many people are experiencing strange happenings in a similar vein; but I don't find any answers.

I watch the traffic mow tentatively through a thick, slippery, white carpet laid afresh through the night. Stark statues, which were yesterday's trees, stand stiffly to attention, while my roof and lawn are coated with thick wedges of snow, like icing dripping from a Christmas cake. Pink light streaking from the east casts a warm glow over the pearly landscape where the blackbirds forage for food. I sigh, exhaling warm breath, which circles like smoke around my head. Sheba has been missing for two days. I wonder where she is? My mind tells me that she is warm and curled up somewhere in someone's house and being fed, looked after by a kind person, and that soon she will appear on my doorstep meowing to be let in. But my heart tells me she won't return.

It's so cold, even colder than it was when we had a month of snow. Everything remains frozen. There is no sign of her and I go home disappointed. All I can do is wait and hope. The day passes in a bland quiet and the evening light fades as I walk in the garden. The moon is out and my roof sparkles, glinting like tiny Christmas tree lights. I open my front door and the ice inside sticks around the edges, so I have to force it open. There is a layer of ice inside my bedroom window. The opaque coating sticks to the curtain, which is frozen stiff like an ironing board. I am not hungry. Tomorrow is Christmas and I do not feel like feasting. The moon smiles a shiny, silver-ball welcome and I remember a strange happening from twenty-five years ago.

I was teaching at a famous acting school and during one of my dance classes when I leapt into the air, something twanged inside my stomach and I began to bleed. I thought it was the contraceptive coil, which might have become dislodged but when I went to the doctor he couldn't find anything amiss. It was September and I ploughed on through the new term but the bleeding grew worse, and the doctor thought I had suffered a miscarriage. By the October half-term I was still bleeding but soldiering on, since I had been told there was nothing wrong; but the bleeding continued. For the half-term break, as a family, we had booked into a friend's house on the Yorkshire moors where there were no television and no outside communication, only fields and sheep. One night in the cottage the worry about my health kept me awake. As I lay down in bed, I turned my head to the right and saw the moon in a beautiful clear sky. I watched it glide towards the cottage, coiling silver waves through the window towards me and I became entranced by the hypnotic motion. Through the window its fronds of energy glowed reaching out towards me as it entered through the window. From the shiny tentacles, a couple of glowing beings emerged and stood in the doorway opposite the bed. They seemed to hover halfway through the green door where there was a black tunnel-like denseness behind them. They emanated total peace, happiness and love beyond any emotion I had ever experienced. The feeling was all embracing, all knowing, infinitely powerful and all encompassing. I wanted to go with them. I felt they were taking something away from inside me. I desperately wanted to go with them. I sat up pleading with them, but they said I had work to do on earth and that one day, they would come for me; but it wasn't time. I pleaded again, but they made me lie back very slowly, and as if in a trance I drifted into a deep sleep.

The next morning when I woke the cottage was covered in a blanket of thick snow, and a strange silence filled the bedroom. I had overslept and everyone was outside enjoying the snow. Suddenly I remembered the happening. Fear swept through my body and I began to shake, as I realised there was not a window to my right or a door opposite the bed, only thick, strong walls. I sat up going over the incident in my mind, for I knew I had not dreamt it. I didn't say anything but kept it secret. By December I was very ill and was rushed to hospital. It was Christmas. I was immediately operated on and was surprisingly found to have two foetuses growing in my fallopian tube, the size of two grapes! A friend who was a doctor was furious with my own GP because, he said, "You could have died at any time if the tube had ruptured! It's a miracle you've gone this long without it being detected; you are one lucky girl!"

I felt too ill to feel anything, especially as a choir of little children came into the ward to sing Christmas carols, and I struggled to heave myself to the bathroom to lock out the sound. I was empty inside where two little babies should have grown, and I wanted to lock out the world; but through my misery a remembered joy floated in through the crack in the bathroom door, and I recalled the beautiful shiny beings from the moon that had visited and the love that emanated through them. I suddenly realised that they must have come to take the little beings away as their passageway to earth was blocked. I mourned the loss of my twins; but a few years later, although my body was only working on one cylinder, I became pregnant with a precious daughter. The moonlight twinkled through the tiny mirrors in my cherry tree, and my boots squeaked on the icy path. I mused how time forges ahead in a diurnal round of daily doses of ritual routine and how my baby girl was already grown up.

Christmas passed and there was still no of sign of Sheba. New Year's Day came and went, and I knew she was alive as the neighbour was still feeding her. The snow was just beginning to melt, but it was still bitterly cold. I held out hope that after her adventure she would appear on my doorstep as though nothing had happened. A voice from afar advised: "Don't let your dreams go cold."

She was found today; a neighbour reported her whereabouts and she was brought back home to me in a black plastic bag that had been put in the dustbin. I stood in front of the dustbin unable to open it for a while, afraid of what I would find. I didn't want to see she had been hurt. When I plucked up the courage to lift the lid and heave out the bag, I laid it on the path. With rubber gloves I tipped her out, and her wet slippery body slumped onto the gravel. To me she was still beautiful and sleek. Her eyes were shut as though she were sleeping and at any moment would wake up and spring into action. I checked her body and there was no sign of injury. She wasn't thin; she looked in wonderful condition. A neighbour reported that a carcass, perhaps a turkey, was found next to her. Maybe she had stolen it. She was a very proud creature, and I was glad that she had maintained her dignity; for in death she was still a magnificent being. I loved her for the little part she allowed me to play in her life and now she was free. I wrapped her in a blanket and buried her in the garden and planted a little fir tree where she lay. That same night I heard her meow twice, but maybe it was my imagination?

From my experience of the animal spirit world, it is possible for the owner to feel a close relationship with the deceased animal for a long time after death and in some cases to see, feel and hear the pet. My first pet dog had died very young from distemper, which she had caught when she was kennelled while we were away on holiday. My father had spent many sleepless nights nursing her before she died. A week later, after having an argument with my mother, he was sleeping on the sofa downstairs and was awoken by something washing his face. He opened his eyes and our pet dog was licking his face and wagging her tail. The vision lasted for a few moments before it faded, but my father was so shocked by the experience that it sent him straight back to bed!

On another occasion, in my early twenties, I was staying in Scotland with a friend's family. It was the first time I had met them and I had no previous knowledge of their family life. When we sat down to dinner, I thought someone was slapping my leg under the table as a joke. I didn't like to say anything, as I didn't know the family. The slapping continued at varying intervals until I became agitated and had to look under the table. I saw a large black Labrador dog playfully wagging his tail against my legs. "Oh, it's your dog," I laughed. Everyone was silent and looked at me. "Your dog—it keeps slapping my legs!" No one spoke. "Your black Labrador." Before I could finish the sentence, however, the mother ran out of the room crying. The father apologised saying that their dog, a black Labrador, had recently died and had always been under the table while they ate and slapped peoples' legs in the same manner. When I looked under the table again, there was nothing.

A few nights after Sheba's death, I was lying in bed trying to sleep and I felt her jump onto the bed, just like she used to do. I wasn't shocked. I waited to see what she would do, but it was as though her little paws disappeared into thin air and she was taken over by a whirring energy that travelled up my legs. I immediately recognised the spirit invader. It was the same shaking of my limbs that I had felt in India. My feet were massaged and it wasn't unpleasant. A voice asked: "Is this frightening?" Strangely enough while it was happening, it wasn't! So I allowed the manipulation to continue until my reason took over and I thought, No! I don't want this and I sat up, by which time I was frightened again and the thought of something tricking me into accepting its will was horrific. It's difficult to explain night terrors and to know what it's like to get to sleep shaking with unimaginable fright.

It was early January and I had been back from India for five months when the "thing" returned. Night became something I dreaded, and I tried to seek as much information as possible to learn how to deal with the entity. I didn't know whether it was a good energy that was trying to help me or something totally evil. I had never had to deal with such a spirit and prayed for help from the goodness channel. After experiencing another attack, I was resolved that the next time it happened I was going to stand up to it and not show any fear, as my research was suggesting that the entity was probably from a lower dimension, which usually fed on a subject's anxiety. I went to bed with the feeling that I was being watched and had a premonition that something was going to happen. I lay down in the dark and drew the covers up over my face; my heart raced. As much as I tried not to be afraid, I was terrified and in desperation, I asked for help from Angel Gabriel and Archangel Michael. I had a sensation of protective wings covering my chest and I began to breathe with a steadier rhythm. I was told a mantra: "I seek light, love and knowledge in the highest realm." I repeated this again and again waiting in the blackness for the invader to attack.

The air above me changed and grew colder, and I knew it was approaching; but there was no initial preparation—the "thing" went straight into a heavy attack on my legs. The massage was stronger and rougher than before as though it was rushing. It was racing to get to the top of my legs when from inside my chest, I drew an amazing amount of strength and felt myself rise up and stand before it. Fear drained away like sand in a timer and I felt the thing pause. It seemed shocked by my strength and I watched an ugly little being draw away from my body and stand in sheer surprise at the bottom of my bed. With mocking disgust, I looked at it and it cowered away. A sense of triumph overwhelmed me, and I was relieved to rid myself of a repulsive monster; with a deep feeling of gratitude, I thanked the great ones for their assistance. I vowed never again to be uncertain of such a being, but I had no idea what was to challenge me next.

CHAPTER 17

Beyond Knowing

Thank you for your company on my journey back to India, for all your interest in *The Eden Trilogy* and for your letters and e-mails. I hope in all cases I have been able to answer your questions. Now, when I take you into a world beyond worlds, where different beings of multidimensional heritage exist, I fear that my experiences will test your belief to the breaking point. I can only relate the truth. What occurred truly happened, and my purpose in making you aware of existence beyond your routine world is to expand your higher consciousness and show you that all is not what it seems. Please stay with me, for everything is part of our journey.

I do not have answers to what I am about to relate, but only wish to share what is being shown to me. I don't claim to understand the teaching that is being revealed, but I take comfort in sharing the ideas with you. Confused, I am marooned and drowning in a sea of uncertainty. The latest strange experiences and the visions, together with the voices and the new teaching, are baffling beyond my understanding; I struggle to swim back to the safety of yesterday's acceptance. The new ideas and visions are a heavy burden, and I cannot return to the security of old knowledge; instead, I must begin a different journey to seek the truth.

After my unexplained experience on my last night at Diana's and the return of the malignant energy in my home, I was sure

Return: To the Land of Durga

that nothing more would disturb my inner peace; but I was wrong. What I am about to relate is unbelievable in the extreme; even I struggle to come to terms with the events, and to this end I have kept a record of the happenings as a diary throughout the eight months in which the events occurred. Before I share these with you, however, I need to tell you about my "blue" experience, as this has a bearing on what is to follow.

My blue experience happened when I was living in a small house in a tiny village where King Richard III had resided in a magnificent castle. As you might expect, many extraordinary things occurred in that village, which was an ancient site where many bloody battles had been fought.

This was also a time when I attempted to write my time travel experience in Crete at Knossos Palace and was thwarted by a malignant force, which strove to prevent me from documenting my account. It was also where I asked to be shown a sign in the night sky that would give me the confidence to continue my search concerning a little princess, Izatah, who had been murdered and whose body I had entered during a visit to the island where I had time-travelled back into her experiences. (*Beyond Belief in the Land of Rhythm*—the second book in the Eden Trilogy).

It was a Sunday evening and I had taken my two youngest children back to their father's house; I was sad, missing them after a weekend of laughter and fun. I had lit a fire with the kindling we had collected during the day from the forest near the castle where the late autumn sunshine had allowed fruitful forage into secret bushes and hedgerows. Like ancient gatherers, we had collected nuts and berries to make a harvest festival feast and enjoyed the fruits of our labour. As night nestled around my little house, my dog sat faithfully at my feet as we watched the dry kindling spark flashes of blue and yellow flames up the sooty chimney. I poured myself a glass of Burgundy wine and listened to the silence. I was tired and decided to retire early to bed. I snuggled up under the duvet as my little dog curled up by the side of my bed and just as I was drifting off to sleep, I heard a light tapping on my tiled roof. I thought it must be raining;

as my bed was tucked under the eaves, I rolled out on my left side to take a look out of the window. The night was bright and clear with no sign of rain. Back in bed the tapping grew louder and something burst through the eave wall on my right side. My room was bathed in an electric blue light and everything became blue. The buzzing noise in the room was glaringly blue; the energy smelt and tasted electric blue; everything in my head was blue. Then I blacked out as I was smothered in the blue electric light.

    I don't know what ensued; but when I came to, there were strange beings at the foot of my bed. I was sitting up facing them, and they were coaxing me to lie back down. They told me to think of something peaceful—a memory that was tucked inside my head—and coaxed me to lie down and relax. I jumped into the memory of when I was about three years old watching my great grandfather sitting on an old wooden bench in his garden, which was overgrown with wild flowers, weeds and grasses taller than me. The sun was shining, the birds were singing and from over the hedge, I could hear children calling to each other in play. My great-grandfather was totally still staring into space, with his face white as a monumental statue and his rough, gnarled hands resting on top of his walking stick. It was an odd moment because I don't know if I appeared to myself from the future beyond the moment, or whether it was a spark of sheer enlightened awareness with a feeling of something greater happening, like a pause of infinity when time stands still and the emotion is frozen, locked in a time warp. As I relived the scene, hypnotically I became peaceful and fell asleep while the blue beings left through a tiny hole in the window.

    In the morning when I came out of the forced sleep, I was horrified to remember the blueness of everything and was afraid to see anything with the same intense, electric blue sheen. Repeatedly I traced the events trying to discover what exactly had taken place. I went downstairs and ran a bath and as I climbed into the tub, I noticed a circle of dried blood over a cyst that had appeared directly on a vein on my right ankle. In the bath I tried to remove it with my sharp nails, but the thing had a hard almost metal shell under the surface of my skin and couldn't be budged; it was lodged into my vein. I knew instinctively that the blue experience had to do with implanting a device into my body. It was possibly a tracking gadget.

I have had the implant in my body for about eighteen years. Recently when I woke up, there was a circle of dried blood around the spot, and I knew that the device had been deactivated. Recent research and reliable investigations have shown that many people have been the victims of the same type of blue experience. I have been in touch with people who have had similar happenings, and they also find the electric blue colour disturbing and frightening. For many years I could not tolerate an electric blue light or look at one or walk near one or drive near one. During the blue light encounter people describe being incapacitated and unable to defend themselves. Many have no idea why the event took place, but some think that under the blue light, devices were implanted in their bodies. A while ago I was greatly comforted by a BBC programme that investigated people who had been implanted with odd devices. It presented an American surgeon, Dr. Lear, who had been removing these objects for a long time. The objects were unlike anything that could have been made on earth, and all the victims instinctively knew there was an alien object in their bodies. There is interesting evidence documented on You Tube on the removal of the implants.

After my "blue" encounter, I researched the properties of the colour and came up with some fascinating facts. The colour blue has natural antiseptic qualities and is often used in public places such as swimming baths and spas. Apparently the colour blue slows down the human metabolism. The colour blue is also used for technical excellence and precision work, which would be vitally important for injecting a victim in the right place and implanting the device into the correct target. The colour blue pacifies the nervous system and reduces blood pressure and has also been found to help reduce pain. The colour blue is also associated with generating new ideas and freedom and is used for enhancing and strengthening new beginnings. It also symbolises excellence, as in awarding blue ribbons for achieving the greatest expertise in a given field.

I never had the blue experience again, but in January 2011, strange things began to happen. I don't like to use the word "alien," as it has negative connotations; and I don't wish to refer to "abductions," since I can't explain the process; so I will try to describe what happened to me as best I can, in the hope that you come with me on my journey and share what I went through. Moreover, if anyone can shed any light on these "happenings," I would be grateful to learn more. The following is my diary of events.

Sunday evening, January 23, 2011: I went to bed tired but woke in the early hours of the morning to cold air blowing across my face and left hand. Half-conscious, I felt the atmosphere above me change as though the air was racing, similar to a film in which clouds are speeded up whilst moving across the sky. I was lying on my left side and facing the left wall of the bedroom. The cold air roused me into a more aware zone of consciousness, and I felt a sensation of something sharp pricking into a vein in my left hand. I was cognizant of a grey/blue entity kneeling by the bed and almost at the same time as the needle went into my vein, I simultaneously agreed to have the treatment. The being said it was for arthritis. Substance was injected into my vein. At first it hit a blockage; then something touched my lower arm and the flow was unblocked. It was cold. I envisaged it as a thick, white liquid with a purple luminescence travelling through certain parts of my body. It passed below my chin and didn't go into my head. A voice told me it wouldn't go into my head. Then it travelled down into my lower gut, tipping over my pelvic girdle, trickling through my hips and racing down my legs with a sensation of a cold tingling that was not unpleasant. The voice said the medicine would make me stronger and that I needed to be tougher for the changing vibrations to come, which would affect our planet. It also told me that I had to be aware of what I ate, as too much heavy food after the injection would make me sick, and that I had to avoid alcohol. I fell asleep.

When I woke, I instinctively looked for an injection mark. It was prominently there. A red dot marked the spot where I had been injected, and it was sore. When I pressed it, there seemed to be something under the skin; I tried to cut it open but couldn't. It remained visible for three months.

Tuesday evening, January 25, 2011: I was awakened around the same time as the first night. I heard a thudding sound on the landing, and my door handle rattled a couple of times. (There is often a strange noise upstairs before something unusual happens.) I was half-asleep and lying on my stomach when I had the sensation of the bed covers lifting. Something hard slipped under my stomach, like a hard stretcher used for lifting bodies. Then there was pressure on my feet as though my legs were being tied down. It felt like I was being lifted up to be carried somewhere. In my mind I screamed: "I want it to stop! Please stop!"; and it did. Horrified I sat up to see something but I couldn't see anything, and the air around was charged with an unusual energy.

Wednesday, February 9, 2011: In the early hours of the morning they came again. The grey/blue beings made a noise near my door and I knew they were coming. I was not fully conscious but aware of the change in the air around me. They said I needed another injection; they used the same spot as before, into which they injected a thick, white substance, which had an iridescent, candy-green tinge and glowed as it was pushed into my vein. A few inches from the crease in my arm, the substance hit an obstacle, so the beings decided to puncture another vein; this time the liquid flowed along the same route inside my body as before, avoiding my head, but it seemed heavy in my right arm. They said it was to help to change my body vibration to receive information. They told me not to drink alcohol and avoid normal meals but to have soup and other sloppy baby foods. As the treatment was underway, I began to feel sick in the pit of my stomach, like the overriding nausea felt after an anesthetic. They turned me on my side to relieve the sickness and something incredible happened inside my head. It was like Blackpool Illuminations lighting up every nerve in my head. Involuntarily the roller coaster flashing played itself like a pinball machine, lighting up parts of my brain as the electric impulse surged and bounced until it faded and I blacked out into a deep sleep.

In the morning I had marks on my arm where the needle had been inserted. It left a tiny, brown triangle, which remained for approximately a month. I didn't take their advice to avoid alcohol, nor did I change my diet and I had an odd feeling that the beings were not pleased. Perhaps I felt guilty at not following their directions, but I had a notion that they were trying in some way to manipulate me. It was also around this period that I began to get, at odd times, horrible, sharp burning pains like needles poked into my feet. Sometimes I would be quietly watching the television when something would jab me making me jump and cry out in pain. I have recently discovered through my research that I am not alone in this. A document, "Chemtrails, HAARP and Mass Mind Control, reveals the most terrible and frightening information by someone who has had access to classified information and has dared to make public his findings. He states that psychics have been a target for mind control research projects, because they have a psi-gene and a more complex molecular brain structure than those who do not have psychic ability. He states that:

"A secret programme has been carried out by the Illuminati to identify every person on the planet who is capable of being psychic. They are identified and then assigned to people (a male and a female) who monitor them. They have been identifying people with psychic abilities and then trying to track and/or control them. They also will try to recruit these people or place them under mind control or both."

He relates how *torture or nerve and muscle stimulation implants* are used in people and states:

"An implant in the middle (square in the heel) of the foot is activated like a sparkler, causing pain, anxiety and discomfort. Some describe it as a hot pin prick in the foot."

That is exactly what I experienced and still do from time to time. The incident is described as a form of torture, but I can't accept that someone is deliberately hurting me. It is too horrific to accept that idea. I just think that when it happens, they are testing the connection to see if it works. (Recent investigation shows that an electromagnetic weapon is being tested for the use of crowd control, whereby waves of electric pulses are sent through the airwaves to burn the surface of the skin.)

I was appalled to read the full document, as what it implies is an Orwellian network, which is greater and more knowledgeable than any sci-fi movie could ever conjure up; and we, like ants, follow vibration signals to such an extent that we have become accustomed to living enslaved and manipulated lives controlled by energy forces sent out through television, film, radio, music and cell phones.

A few weeks passed without any contact and, strange as it may seem, I felt almost bereft, as though I had been dumped and forgotten. I found it very peculiar to go from being in abject terror of the beings' presence to feeling lost without them; or maybe that's what they wanted me to feel. Whenever they made contact, my body grew unusually hot, and even in the coldest night I would find myself waking up without covers.

On Saturday evening, February 26, 2011, my body began to tingle and become overheated. I knew they were coming. I wasn't afraid. This time when they came, I was alert enough to ask for a name, and they showed me a long line of letters and figures with signs and symbols; but I couldn't understand anything. I asked if they had done something to my head or brain or if I had imagined it, but they explained, "Necessary for better communication!" I was shocked at the prompt response. I enquired about others and was told that there were masses of others who had been treated, but these people were mostly afraid to talk as they might be imprisoned in a mental hospital. I asked more questions, but on waking in the morning I couldn't remember the rest of what I had been told.

A few days later I went to the hairdresser and was concerned to see my young hairdresser upset. We usually chatted about any topic; but when I asked her what was wrong, she looked around furtively and whispered that her father had been taken to a mental hospital. Immediately I was intrigued and pressed her to tell me the story. When we were alone, she told me that her father had described alien visitors whom he said had come out of the television. He had a problem shoulder and had been told by the beings that they could heal it. They also said they had given him a new stomach lining and that he was only to eat soup or sloppy baby food and avoid alcohol. I was shocked to hear her describe what I had been told by the beings and pressed her for more information.

Apparently her father had become a different person, going from his usual happy-go-lucky self to being depressed, agitated and upset and unable to eat normal food. On visiting the doctor, he was referred to a mental hospital; after drug treatment, he was made to believe that he had made up the whole story and that if he took pills for the rest of his life, he could live a so-called normal existence. He was put under the pressure of thinking that he would be admitted back to hospital if he ever spoke of it again. Many, many people have been labelled and diagnosed with all kinds of disorders and locked away in mental institutions because of their experiences. Patients diagnosed as schizophrenic must live a life trapped inside a head comatose from drugs that prevent them from seeing the real world. Many psychics, who see the "real world," remain silent, because they are afraid to speak out for fear of being whisked off to a mental hospital. I too have been afraid to speak out, but now I know I must.

Sunday, March 7, 2011: I was asleep, but I was conscious of being either lifted up by my arms or put back down on the bed with my arms held up in front. As I became more aware of what was happening, something cut open a flap in my right arm a few inches from my shoulder and put something inside, then sealed the cut quickly. It seemed to happen in a flash, but it sliced into my muscle and the pain was intense. Then I rolled onto my stomach, and they showed me a tablet with scribbles in the colours orange, pink and purple with symbols written in pencil-like drawings. I couldn't even comprehend any of it and became frustrated when I couldn't make sense of any of it. (Through research I have seen similar designs, which are on skin implants devised as tracking gadgets that will be used on all humans in the future. Recently in America I saw similar designs used on bar codes.)

After the implant in my arm, the pain is like a nagging toothache, especially at night in bed when I can't even lift my arm. I battle with the pain and refuse to let it stop me from teaching dance. Something is not right, and I think they have cut into my muscle; but I cannot go to the doctor because I fear the outcome.

Wednesday, March 23, 2011: in the night, they came. I think they gave me something in my brain. I am not sure; but it feels good, light and floating like a gentle sail in the wind. It is on the right side of my brain. I am not sure why, but I feel detached from reality. I am not stressed; I feel at peace, but I don't remember what happened—I was only vaguely aware of a disturbance.

Sunday, March 27, 2011: I deliberately waited for contact but slipped into a sleepy meditative state while waiting and then felt several injections through my left big toe. For some time I had experienced a strange metallic crack, which came from my nose into the top of my head and exploded at unusual times, mostly when I was about to go to sleep, reverberating through the back of my throat (I have since read that this is another tracking device planted in the nose). Then a purple line, like a fishing line, was pulled through my left ear and I was told: "The brain is the engine room of the body and is responsible for the running of the body; all things come from the brain, so it is important to be healthy, and allow the brain to respond and lead the body. It is an amazing piece of machinery and should be used and stretched. Most people don't use the brain to its full potential. Use your brain to listen to the vibration of the universe attempting to communicate to your mind, which is like a tunnel that has many different channels, making it very difficult to steer a straight line through the maze, so you must train it to obey straight thought lines. Your mind has a different job from the brain, since it records memory, stores learning and initiates things but does not necessarily run the show. The mind also has to be trained and can be very willful at times; you have to take control of the reins and make it do exactly what you want."

Then I had the weirdest experience of all. I can only describe what it felt like, even though it seems impossible. I was lying on a lab table and there were grey beings around me. My head was unhinged and I couldn't breathe. They struggled to put my jaw back together and realign it inside my head. My mouth was opening and closing like a fish out of water gasping for air. My body was flapping and wriggling on the table; a being next to me saw that I was in pain and called someone in authority to see me. It told me to take two deep breaths. I obeyed, but my breath was not coming from inside of me; instead, it came from a distance and was not part of me. The being replaced my jaw, and I was fine and was somehow transported back to myself lying in bed.

The experience was horrible; and after that I seemed to have something stuck at the back of my throat, like a tiny hair that I couldn't swallow. I was afraid to go to the doctor.

Sunday, April 3, 2011: I woke with pain in my arm where they had sliced open a flap and planted something inside. I struggled to breathe. I felt something cold pouring from my arm into my chest and the weight of it was suffocating. My lungs were collapsing under the weight. I tried to move to alleviate the strain, but the pain was intense. I called out to them to stop it. After a few minutes the pain faded, and I was able to breathe again. I was still aware of something stuck in the back of my throat, but eventually I drifted into sleep.

Thursday, April 14, 2011: I was asleep and was woken by strange sound vibrations echoing across the room. I fought to recognise the noise, but then there was a huge crash on the left side of the bed. "Oh they are back!" I thought, and then I turned over and went back to sleep. But I didn't remember anything else.

Monday, April 18, 2011: I thought I went to sleep but I seemed to stay half awake. I was conscious enough to be able to move and turn to scratch my right ear. I was lying on my left side; my right ear was exposed to the air, and I felt something wriggling inside my ear. I poked my finger inside to alleviate the sensation and to convince myself nothing was there, but the sensation grew stronger. It was like a thin wire going through my ear. I relaxed into it pondering the feeling, knowing it was not a dream; but I was in a daze. Then I felt pressure on my right temple. Something was squeezing or easing a thin plate into the side of my head. I grew uneasy, not sure what to think. I asked about the chest pains I had previously suffered, and they rubbed my ribs; but I fell into a deep sleep and began to panic in my dreams. The panic attack grew worse and I couldn't breathe. My chest felt as heavy as lead and my heart hurt. The pain woke me up and there was no one there. I got up and took painkillers. The odd thing was that through the pain I felt intensely alive.

Sunday, May 15, 2011: Before I went to sleep, I heard voices. It seemed as though my hearing, which is poor, suddenly became heightened and I could hear the woman from next door so clearly. In the garden there were strange sounds, like a chair scraping and ducks hooting. My arm that was sliced hurt intensely, and I struggled to get comfortable but eventually drifted into sleep.

Thursday, May 19, '2011: My skin grew cold and clammy, while inside my body I was boiling. It felt as though I was brewing a high temperature. Shooting hot needles pricked both big toes, and my heel itched incessantly around the implant. The pain in my arm began to throb and I couldn't lift it. I asked for it to stop and somehow I drifted into sleep.

Sunday, May 29, 2011: In the early hours of the morning I slightly woke. I turned on my back and I didn't see them, but I spoke to them as though I knew they were there. Then without any warning the pain in my right arm became shockingly intense, almost unbearable. It seemed they were injecting something into me by way of what they had implanted previously. This time the substance was thin and bright red like blood, but it wasn't blood. Halfway down my arm the pain was terrible and the stuff seemed to hit a block, but then they pushed harder and it began to flow around my body. I had a sensation of floating. The pain came in spasms and when it was there, it consumed my body. There was no escape; I was allowed to turn on my side to alleviate the agony, but it continued. Then I rolled onto my stomach and felt sick, like being dizzy from a roller coaster ride. I asked what it was for and they said to rejuvenate all cells. In the morning, as I sat up, I noticed my hand was different. It was plump, moistly damp and rubbery. That effect didn't last long; but the experience, although extremely painful, left me wanting more of the youthful effects!

Saturday, June 23, 2011: I went to bed, but the pain in my arm was intense. My body was feverishly hot. In half sleep I felt they were talking to me and doing things to my face, pummelling the muscles. They seemed to be changing something in my ear. They spoke about the changing world and how food would be very different and that I had to start changing my diet in order to acclimatize my body for the New World changes. Then I lay on my stomach with the left side of my face on the pillow. I was shown an X-ray of a skull lit up in red, and my head and throat began to burn. I could feel myself coughing from a distance. Then I blacked out.

Wednesday, June 29, 2011: I had terrible pains in arm again but was not conscious of anything else.

Wednesday, July 20, 2011: I woke up with bruises on each arm just above elbow. Both bruises were in exactly the same place on each arm and were the same colour and size. It looked as if someone had tried to restrain me by using force on my arms. I don't remember anything, not even dreaming anything. The bruises hurt. My right arm aches constantly. I have had things in my throat for a long time now.

Friday, July 22, 2011: I had just got into bed and was getting comfortable when a sharp pain jabbed up my vagina. I called out in pain and sat up, but I couldn't see anything. I was really angry and shouted at them. I had endured all kinds of pains and the worst was in my arm, but that intrusion was too much. Then I lay down and was almost asleep when something held my hand. It was a lovely gesture, and I warmed to the feel of it, except

Return: To the Land of Durga

that it felt cold, moist and clammy with a rubbery texture and was thin and bony. I had the sense of a blue/grey being standing by my bed. It was bizarre and seemed out of character, as the beings had never shown emotion or caring and to hold my hand was very peculiar.

Saturday, August 27, 2011: I was just about to go to sleep when everything in my head lit up behind my eyes, as if someone had turned on a switch. My head was filled with information either being taken out or put in—I'm not sure which, but I could see writing and other information rolling like a slot machine when the plums or apples circle round until everything comes to a standstill. Then I blacked out. In the morning my ears felt wet inside, and I discovered that the wax inside had melted and was running down the side of my cheek. The light inside my head must have been very hot in order to melt the wax in my ears. The next morning I cleaned the inside of my ear with a cotton bud, and something dropped out. It was tiny and looked like a rusty old wheel with jagged edges coated in blood.

It is now early October and nothing has happened for a while, except that recently in America, in Missoula Airport while waiting in the early hours of the morning for a flight, I was trying to sleep on a bench; I was accompanied by a friend, who in the few hours quiet before the airport burst into action, was also trying to rest. There was only a handful of skeleton staff around cleaning and all the lights had been turned off. Suddenly in my right ear I heard the voices of a man and a woman talking. At first I thought it was the radio and got up to look around. There was no one about and the lounge was dark, with no television or radio blaring out. When I got up to walk around, the sound stopped, but when I lay down again and had my ear in a certain position, the voices were clearly audible as though they were in an office talking about mundane things like the weather. They had American accents. I was terrified and woke up my friend asking if he could hear voices; but, although he had extremely sharp hearing, he heard nothing. In a panic I lay down in the same spot and clearly heard the couple discussing the news. I knew then for certain that I had definitely got an implant in my ear that was tuning in to a nearby frequency and that terrified me. I moved away from the spot in which the frequency was strong and I tried to forget the experience.

Back home in England, time rolls on in the mundane routine of work and sleep. Nothing happens. They do not make contact. At night I have the occasional hot pinpricks in my foot, but apart from that everything remains quiet. Last night, however, I had a strange experience, which fills me with hope, reinforcing the fact that we are true spirit and that our bodies are merely suits in which our true identity is disguised.

I had woken up in the middle of the night lying on my right side and wanted to turn over to my left. I couldn't move; my body was rigidly set in position and wouldn't budge. I tried and tried to turn myself over but couldn't. I thought I was held captive in their grip again and they were holding me down, as I had no control over my body until something clicked in my head and unleashed my imprisoned self, and I was back inside my body where I was able to roll over quite freely. Once my spirit was back inside my shell, I thought that if I could perfect the technique of dissociating that part of my brain, I could stand back from outside interference and I would have the key to freeing myself from their invasive intrusion. The realisation that I was truly spirit made me fearless and totally free. The revelation was wonderful; but when I was liberated, I was given a horrible, sharp prick in my right foot and I jumped with the pain. I was not free from them and they wanted me to know it!

I knew they were tracking me and had given me the pain to remind me that I was under surveillance and not free. I was angry with them for inflicting the pain, but thought that's what they wanted. Anger is a base feeling, an emotion that ties the human spirit to a lower level. So I decided not to be angry. I tried to conjure up all things that made me feel good and happy and surround myself with those thoughts. In doing this I was set free from their influence and was given an insight into what had happened. I was shown that I was outside my body, hovering above, so that the feeling I had was the awareness that I was awake. In fact, my body was sleeping and I couldn't turn myself over as

I wasn't inside. However, I was predominantly myself without my body and nothing had changed. The click I felt was my spirit reentering my body and allowing myself to move. The revelation of existence without my earthly body was a fantastic relief. I felt exulted and freed beyond imagining. Although I had travelled out of my body many times before, it was wonderfully liberating to know the truth again. In the light of the new day, I knew I could face whatever was necessary, as I know there is no death.

Sunday, October 16, 2011: During the day I noticed directly outside my house a white van parked next to the boundary fence between my garden and the factory grounds next door. I became suspicious of the driver when he didn't seem to be serving any real purpose other than talking on his mobile and looking furtive. I had been given warnings about vehicles parked near the house without permission, especially white vans and any people pretending to be household appliance technicians or council workers who might be planting tracking or surveillance devices. After my scary strange experiences, I was edgy about anything out of the norm. By nightfall I became slightly nervous anticipating something was going to happen, especially as I had seen workmen tampering with a neon light opposite my house. They were wearing white, all-in-one suits and seemed out of keeping with the usual council workers; furthermore, it was after their work hours, around seven o'clock, when they appeared in a truck. I had read that street lamps were being used to track and monitor people and even transmit electromagnetic vibrations to affect the surrounding populace. As I walked up the stairs, an idea came into my head that I should listen to some music on my headphones. I didn't usually do that as it made me restless and was not conducive to sleep. The fence where I had seen the white van was outside my bedroom, and in retrospect I think that the idea of listening to music was a ploy to get me to ingest energy vibrations into my mind and body so that I would be more receptive to their communication.

I listened to the music and felt good, but after a while I decided I should try to sleep. Almost immediately after I put down the earphones, the beings were there. I don't remember too much about it except that their presence was very strong. I drifted into a deep sleep while fluttering breaths of air hovered over the deactivated implant on my ankle. Then, through a muzzy haze, terrible pains in my heels, like sharp electric dentist drills, sent shock waves up my leg. My right arm, where a flap had been sliced, hurt like a dull, thudding toothache as something was being injected in the veins in the crook of my arm. I was in a tornado of pain, not able to free myself. After a while it stopped, and I lay on my stomach waiting for the next round of pain. There was something addictive about the sensation. In my mind I was questioning whether I was inflicting the torture on myself; but when it began again, I knew I wasn't. The pain was definitely inflicted from an outside force. Once it was finally over, I fell into a heavy slumber.

As I woke the next morning, I gained consciousness through a veil of remembered pain. Perhaps I was becoming accustomed to the visits, because I was not afraid, feeling that everything was happening for a reason. In many cases like mine, I have read that the victim is abducted and taken elsewhere, but I cannot verify this in my own situation. I can't say I have been abducted, since the operation always seemed to be in my bed; but then I don't remember everything. My arm hurts and I am certain there is something implanted under the skin a few inches down from the shoulder of my right arm. I try not to think about the strangeness of it all and keep on with my daily routine, struggling to maintain a normal existence.

While I work at my computer sipping coffee, I am drawn to a news report. It states that a new microchip has been invented to keep track of people, containing a dosage of cyanide, which can be released by those in control, if necessary, killing the person instantly. The implant is inserted in the right arm a few inches down from the shoulder. I am horrified to read the details; although it is the latest news from America, as always, Britain will soon follow suit. I know my implant is a tracking device but can't accept the cyanide possibility; even if it were true, I have reached a point of total acceptance of whatever is happening to me because it is beyond my control, but I do know that my stubbornness and my inner strength prevent them from totally taking over and my spiritual power is a constant source of comfort and protection knowing that whatever they do to me, I cannot die.

CHAPTER 18

Return

My strange experiences pose many questions, for example, what if we have lived side by side with nonhuman beings ever since man roamed the earth? What if everything we have ever been told or learnt about our life is a lie? What if our thoughts are not our own? What if an outside force monitors everything we do, or say? What if an invisible network controls us constantly day and night? What if we are heading towards world dominance by a small minority, who have been engineering the end of the world as we know it? I am plagued by these questions and many others arising from my weird experiences. I do not know the answers, but I have glimpsed through a tiny crack in the universe and seen a vastly different higher consciousness, which exists beyond the realm of our understanding. I have been privileged to share my journeys and my amazing experiences with you, but my conscience won't allow us to part until I have disclosed what has been shown to me. I hope with all my heart that the visions are merely fantasy; that we will be victorious in our quest to defeat the invisible controllers; and that armed with the truth, we can return to our real identity, regardless of what is waiting for us in the shadowlands.

For a long while I have had a recurring nightmare. Sometimes it returns during my waking hours as a moving meditation; sometimes I see flashes of the vision appear inadvertently and I catch hold of a half-truth; then it vanishes. Sometimes the nightmare creeps from the back of my mind, stealing into my conscious thoughts, and disturbs my concentration. Other times the nightmare takes hold all night long and I wake in the morning shaking with terror. The vision appears real and I am given information about our state of living that is truly unbelievable. I am fearful for what I am shown, for I see the beginnings already taking shape in the wings, rehearsing for a grand entrance to steal the show and bring down the house with a dying call.

The nightmare begins with a normal day—well, normal in the sense that daily existence chugs on and I am on the treadmill routine of work and sleep. A deadly virus has hit the country; and we are trying to cope with a skeleton staff, teaching hugely depleted classes. The government fears that if they close schools, people will panic. Hospitals similarly are strained to breaking point, so people are told to stay at home and administer self-help, using pain killers and aspirin to reduce fever, and to drink plenty of tap water. Although I suffered with a heavy cold, I feel lucky not to be more seriously ill.

I switch on the news as I drive unhindered through quiet roads, which are normally heaving with early morning traffic. I am disturbed to hear that thousands of people across the world are dying from the rogue strain of flu, and it seems that there has been a dreadful mistake made by the pharmaceutical companies, who have developed a lethal cocktail of viruses, which instead of combating the normal flu, has given patients a dose of an unknown, untreatable strain. The truth has been uncovered that the amalgamation of drug companies across the world conspired to test out illegally, on unsuspecting patients, all kinds of viruses concocted during the bird flu epidemic; but because people fought against it, the vaccine was taken off the market. Another, which has the effect of reducing the immune system's ability to fight infection, was furtively introduced in its place. Suddenly the normal news is interrupted by crackling interference but clears as a woman's voice breaks through. "They are killing us!" she shouts. "They are killing us! Don't drink the water!"

Lesley Ann Eden

I shudder as the normal station resumes playing music from *Hair*—"This is the dawning of the Age of Aquarius." There certainly is a new dawn emerging, but it is sour and unclean. As I turn into the city, where I normally see flocks of school children, the streets are empty and I feel a twinge of guilt because my voices had warned me that all the vaccines being foisted upon the children were dangerous and I never spoke out. I was afraid of ridicule. I had wanted to shout out to friends with babies and young children to reject the thirty toxic vaccines inflicted upon their offspring before school age, as I was already witnessing as a teacher, the damage caused to a child's level of concentration and intelligent ability to take in information. But I didn't!

I was appalled when, in America, they wanted to inject children with a strain of anthrax to test their reaction and was glad when it was rejected in Britain; but I knew that somehow the medical profession would follow our American cousins down the same road. I had dared to warn people about aspartame and chemical additives in food and drink, and I had even dared to alert them to the terrible effects of chemtrails across our sky; but I knew people thought I was quirky. I felt I was becoming paranoid when all I could see around every corner was a lie, which was projected daily through the media. I thought I was going mad! In the nightmare I see myself driving to school through a haze of a terrible dawning of truth, knowing that I knew it all from the beginning; what was taking shape was the monster that had lurked in the shadows waiting to destroy everything.

Like a film, the dream switches to an amazing office at the top of a massive skyscraper, which is rich and luxurious, dripping diamond chandeliers and extreme technology. Invisibly I walk through the high security doors and enter the main office where an elderly man in a dark suit is talking on the phone. Behind him covering the whole wall is a massive map of the world, replete with secret signs and symbols. He nods to a man on his right, who blots out a part of the world with more symbols.

"And so, Jake—food supplies?"

"Taken care of, Sir—nothing is getting through!" The men laugh.

A beautiful woman with long auburn hair and dressed in a tight blue dress, interrupts: "Time for the news!" She switches a button, and a thin, flat screen rises from the wall and juts out a few feet, presenting a 3D image of a man as though he is in the room.

He delivers the latest news in deadpan professional tones: "The death toll across the globe is rising drastically as news from all the major cities of the world attempt to tackle the mystery of the unknown virus. Millions of people are dying in their homes as the epidemic affects all the main social services. Millions of people are dying of starvation, and there is devastating evidence that water supplies have been contaminated!"

"If the left don't get ya, then the right one will!" sings the man behind the desk as he lights up a huge cigar. "Just tell 'em to drink the tap water; it'll get 'em out o' their misery fast; hey- what do you say, Jake?"

"Precisely, Sir!"

"Message from headquarters—all is in place for the EMP finale!" shouts the woman.

"Tell 'em we'll evacuate as planned. They must wait till I give the all clear when everyone is positioned and we've battened down the hatches, so to speak—hey what, Jake? All undercover and then we'll let 'em have it. Not one single city in the whole goddamn world will survive. Blackout, Jake, sheer genius blackout! Stroke of luck to wrap it up with a solar attack! What a finale! Good-bye, sunshine; hello, 'star shine.' Wanna know what a weapon of mass destruction looks like, Jake? Well, take a look!" He wiggles his index finger and both men laugh inanely.

Then the scene switches as I arrive at school. The car park is quiet. There are only two cars in the whole of the school, and one poor child waits by the main entrance. She is handicapped and struggles to walk towards me.

"What's happening today, Miss?"

I smile and tell her that I will let her know. Inside the school, there is a deathly hush. A solitary secretary makes a cup of tea in the office and I ask her the news. She shrugs her shoulders and says she hasn't been told anything, but she supposes that we have to carry on until we're told differently. The staff room is empty. I run up the stairs to the Headmaster's office. No one is around. I run to the drama studio, but there is not one single child or teacher to be seen. I feel totally lost. I check all the classrooms—bits of paper left strewn on the floor and piles of books left haphazardly balanced on a table are the only evidence that the place was once occupied by the living. I pass the office. No one else has arrived. The secretary has fallen asleep at the computer and I tiptoe out into the sunshine. The child still waits. I suggest she phones home to get her mother to collect her; but she says her Mum's not in, so I help her to climb into the car so that I can drop her off.

As we drive into the city centre, an acrid smell oozes in through the window. The streets are empty but littered with filth and rubbish. I notice a couple of brown, fat rats scamper down the drain as I drive past a mound of rotting refuse. It's only been a week since the council announced that being understaffed, the dustbins, until further notice, could not be emptied and people had to be responsible for their own waste disposal. Near the child's door I stop to let her out, and I falsely reassure her that things will soon be back to normal when the flu epidemic dies down. "Did you have the flu jab, Miss?" she enquires.

"Er—no, I didn't!"

"Neither did I," she smiles. I watch her let herself in and am about to pull away when I catch sight of something slumped behind a mountain of ripped, black plastic bags. Its head is lodged against some discarded tin cans; the eyes are open like a dead fish and the mouth gaping. The body has been abandoned. I realise the smell is more than just discarded refuse. With nowhere to bury the dead, the city is fast becoming overrun with the carnage of rotting bodies.

I zoom away quickly, averting my eyes from other bodies thrown in street corners. Outside the city, where I live, things have not deteriorated as rapidly, although I notice many neighbours have left and there are no cars in the lane. Back at the house my little cottage is forlorn and cold; and as my footsteps echo across the hall, I feel a deep sense of aloneness. I tamper with the television in an attempt to find some news. Most of the major channels are down, but I find a minor one fighting to transmit the latest news. I listen through a crackling transmission relaying how services in major cities across the world have reached a standstill. Survivors are told that they will be taken care of by a re-organised police force wearing new black uniforms with a red triangle on the left breast. A fuzzy photo appears on the screen showing a black crash helmet and reinforced black fighting gear. A voice states that due to the circumstances, normal trading cannot take place, because the monetary system, as we know it, is obsolete and a new currency is being introduced- a new world currency, designed to create a prosperous new global state. In the meantime, anyone found looting would be shot on the spot. People should not worry about their financial status, as everything will be re-organised and the new currency will be reissued at a future date. People should stay in their homes, as the new police will deliver provisions from door to door; the drinking water is still perfectly safe. The transmission flickers and fails leaving me in a strangled vacuum of nothingness. Outside communication is finally severed. There is no signal on my phone or radio. I switch on the electric light that sputters and cracks out.

Momentarily I panic, searching for my car keys. I tell myself to be calm and think rationally. They said help would come, but I know differently. I need to get bottled water, candles, matches and anything in tins. I stupidly search for my purse and realise that money, any money, is worthless and that nothing is worth anything anymore. I decide to drive to the nearest supermarket and get what I can before the police arrive. I am sure I still have time. I race to the car and with shaking hands, I start it. My heart is pounding. Within minutes I arrive at the massive supermarket and am overcome by a disgusting stench. There are a few cars parked by the entrance, and people are rushing to fill their vehicles with anything they can carry. No one is taking any notice of anyone else. All is strangely silent. Inside it is dark and gloomy; people are scurrying around with their faces covered to block out the venomous smell of rotting vegetables, fish and meat. I grab a trolley and begin filling it with anything that is available—candles, matches, chocolate, water, tins, any tins, whiskey, wine and painkillers. In a daze I grab handfuls of goods, not caring what I take. When the trolley is almost full, I turn to go to the check out and then, realising my mistake, veer away to the door. I have to hurry to offload the goods into my car before the police arrive to shoot looters.

I throw everything into the back seat not caring where it lands and drive hysterically out of the car park. My heart thuds and my mouth dries. I wonder where my children are and what they are doing. The last I heard they were not affected by the flu, but that was yesterday. Back at the house I rush like a lunatic transferring all the loot to the kitchen where I pile things up haphazardly on all available worktops. The light is dimming and the wintry, watery sun is dipping low. The sky is creased with white trails, scarring the horizon with crisscross blotches; and I know something is going to happen. They are preparing the scene for something terrible—I feel it; I know it; for in my nightmare, I have already dreamt it repeatedly. The mass culling through an electromagnetic pulse will wipe out humanity, and there is no escape.

Standing alone in the kitchen, I shake uncontrollably. There is no one to turn to, no one to share the terror. I wait, but what am I waiting for? I decide to store away all the goods and make myself busy tidying the kitchen. I am cold. I am still shaking. I run up the stairs to put on extra layers. The night is creeping in with an eerie darkness and a silence that chills the soul. I make several attempts at lighting candles that I place around the kitchen. Shadows surround me like a midnight posse sneaking up on its prey. I am not used to my house being hostile to my needs. I walk into the sitting room where all is shrouded in a bleak, black veil. I cannot turn on the heating; I cannot turn on the light; I cannot turn on the television; and I cannot cook. Already my fridge and freezer are defrosting. I am hungry and decide to eat the leftovers from yesterday's meal. It is palatable and washes down with a glass of champagne. How I laugh to myself—champagne—what luxury in such desolate conditions.

I sit in the sitting room listening for sounds of the living; and through the window the moon strikes a silver beam across the lawn and a bat dips under the eaves, its wing momentarily silhouetted in the shimmering light. I walk across to the French windows to peer at the moon as it slides behind a cloud. Oddly I notice three places in the night sky where the moon hides. It can't be so—there are not three moons and yet as I scrutinize the sky, there are three distinct halos of light peeping through the clouds. As I ponder this anomaly, the first moon pops out like a puppet on a stick and travels backwards through the clouds like a theatrical illusion. A voice in my head talks softly: "Seeing is not necessarily believing- it is merely being, for the illusory nature of the holographic reality projected to you by the moon matrix has held you captive in a bubble of ignorance and your brain is switched off. Wars are won through peoples' minds not their bodies. Repetition is a weapon. Power seeps away from the people when fear makes them cling to the wreckage of the dying."

I do not want to listen and petulantly march through the conservatory out into the cold night air. Where are my children? I whisper hot breath through the freezing air: "I leave you my soul in the footsteps of the last leaves frozen in the earth, my children, my babies!" The sun has set in the wrong place. I thought I had made a mistake; but I have noticed for a while that the sun has been going down, not in the east but more towards the northwest. I look up and am horrified to see the night sky begin to bleed and blister, changing shape as I watch, like a fine face mask peeling away to reveal a vulnerable new skin beneath. The night sky wrinkles and burns tearing back a veneer, and in its place is a hidden galaxy of bright beings. A sudden, sharp electric shock spears my upper arm where I have suffered intermittent pain for many months. My brain is squeezed. My thoughts are jumbled. My body is limp. I need to sleep. I need to sleep. I need to sleep. I walk up the stairs and climb into bed pulling the covers high over my face and disappear into oblivion.

I see myself controlled from outside, and the implant in my upper arm has the power to switch down my body in a comatose sleep. From somewhere above myself I watch helplessly as a vibration of electric energy sweeps across the world. It burns and destroys everything. I see my car disintegrate in a mass of molten metal. Everything is decimated. I have a strange vision where I see above the earth and below. On top of the planet there are only black charcoal remains. Smoke and toxic fumes swirl across the land. The seas are red like the scarred sky and radiation poison continues to leak through the air and earth, so that whatever has not been killed by the electromagnetic pulse is destroyed by radiation, the process of which was begun long before it could be detected.

In my head I hear laughter from the past of how genetically modified food was introduced to help mankind win the battle of world starvation; but it was a trick to kill more people, and I wonder how they managed to dupe the population into believing that protein was poisonous and how governments had introduced a new law forbidding people to eat any form of protein. They didn't specify that protein was not poisonous to the rich. Underneath the earth's crust are thriving cities existing in a warren of underground tunnels connecting cities to cities, even countries to countries. Monorail high-speed trains whiz through a honeycomb of stations, and the New World's police force keeps watch, keeping guard in the new sterile zone. There are other beings too, strange creatures that walk side by side with humans who are working in all the main sections of the cities. People are different in an inconspicuous way, almost as if there is no emotional connection, and there is a new gender that is both male and female. All is solemn. There is no laughter.

I float inside a control station in the underground city, where men in grey uniforms are busy watching monitors and controlling dials. Invisibly I wander into a massive store-room where alien blue/grey outfits are hanging on rows upon rows of hooks. I recognise the shape. I am shocked to see the being that visited me at night and injected me with implants. I begin to understand. I had read that scientists in America, just after the Second World War, contacted alien life forms and made a pact with them. The aliens were allowed to use earth as a base if they shared certain knowledge with the scientists. A massive scheme was evolved across the world to introduce the idea of UFO's entering our atmosphere whereby curiosity and fear of alien beings was generated. The scientists found that the vibration on which the beings existed could be channelled and used to infiltrate the minds and bodies of humans. Suits of alien grey and blue were made to protect the beings so that they could enter undetected by humans and perform all kinds of operations and mind control techniques invisibly. I had not wanted to believe the stories I had read, yet the evidence was clear. Many humans who complained of being abducted were made to appear insane, and seeing the suits hanging limply made me so angry that I wanted to slash and tear them to pieces

I wandered unseen into another office where there were monitors receiving communication from other planets. I recognised the moon but was amazed to view the actual picture. It was a fantastic place full of intricate buildings, which seemed to hang in the air without much support, almost like Gaudi's architecture. I had always loved the moon and felt as a child it had protected me. I thought it was my home; and looking at the screen, I recognised a temple where I often visited in my mind. In a strange way, it was comforting to know that my roots really were embedded in another sphere and that my unusual connection with the moon, which I had been afraid to speak about, was real. My true nature was there, my real family was there and I knew that someday I would return to where I really belonged.

A man sitting at a monitor spoke into a microphone: "Schedule as usual."

Another man sitting next to him laughed, "I could do this standing on my head; don't know why we have to oversee the schedule—they know what they're doing. Hell, we've been sending our crew to the moon twice a week for at least fifty years!"

I was shocked to hear his words. It was another lie that had been fed to the populace. We were told there was only dust on the moon! I remembered how I felt when I first heard it, for I knew that wasn't so.

As I was sneaking through the underground city, everything began to make sense. I understood how the mind control system had held the world captive. People were warned by the brave that television, street lights, electrical goods and cables in houses were emitting electromagnetic pulses, which were dulling the brain, rendering intellect incapable of organising intelligent thoughts. Combined with chemical poisons in food, drink, drinking water and medicines, these were ideal methods of wiping out the masses. World disasters engineered by the massive microwave weapons were powerful instruments of mass destruction. People were so blinkered that the death of thousands of birds, fish and burnt shoals of dolphins were never recognised as pre-run tests for mass annihilation.

All the evidence of our stupidity as human beings lay before me as the men discussed how easy it had been to put in place all the last details to enforce the New World government. People had stood back and allowed the world currency to dwindle into thin air; it was, the man at the desk said, "Like taking candy from a baby!"

"Ych!" laughed the other, "make 'em scared, make 'em scared! That's the way to do it!" They both laughed as I drifted invisibly back above my body. Why was I there?

A being close to me soothingly spoke: "You have special psychic gifts, which they want to use. A programme was introduced many years ago to seek out those with extra sensory ability, who would be of use in the New World system. You have the mechanism to communicate through thought and mind transference of energy. You have been implanted with a bodysuit of tracking devices. There are many like you who will be needed under the transformation process."

I wanted to cry with shock, relief and horror. Everything I had felt and gone through was real and not imagined. From the time when I was very tiny and my mother had taken me to the doctor's because she thought I was mad, in that I talked for hours on end to invisible beings and it was explained that I was under surveillance from this time onwards, as doctors had been asked to report children who they suspected had psychic talents. The soothing voice continued: "Children with this ability have special psi-genes and were used in Nazi Germany to help the scientists in their experiments, which were later continued in America after the Second World War."

I suddenly realised why a memory kept haunting me of when I was six years old, being taken to have my eyes tested. There was something about the experience that wasn't right, but I couldn't remember what. I just knew that my mother had to administer drops in my eyes for a week before I had the examination, which made my vision blurred and I felt dizzy. When I went for the so-called eye examination, it was strange. My mother wasn't allowed to go with me and I entered a dark room with strangers; a man in a white coat, with dark hair and black eyes, asked me to sit in a big chair. He put something in front of my face and I don't remember much else."

The voice continued: "Implants were put in children behind their eyes!" I was angry, yet it made sense; I understood all the sounds and noises in my head as a child, which had interfered with my mind, like a radio being tuned into different stations.

Throughout the nightmare a flood of information whirled and turned like a tornado whipping up everything in its path. Entrenched in the dream, I could see myself waking from the enforced sleep while the earth was being been destroyed.

In my dream vision, I wake. I scramble my thoughts to remember. Little by little my mind assembles memory and I regain consciousness. I remember the fear. I remember the confusion. I sit up. My head is fuzzy; and when I try to stand, I am dizzy. The light is odd. It is twilight, yet I know it is morning. I am horrified to see the sky scarred like a little boy's knees, cut and grazed in a gravel playground. It is not blue and beautiful, but perhaps it never was; perhaps it was a dome concealing secrets. I manage to walk down the stairs, and a terrible smell knocks me backwards; I cling to the rail. I hold my hands over my mouth and nose and see that sewage has leaked through the kitchen sink. The floor is water logged. There is rotting food in the fridge and freezer, and my plants have shrivelled and died. Could all of this have happened during one night? I feel uncomfortable with my clothes stuck to my body, and I realise I smell.

I open the front door onto a world that is not mine. Everything is dead. I turn towards my house, shocked and awed that parts of it still remain, while the whole row of cottages in which it stands, have all been decimated. My lawn is ash, my flowers, shrubs and trees all brittle charcoal. My car is molten metal lying in a cartoon heap of rubble. The air is acrid and I rush back inside, instinctively knowing that outside is not safe. I slosh through the disgusting puddles and find the bottles of water I have stashed away. I go to the bathroom where I discard all my clothes and stand in the bath, pouring the cold water over my body to wash away the filth.

I feel better in clean clothes and after drinking bottled water, I am fully awake. A song enters my head, "If you were the only girl in the world . . ." It seems I am the only girl in my world and it feels horrible. I want to die. I ponder the idea, but a voice blocks my thoughts. My arm hurts again, and a voice clearly tells me to wait; for it won't be long before I am rescued. I sit on the bed that is still in tact and wait and wait. Suddenly the stillness is broken, as the door downstairs crashes open and footsteps swell and slosh through the flood. I stare in horror at two beings in black suits of armour. They breathe through a tank on their backs and hand me a mask. I put it on and am lead out to a black, armoured vehicle.

I climb in and sit in a black office with a swivel chair facing a flat screen. I am told to watch. I am shown all I need to know. I am being taken to a substation where I will receive further orders. The substation is below ground in an underground city. I watch the screen in terror as I witness a recording of the effects of the electromagnetic pulse that is timed to coincide with a solar explosion. I have the same feeling as when I saw the "twin towers" in New York City fall. It can't be real! Information Station, a new teleport channel, reveals the workings of the New World government. The opening lines of my play *Uranus Ureingus* come to mind, "Self, self, there is no self. Self has no identity." I feel stripped naked of all emotion. I have no self; it has withered away. Where are my children, my children?

The vehicle stops and I am a shell. I am nothing and I don't care. I am hauled out into a whirlwind of activity. It is like a landing strip where helicopter-like transit vehicles are whirring and buzzing. People in black uniforms are scurrying everywhere; I stand in bewilderment. A vision returns of when I was eleven years old. I see myself in the future wearing a black uniform. I have short, white hair and am standing in front of a large group of recruits. I am instructing them in movement and mind energy. My vision blurs as a being moves forwards and I am escorted inside, where there is a vast array of super technology with 3D flat screens projecting all manner of communication and rows of people at desks formulating the information. I am placed in front of a desk where a being talks to me. He/she/it tells me I have a choice. I am amazed to be given a choice. The being registers my surprise and states, "We are not evil beings. You have, how shall I say, an old-fashioned idea of good and bad. You have lived earthly life under a structure that in our new zone does not exist and never has. It is an absurd way of existing. There is only one law and there always has been; it is only humans who have distorted the way of being. All is as it will be; there is no good or bad—we only are." Somehow in the nightmare it made sense.

"What are my options?" I asked tentatively.

They showed me a vision of myself, which I had seen before, instructing young recruits and then a shimmering image, like a mirage in the desert. It was a spacecraft waiting to ship me back to my people—how I longed to return!

Always at the same point in the nightmare I wake. I never see the choice I make. Whether I have been asleep or whether the visions are part of a moving meditation, I never know the outcome; I am left hovering in a dilemma. Whenever I have the experience, I return to the knowledge of the present with a greater sense of injustice and desire to share what I have seen, for the sense of impending doom is reaching fever pitch and all that I have seen is slowly unravelling too close to reality. I fear for humanity that we are all slumbering under delusional security and that while we are lulled into a comfort coma, a monster is busy in the shadowland waiting to pounce.

Where is the now? It is a bright, crisp, late autumn morning and the world appears beautiful and serene. Summer roses cling precariously to withering branches, and the last of the leaves on my cherry tree quiver in the gentle breeze. I take down another batch of costumes in preparation for the next show and sigh remembering all the heartache, tears, triumphs and joy that the shows bring. A small, pink, sequinned tutu slides from under the pile, and I smile remembering a very special moment from the last show.

Two friends stand in a hushed pause on an empty stage just before the curtain rises. The atmosphere is charged with excitement, as adrenalin pumps. No one is around and there is a rare moment of quiet as everyone prepares. There is no sound as the two friends smile. One is a professional photographer and takes photos of all the shows and the other the choreographer. Together they hug in a last minute embrace before the music begins and reminisce about all the years that have emptied out like a slow trickle of good wine.

"Where have all the years gone, Lesley?"

I smile. "Do you remember when your Mum used to dance?"

"Oh yes, she loved it!"

"She was a wonderful lady."

"Thank you!"

"You know she's still around?"

"Yes, I've often wondered what happens after death?"

"She is not gone; life is like electricity—it cuts through; it does not die; it just changes direction. She is still around."

In the silence from the steep rafters high above our heads, from nowhere, like gentle snow, falls a little pink, fluffy, fun feather. The two friends watch in amazement. No one has a pink-feathered costume. There are no pink-feathered bowers or pink-feathered anything. Kate, the photographer picks up the sweet, pink feather and smiles. Our eyes glisten under the stage lights. We know where the little pink feather came from.

"Yes, she is still around!" smiles Kate with glistening eyes.

I gather up the costumes and wonder where my travels will lead me next? I am filled with gratitude to have returned to the Land of Durga, which formulated so much of what is my present; but the nightmare visions from the potential future are never very far away. I ponder the choice that I might be given in the future and feel the yearning to return to my people. From my future visions, I see I am teaching a whole new spectrum of knowledge, which is beginning now. I am being taught and guided towards gates that hold specific knowledge in sound, colour, vibration and movement, which are to be passed on as self-help and mindscape skills to increase peoples' ability to reach a higher level of consciousness, expanding their spiritual awareness.

I am still uncertain what the visitors' purpose is in my life or why they have done the things they have. I am open to the realisation that it is a preparation for things to come; and if I am to be used in a specific way, then so be it. I am learning new information, which I am formulating to be passed on. I am told the new knowledge will be very important, and so I wait to be instructed and guided in complete acceptance of what I must do. On my bedroom wall is a print of Durga and I smile to think that I have played a small part in nurturing children, knowing that I am following my earthly purpose and that the Mother Goddess will shine a light for us all to embrace our rising consciousness and that whatever follows, we will have the strength to face it with clean hearts.

Thank you for travelling with me and for sharing my incredible and unbelievable events. I hope we will find a new adventure together at the Gates of Eden. If my travelling has taught me one thing to pass on to you, it is that it is not the returning home or going back to family or loved ones that teaches the most important lesson; it is finding your true self in all situations and however far you travel, you must always return to yourself in the full knowledge that all you have is who you are; who you have been and who you will become.

—*Lesley Ann*

Lesley Ann Eden

Cuban musicians. Book 2, page 80 . . . "imbibing the rhythm, feeding the people with light of their sowing, forever in creating the music of knowing."

Backstreet of Havana. Book 2, page 42 . . . "yet amongst it all cars of character sat back preening in the poverty-ridden backdrop of chaotic decay."

Return: To the Land of Durga

Cuban mountain village. Book 2, page 184 . . . "Somehow I felt close to Che in that lonely village where time hung still, caught in a web of tradition."

Cuban market in the mountains. Book 2, page 183 . . . "I thought it was wash day - it was the women's way of displaying their handicraft."

Lesley Ann Eden

Temple at Palenque: Book 1, page 45 . . , "having climbed to the top of the temple I became frozen with fear when I had to step over a gaping hole-"It seemed easier just to fall. I wanted to fall!"

Chiapas Mountain women weaving: Book 1, page 54 . . . "On the dry dusty ground the women sat working a primitive loom."

Return: To the Land of Durga

Jungle Hut in Belize. Book 1, page 135 . . . "Back in the small round hut in the jungle, I was a million years away from West Sussex."

Hurricane disaster on Caye Caulker Island. Book 1 page 145 . . . "We paused near a dilapidated wooden hut with blue paint hanging off in strips."

Lesley Ann Eden

Car art in Dune Hotel, Book 3, page 52 . . . *"Turning a corner a Cadillac car blazoned a Hippy era.."*

Tsunami destruction of shore line in Elephant valley. Book 3, page 65 . . . *"Dead wood and trees lay dry and sterile in a brown parched mass along the seashore."*

Return: To the Land of Durga

Coconut seller in Pondecherry. Book 3, page 68 . . . "hot and parched with the heat we stopped to buy a drink of coconut milk with 'a cornucopia of aromatic smells.'"

Discovering Granny's grave on Tiger Hill. Book 3, page 133 . . . "Branden and I followed the chokidar to the hallowed ground where a soft chorus of birdsong filled the air with an ancient hymn."

Lightning Source UK Ltd.
Milton Keynes UK
UKOW050608040812

197055UK00003B/1/P